"To say that the fourth edition of *Identity in Adolescence* has been updated is an understatement. Although Ferrer-Wreder and Kroger have retained the coverage of seminal work by Erikson and Blos, the book has been expanded to include many new and exciting developments in adolescent and young adult identity research that emerged since the last edition. This new edition includes chapters on narrative studies, sociocultural approaches, intersections of gender and sexuality, and technology and virtual identity. At its heart, this book embraces a lifespan and life-course approach to understanding where adolescents have 'come from' and are 'going to'. It also takes very seriously the contexts in which adolescents are developing, holding onto the original theme of the balance between self and other, even virtual others. Infused with stories that illustrate the processes of adolescent identity development, this masterful revision provides students of adolescence and professionals working with youth a stimulating and rich resource."

– Sheila K. Marshall, University of British Columbia

"This fourth edition of *Identity in Adolescence* not only provides the most comprehensive review of the theoretical landscape of identity development in adolescence, but it also highlights critical contemporary issues facing identity scholars in our modern digital and global contexts."

– Renee Galliher, Utah State University

"The new fourth edition of *Identity in Adolescence: The Balance Between Self and Other* addresses and critiques the foundational theories of identity (Erikson, Blos, Marcia, and others) while also looking ahead to contemporary themes, including life in the digital world, intersectionality of identities, and neurological underpinnings of identity. The volume is an important resource for professionals working with adolescents, as well as for parents and those setting policy affecting adolescents. Throughout, it takes a sympathetic view of adolescents and argues for greater understanding of the complex task of identity development in our increasingly identity-conscious world."

– Harold D. Grotevant, Ph.D., Rudd Family Foundation Chair in Psychology, University of Massachusetts Amherst

"A re-written and updated version of a popular and authoritative book on the most important psychosocial challenge of adolescence: identity formation. New multi-cultural research and practical implications are presented, providing a useful basis for understanding and working with youth as they face the challenges of this crucial developmental stage."

– James E. Marcia, Simon Fraser University

D1595312

Identity in Adolescence

This fully revised fourth edition of *Identity in Adolescence: The Balance Between Self and Other* presents four theoretical perspectives on identity development during adolescence and young adulthood and their practical implications for intervention. Ferrer-Wreder and Kroger consider adolescent identity development as the unique intersection of social and cultural forces in combination with individual factors that each theoretical model stresses in attempting to understand the identity formation process for contemporary adolescents.

Identity in Adolescence addresses the complex question of how adolescent identity forms and develops during adolescence and young adulthood and serves as the foundation for entering adult life. The book is unique in its presentation of four selected models that address this process, along with cutting-edge research and the implications that each of these models hold for practical interventions. This new edition has been comprehensively revised, with five completely new chapters and three that have been extensively updated. New special topics are also addressed, including ethnic, sexual, and gender identity development, the role of technology in adolescent identity development, and ongoing identity development beyond adolescence.

The book is essential reading for advanced undergraduate and graduate students studying adolescent development, self and social identity within developmental psychology, social psychology and clinical psychology, as well as practitioners in the fields of child welfare and mental health services, social work, youth and community work and counseling.

Laura Ferrer-Wreder, Ph.D., is a Docent (Associate Professor) in the Department of Psychology at Stockholm University. She has published widely and her current research focuses on advancing the study of positive youth development from a global perspective. She is one of the co-developers of an identity intervention called the Changing Lives Program.

Jane Kroger, Ph.D., is Professor Emerita of Developmental Psychology at University of Tromsø, Norway. Previous books include *Identity Development: Adolescence through Adulthood* and *Discussions on Ego Identity*, along with numerous research investigations on identity development during adolescence and adulthood.

Adolescence and Society

Series Editor: John C. Coleman

Department of Education, University of Oxford

In the 20 years since it began, this series has published some of the key texts in the field of adolescent studies. The series has covered a very wide range of subjects, almost all of them being of central concern to students, researchers and practitioners. A mark of its success is that a number of books have gone to second and third editions, illustrating its popularity and reputation.

The primary aim of the series is to make accessible, to the widest possible readership, important and topical evidence relating to adolescent development. Much of this material is published in relatively inaccessible professional journals, and the objective of the books has been to summarise, review and place in context current work in the field, so as to interest and engage both an undergraduate and a professional audience.

The intention of the authors is to raise the profile of adolescent studies among professionals and in institutions of higher education. By publishing relatively short, readable books on topics of current interest to do with youth and society, the series makes people more aware of the relevance of the subject of adolescence to a wide range of social concerns.

The books do not put forward any one theoretical viewpoint. The authors outline the most prominent theories in the field and include a balanced and critical assessment of each of these. Whilst some of the books may have a clinical or applied slant, the majority concentrate on normal development.

The readership rests primarily in two major areas: the undergraduate market, particularly in the fields of psychology, sociology and education; and the professional training market, with particular emphasis on social work, clinical and educational psychology, counseling, youth work, nursing and teacher training.

Also in this series:

Identity in Adolescence, 4th edition
Laura Ferrer-Wreder and Jane Kroger

Youth Civic and Political Engagement
Martyn Barrett and Dimitra Pachi

Adolescent Mental Health
Terje Ogden and Kristine Amlund Hagen

Adolescent Coping
Erica Frydenberg

www.routledge.com/Adolescence-and-Society/book-series/SE0238

Identity in Adolescence
The Balance Between Self and Other

Fourth edition

Laura Ferrer-Wreder and Jane Kroger

Routledge
Taylor & Francis Group

LONDON AND NEW YORK

Fourth edition published 2020
by Routledge
2 Park Square, Milton Park, Abingdon, Oxon, OX14 4RN

and by Routledge
52 Vanderbilt Avenue, New York, NY 10017

Routledge is an imprint of the Taylor & Francis Group, an informa business

First edition published by Routledge 1989
Second edition published by Routledge 1996
Third edition published by Routledge 2004

British Library Cataloguing-in-Publication Data
A catalogue record for this book is available from the British Library

Library of Congress Cataloging-in-Publication Data
A catalog record has been requested for this book

ISBN: 978-1-138-05559-9 (hbk)
ISBN: 978-1-138-05560-5 (pbk)
ISBN: 978-1-315-16580-6 (ebk)

Typeset in Times New Roman
by Swales & Willis Ltd, Exeter, Devon, UK

For my parents, Alice and Tony Ferrer; and for my husband, Richard Wreder and for my children: Sara and Patrick Wreder

– **Laura Ferrer-Wreder**

In memory of Emmy Werner, dear friend, former mentor

– **Jane Kroger**

Contents

Figures and tables

Figure

Tables

Preface to the fourth edition

Like identity, this fourth edition of *Identity in Adolescence: The Balance Between Self and Other* has a long, slowly evolving history. Many years ago, on a cool autumn day in London as the leaves where beginning to turn, I (JK) was on sabbatical leave for the semester. I had just completed replicating some of John Coleman's work in New Zealand, where I was living at the time, and I had been in contact with John during this process. During my London stay, he and I met over coffee one morning when he was in the city for the day. At the conclusion of that meeting, he raised the possibility of my authoring a new volume on identity in his newly developing Adolescence and Society Series. I was both delighted and overwhelmed with this opportunity, and so the first edition of *Identity in Adolescence* came into being in 1989. Over the next several decades, editions two and three were undertaken and appeared (1996 and 2004, respectively). These volumes explored a number of different developmental orientations to adolescent identity formation and the implications that each held for social response in facilitating that process.

Readers familiar with these earlier editions will have noticed a significant gap between the last and current fourth edition (15 years!). What can I say, other than that "life happened." Following the second edition, I had become heavily involved professionally in several large and demanding identity-related investigations, had written or edited two other identity-related volumes, had moved to a university setting in northern Norway (200 miles north of the Arctic Circle!) from New Zealand, learned to function in a new language and cultural setting, but thought I would undertake a third and final update to the Identity in Adolescence series. In the fifteen years since that last edition, I have partially retired, returned to my native country (the United States), and become settled in new and broadening life style commitments. Over this time, I was also becoming aware that identity research had mushroomed, drawing many new scholars into the field and inspiring hundreds of new studies as well as several new journals and societies devoted to identity studies. The publishers had approached me for some years about a new edition, but the time seemed right at this point, and I somehow felt the need not to let the volume rest without capturing many of these new and exciting developments in the field.

In the meantime, my colleague, Laura Ferrer-Wreder, at University of Stockholm, expressed interest in undertaking a new edition, and we discussed the possibility of jointly contributing to this enterprise. We realized that this fourth edition would need to be largely re-written, and over the past two years, we have been working toward that end. Laura's interests in issues of identity interventions as well as the importance of intersectionality, ethnicity, gender, sexuality, and technology to the study of adolescent identity development have added greatly to the expansion of work covered in this fourth edition. This volume now includes growing elaborations of Erikson's psychosocial orientation to identity, Blos's views and expanded research on adolescent separation-individuation processes, narrative studies of identity, and sociocultural issues and their applications that form the introductory theoretical chapters of the present edition. It also includes special issues of ethnicity and the intersection of gender and sexuality as well as the role of technology, all in relation to adolescent identity development. The volume concludes with a chapter on the evolution of identity beyond adolescence, for the foundations of identity normatively crystalized during adolescence have some rather long-term implications that we felt it important for readers to appreciate.

This new fourth edition of *Identity in Adolescence: The Balance Between Self and Other* is, again, first and foremost, a book about identity development during adolescence, and the implications that this development holds for practical response by parents, teachers, youth workers, and others interacting with youths during the second and third decades of their lives. In this book, special care was taken to have a culturally informed perspective on how adolescents in various parts of the world meet the challenges of identity development as well as thrive and contribute to their life contexts. In part, the book aims to capture the many new theoretical and research innovations both to some of the existing models of identity development covered in earlier editions of the volume as well as newer approaches in the field of identity studies during adolescence. It has also been sparked by our concern over adults' frequent failure to recognize, meet, and respond optimally to the special needs of adolescents in their various phases of identity development. The wealth of research data that now exists about what constitutes an effective identity intervention during adolescence offers even clearer answers to questions of how effective intervention can be a planned event rather than chance occurrence. Now, more than ever, it is vital for the adults of today to recognize the strengths and promise of the current generation of youth and to support them in their identity development, as a way to better ensure that the next generation is fully equipped to meet the challenges of today and the future. It is hoped that the results of our work with this fourth edition will help promote interests in identity studies, either as a supplementary emphasis to courses on adolescent development or as a field in its own right.

Jane Kroger
Bellingham, Washington, USA
Laura Ferrer-Wreder
Stockholm, Sweden

Acknowledgements

We are grateful to the series editor, John Coleman, our editors, Lucy Kennedy and Helen Pritt, and editorial assistants, Sophie Crowe and Charlotte Mapp at Routledge for their great responsiveness and helpful support during the development and preparation of this volume. We also greatly appreciate those who have read selected chapters and offered their thoughts on earlier drafts: Jim Marcia, Lena Adamson, Carolyn Cass Lorente, and Nele Stoffels. Their suggestions have significantly improved the coverage and readability of all chapters. We also thank Monisha Pasupathi and Deborah Rivas-Drake for agreeing to speak with us and for sharing their biographies and perspectives in this book. And grateful thanks also go to the many students and colleagues over the years whose comments have contributed enormously to the development of the present volume. Finally to those individuals who participated in Kroger's formative research interviews and provided anonymous statements that intro- duced Chapters 5, 6, 7, and 8 about their own identity-related concerns, we express our sincere gratitude.

During the writing of this book, Laura Ferrer-Wreder was supported by a research sabbatical grant from Stockholm University. Her sincere thanks go to Stockholm University's Håkan Fischer and Lilianne Eninger, as well as the University of Bergen's Nora Wiium, Radosveta Dimitrova, and David L. Sam and the rest of the Psychology Department at Bergen for their steadfast sup- port during Laura's research sabbatical, which made her work on this book possible. Laura would like also to acknowledge William M. Kurtines for his mentorship. Special thanks also go to Richard Wreder, Alice Ferrer, and the teenagers in Laura's life (Sara and Patrick Wreder) who were patient and help- ful in sharing their reflections about the post-Millennial digital landscape and gender. Finally, our heartfelt thanks go to other family members and friends who have been patient with the many hours that we have been "lost" to them through the production of this work.

Permissions acknowledgements

of Carson McCullers. Reprinted by permission of Houghton Mifflin Harcourt Publishing Company. All rights reserved.

By Herman Hesse, translated by Hilda Rosner, from *Siddhartha*, copyright © 1951 by New Directions Publishing Corp. Reprinted by permission of New Directions Publishing Corp.

Extracts from *Siddhartha* by Herman Hesse reprinted by permission of Pollinger Limited (www.pollingerltd.com) on behalf of the Estate of Herman Hesse.

1 Adolescence and the problem of identity

Historical, sociocultural, and psychosocial views

"Listen," F. Jasmine said. "What I've been trying to say is this. Doesn't it strike you as strange that I am I, and you are you? I am F. Jasmine Addams. And you are Berenice Sadie Brown. And we can look at each other, and touch each other, and stay together year in and year out in the same room. Yet always I am I, and you are you. And I can't ever be anything else but me, and you can't ever be anything else but you. Have you ever thought of that? And does it seem to you strange?"

(Carson McCullers, *Member of the Wedding*, 1946, pp. 114–115)

F. Jasmine (alias Frankie) Addams's ruminations address a question that adolescents and social scientists alike have pondered over preceding decades: When and how does one develop a sense of identity? While the foundations of identity are formed in infancy through the interactions of caretakers and child, adolescence does seem to be a time, at least in many contemporary, technologically advanced cultures, when one is confronted with the task of self-definition. Frankie can't ever be anything else but herself. However, trying to find out who "she" is and where she "belongs" becomes Frankie's task in Carson McCullers's (1946) novel, *Member of the Wedding*. The process of identity formation is something that scholars have attempted to understand from a variety of perspectives – historical, sociocultural, and psychosocial. While Frankie, herself, is not concerned with all of these issues, she eloquently gives voice to some of the forces that helped shape her "I," her sense of identity, and her place in the world.

Frankie's story is set during the Second World War in a small, rural southern town in the United States during a seemingly endless summer. Frankie is about to turn "twelve and five-sixths," feeling very much betwixt and between meaningful social niches (that summer has a way of exacerbating), and wrestling with the matter of belonging. Given an option, Frankie would have preferred to have been a boy and gone to war as a marine. However, this was not to be her fate, so she decided instead to give blood (at least a quart a week) to the war efforts. In this way, a part of her would be in the veins of Allies fighting all over the world (the reddest and strongest blood ever – a true medical wonder). Soldiers would return, saying they owed their lives to "Addams" (not "Frankie"). But this scenario was not to be her fate either, for Frankie was too young, and the Red Cross would not take her blood. Thinking about the war for very long made Frankie afraid, not because of the fighting but because the war refused to include her, to give her a place in the world, just as her brother's upcoming wedding would not include her in the wedding party. Actually, thinking for very long, at all, made Frankie afraid as well, for it brought up questions of who she was, of what she could do in the world, of why she was standing where she was at that moment – alone. Through the trials of trying to adopt a new name (F. Jasmine Addams), a new family, a new town, Frankie struggled to establish her sense of identity and where she belonged.

The present volume is first and foremost a book about *identity* and its development during *adolescence*. Identity is that which gives meaning and purpose to one's life, allowing one to move with a sense of direction toward expressing one's values and goals. Identity is who and what one believes oneself to be, allowing one to seek and hopefully find meaningful personal expressions of one's psychological needs, interests, talents, and values within a sociocultural context. *Adolescence* has often been defined as the period of life beginning in puberty and ending in culture. By this definition, the biological changes of puberty herald the transformation into an adult body, as well as changes in the emotional, cognitive, and social capabilities that mark the beginning of adolescence. The ending of adolescence has been defined in various ways, but adolescence generally is considered to draw to a close when one is able to take greater responsibility for oneself emotionally, economically, and relationally. One's immediate social and cultural contexts will play an important role in determining when adolescence draws to a close and adulthood proper begins.

The time during which one might be considered adolescent has been greatly lengthening in many parts of the world due to the increased cultural demands for learning the technical skills that are needed to function in that adult world. And so, several decades ago, those who were referred to as "late adolescents" were often young people finishing their educational training and entering the workforce in their late teens or early twenties. However, the current trend toward obtaining further education or training has extended the time of adolescence into emerging[1] or young adulthood, as youth prepare for their future adult roles (Arnett, 2015). The terms "young adult" and "emerging adult" will be used interchangeably throughout the volume. This volume thus focuses on issues of identity as they evolve over the course of adolescence through adulthood.

There is urgency and value in the scientific effort to advance knowledge about identity development. Identity remains vital to the individual psychological experience and it continues to have a social and political function that in some cases can work for the real benefit or detriment of particular groups of people (Hammack, 2014). For example, many of the worst conflicts in the world are fueled by what Wainryb and Recchia (2014, p. 3) called "polarized collective identities"; such an identity is rooted in

> a belief in the justness of one's ingroup goals, along with a simultaneous negation or delegitimization of the outgroup's perspective, as well as a

positive collective self-image (e.g., as courageous, fair, and humane) that is juxtaposed against a negative view of the outgroup.

(Wainryb & Recchia, 2014, p. 3)

Polarized collective identity can work as a shield against some of the harm caused when a young person is exposed to the violence and senselessness of war; however, such an identity may perpetuate conflicts for generations to come and can derail a young person's identity development and adaptation in the long-run (Wainryb & Recchia, 2014). Although finding oneself may at times appear to be a luxury, it is indeed essential to fostering youth development, harmony between social groups, and may even be essential to addressing some of the most pressing problems of the day. In keeping with these ideas, the general aim of this volume is to better understand the essence of adolescent and emerging/young adult identity through a variety of perspectives and special topics in order to encourage informed research and intervention strategies that will facilitate the identity formation process.

Up through the 1960s, much of the literature on adolescent psychology came from psychoanalytic treatment centers. There was often a stress on the "universality of ego weakness" in adolescence, and the depiction of an ego "besieged by the drives and unable to rely on the now-dangerous parental ego for support" (Josselson, 1980, p. 188). Such portrayals lay at the heart of the "turmoil" theory of adolescent development, which presented storm and stress as normative features of the teenage years. It was only when researchers of the 1960s and 1970s (e.g., Douvan & Adelson, 1966; Offer & Offer, 1974) began to find little evidence of psychopathology or even much storm and stress at all among large samples of adolescents in the general population of the United States that attention began to shift from clinical to more normative populations for an understanding of the developmental processes occurring during adolescence.

In the following decades, the millennials (the generation born after 1980) began their entrance into late adolescence and early adulthood. These younger members of society were noteworthy both for their ethnic diversity as well as their competence with the use of technology (Pew Research Center, 2010), which differentiated them from previous generations. General social attitudes toward adolescents and young adults have also been changing over these years, from considerable negative stereotyping about adolescent behaviors – rebellious, self-centered, and even delinquent ("Generation Me"; Twenge, 2006) – to the growing contemporary focus on youth and their many constructive capacities, likely an influence of several positive frameworks that have advanced what is known about youth development – that is, positive psychology, positive youth development, social and emotional learning (Tolan, Ross, Arkin, Godine, & Clark, 2016).

Adolescent identity development figures prominently as a target for intervention change in a diversity of current promotion and prevention intervention efforts with adolescents (e.g., Ferrer-Wreder, Montgomery, Lorente, & Habibi, 2014). Kurtines and his colleagues (e.g., Eichas, Montgomery, Meca, & Kurtines, 2017) have been involved in developing and evaluating positive youth development interventions that have a particular focus on supporting adolescent identity development, while Umaña-Taylor, Kornienko, Douglass Bayless, and Updegraff's (2018) intervention called the Identity Project has shown positive benefits in adolescents in groups with ethnic minority and majority social positions in the United States (Umaña-Taylor et al., 2018).

Literature on adolescent and emerging/young adult development has also mushroomed over the past decades, with the creation of both North American and European journals and societies devoted solely to research on these phases of the life cycle. Additionally, during these life stages, there has been greater specialization in textbook and journal offerings. A number of supplementary textbooks now deal with selected issues of adolescence and emerging adulthood, including the current volume on identity. Interest in identity has also been evidenced by the appearance of several new journals devoted solely to themes of self and/or identity.

It is the intention of this book to examine prominent theories and special topics related to identity development during adolescence and young adulthood. The task of identity formation, revision, and maintenance is a lifelong challenge, and this volume also highlights the role that adolescent identity resolutions play in ongoing development throughout adulthood. While some less than optimal identity outcomes will be presented, the focus of this volume rests primarily on those normative identity changes of adolescence that evolve slowly over time to set the foundations for entry into adult life.

Frankie's own identity struggles that opened this chapter may be understood through a variety of different lenses. Historical, sociocultural, and psychosocial traditions have all arisen to account for various dimensions of identity development during adolescence and beyond. Under these broad labels, a number of specific approaches to understanding identity development have evolved. It is our intention below to note only the general emphases within each basic tradition and to describe aspects of these approaches in more detail in the chapters that follow.

Historical approaches to adolescent identity

Were Frankie born in an earlier *historical* era, her story would probably not have given rise to a literary novel, for self-definition and finding a place in the world would not have been such a difficult problem. Berenice also would likely have held a somewhat different place in Frankie's identity struggles than she might at the time the story was set. As Erikson (1975) noted, the issue of identity holds historical relativity; Lifton (cited in Goren, 2017) has also addressed the power that general cultural values and group pressures have in a particular historical context to influence individual identity. Erikson (1975) suggested that identity only became a matter of concern in the United States late in the nineteenth century because a new generation of immigrants were attempting to define themselves in a land far removed from their ancestral homes. Baumeister (1986, 1987) and Burkitt (2011) have provided excellent and extensive overviews that illustrate the importance of historical times and forces to how identity is conceived and experienced in America and in other Western nations over time.

For example, in speaking to the Western European experience, Baumeister found that medieval adolescent and adult identities in these societies were defined in a very straightforward manner. The social rank and kinship network into which one was born determined one's place for life. While some changes of title or role were inevitable over time, general possibilities were circumscribed by the clan. In the early modern period, the rise of a middle class began a shift in the standard for self-definition, when wealth rather than kinship ties became the new measure of social status and hence self-definition. The later Protestant split and subsequent decline of the Christian faith gave rise to an era in which individuals became able to accept or reject the religious traditions of their forebears. During the Romantic era, most people still espoused Christian beliefs, but these held less influence over their daily lives. Furthermore, society was often perceived to be oppressive, and the need to reject some of its demands was recognized. By the Victorian era, late adolescents and adults increasingly began to reject Christian dogma and a focal concern was on whether or not morality could survive without religion. Thus, Victorian adolescents had to define their adult identities without clear guidelines in the midst of general cultural uncertainty regarding issues of appropriate values (Baumeister, 1986, 1987).

Such difficulties for adolescents in the United States and some Western European nations continued into the twentieth and twenty-first centuries, as the process of self-definition and identity formation became normative developmental tasks (Erikson, 1968). Cushman (1990) further suggested that, at least in the United States, the absence of community, tradition, and shared meaning created the conditions for an "empty self," a state of being in which adolescents and adults alike experienced chronic emotional hunger. Cushman argued that the "empty self" attempted to be soothed, to be "filled up" by consumer products, and that advertising and psychotherapy were the two professions that Cushman cited as being most involved in individuals' attempts to heal the "empty self." Almost two decades later, Damon (2008) was also concerned about the lack of a sense of a purposeful identity for many adolescents. However, there has also been recent movement, thanks to the influence of positive views on youth development to consider and support adolescents and young adults in their efforts to formulate meaningful identities within their social contexts (e.g., Ferrer-Wreder, Montgomery, Lorente, & Habibi, 2014). Thus, in historical terms, the issue of self-definition and identity formation, at least for many adolescents and young adults in the United States and in some Western European nations, is a relatively recent phenomenon (Baumeister, 1986, 1987). See Burkitt (2011) for an historical analysis that traces identity and self-related issues farther back in time, but also from a Western European social perspective.

Sociocultural approaches to adolescent identity

In her efforts toward self-definition, Frankie voiced her intense desire to break free – to be free of her family, town, and many of the sociocultural conditions that constrained her. Berenice, who is African American and the family housekeeper, said the following:

> "I think I have a vague idea what you were driving at," [responded Berenice]. "We all of us somehow caught. We born this way or that way and we don't know why. But we caught anyhow. . . . We each one of us somehow caught all by ourself. Is that what you was trying to say?"
>
> "I don't know," F. Jasmine said. "But I don't want to be caught."
>
> "Me neither," said Berenice. "Don't none of us. I'm caught worse than you is."
>
> F. Jasmine understood why she had said this, and it was John Henry [Frankie's younger brother] who asked in his child voice: "Why?"
>
> "Because I am black," said Berenice.
>
> (McCullers, 1946, p. 113)

Frankie and Berenice are "caught" by their social class, gender, and ethnicity as well as the technological influences, societal norms, and the legal requirements for adolescents and African Americans living in the South at that time. The socio-cultural conditions of society, some would contend, create problems of identity and self-definition in the first place (Baumeister, 1986, 1987).

A variety of theoretical orientations to identity are represented within the general sociocultural approach, ranging from proposals that identity is largely a reflection of an individual's adaptations to social and cultural conditions (e.g., Côté & Levine, 2002), to a focus on the reciprocal interactions between person and context (e.g., Galliher, McLean, & Syed, 2017; Rogoff, 2016), to the more radical suggestion that one's identity is merely an imprint of one's social and cultural surroundings (post-modern positions).

One group of writers working within this general sociocultural framework has focused more strongly on contextual implications that these conditions hold for individual identity formation. Triandis (1989), for example, differentiated "tight" from "loose" societies on the basis of how much opportunity for individual choice a society would allow. Thus, enormous variation may be seen across cultural con-texts in how much latitude youth are given for creating or realizing their identity interests. Adolescents in many collectivist societies are simply not faced with the choices and decisions that youths in cultures that allow for choice must make in defining their own identities (Côté & Levine, 2002). Tupuola (1993) interviewed New Zealand and Samoan-born youths living in New Zealand in focus groups about their experiences of adolescence. One Samoan-born participant summa-rized the responses of many as follows:

> I feel I still can't answer the adolescent thing. As a Samoan born, I had never heard of it [adolescence] until I came to New Zealand. I don't think it was part of my life because it is a western concept, and from a non-western society all those development stages didn't relate to me. All I know is that my *aiga* [family] and my community and my culture are important. They determine the way I behave, think, and feel. . . .

Sometimes I think that we [in Samoa] are children for most of our lives, and it can take a very long time for us to become adults. It does not matter how old you are, [for] if you are not considered worthy or responsible enough by your elders, then you will not be treated as an adult. You really have to earn your place in the Samoan culture. So adolescence as a developmental stage is foreign to our culture.

(Subject #3, Tupuola, 1993, pp. 308, 311)

Cultural conditions for this young woman made the issue of identity formation and finding her place in the social milieu a rather straightforward process. While some of the roles that she was expected to fulfill were not easy, the actual process of identifying suitable roles for herself within the larger society was not, in itself, a complex problem. Tupuola further reported that a number of participants in her study consulted Samoan dictionaries over the course of their interviews and were unable even to find a Samoan word meaning "adolescence."

The most radical of approaches to the person-in-context dilemma has come from the post-modernists. There are, again, many different schools of thinking adopting this general approach, but common to all is the denial of any general pattern of development across individuals, a delegitimizing of anything structural or hierarchical in form, of anything that is consistent across situations. Post-modernists consider the present to be "the end of the age of development" (e.g., Gergen, 1991) and a denial that there is any design to the course of change over time. When addressing issues of identity, post-modernists argue for the existence of multiple identities that are assumed in different contexts. Post-modernity emphasizes fragmentation, discontinuity, and only local rather than general themes. In the view of Rattansi and Phoenix (1997), identity is fluid and fragmented and not something that exists within the individual at all. Thus, we all have a range of identities, each having salience in a different context. Identity is also conceptualized by post-modernists as a culturally appropriated mode of discourse (e.g., Slugoski & Ginsburg, 1989). Many post-modernist thinkers would hear Frankie's narrative as an example of a teenager with fragmented identities, created through the language that she uses to tell her story. That story reflects identities created during the whims of the moment, lacking any central core or continuity across situations. Great discrepancies in the demands of various contexts induce "situated" identities, ultimately leading to a sense of no self or identity at all (Gergen, 1991).

Côté (2006, 2015) has nicely summarized a typology of several different and fundamental assumptions that various models of identity development take in describing the nature of the relationship between individual and society. These differences in approach are based on several factors: (1) whether the focus is primarily on the individual or on society in identity's formative process; (2) whether or not social reality is understood as fixed and independent of human consciousness (objectivism) or dependent on social constructions (subjectivism); and (3) whether or not the existing social order is accepted "as is" and represents a universal process or is viewed critically, wherein the researcher assumes that all identity processes are contextually based. All approaches to identity that are overviewed in this volume may be understood in terms of their answers to these basic assumptions. The sociocultural approach highlighted later in this book, is one that is highly visible in the field of human development and cultural psychology (e.g., Rogoff, 2016), and is focused on how the individual and context, including culture, come together to produce identity development.

Psychosocial approaches to adolescent identity

Social and historical circumstances have left teenagers from many Western, technologically complex cultures with ambiguous role prescriptions to struggle with the problem of identity. A number of social scientists, however, have focused more intently on what Frankie described as a changing sense of "I" – on an internal, psychological transformation of the sense of herself and consequent ways of making sense of her life experiences within changing social circumstances. The beginnings of psychological restructuring during adolescence in combination with societal responses have brought Frankie's identity questions to the surface, according to this view. And while sociocultural factors undoubtedly may accelerate, delay, or even arrest this process, this general view argues that sequential changes in the psychological transformation of the self and its way of understanding the world do exist. Changes in biological, cognitive, and affective processes have been deemed accountable for alterations to the subjective sense of identity frequently experienced during life's second decade – at least in those societies where adult identities for youth are not prescribed.

From psychodynamic beginnings, Erik Erikson's work was the first to appreciate the *psychosocial* nature of identity with the important role played by the community in recognizing, supporting, and thus helping to shape the adolescent ego. As a developmental theorist, he distinguished the identity solutions of *introjection* during infancy and *identification* in childhood from the process of *identity formation* during adolescence. It is during adolescence that Erikson saw opportunities for identity resolution through a synthesis that incorporated yet transcended all previous identifications to produce a new whole, based upon yet qualitatively different from that which had gone before:

> The final identity, then, as fixed at the end of adolescence, is superordinated to any single identification with individuals of the past: it includes all significant identifications, but it also alters them in order to make a unique and reasonably coherent whole of them.
>
> (Erikson, 1968, p. 161)

Here that self of childhood, derived from significant identifications with important others, must, during adolescence, give way to a self, based upon, yet transcending those foundations, to create a new whole greater than the sum of its parts. Significant others now become important not merely as potential sources of identification but rather as independent agents, helping to recognize and support the "real me." Erikson appreciated the importance of context to this process. He saw identity development also as a reciprocal relationship between individual and context, a process of recognizing and being recognized by others.

Peter Blos, more strongly than Erikson, maintained his alliance with classical psychodynamic traditions and focused more heavily on *intrapsychic changes* during adolescence and how they were supported (or not) by others. His portrayal of adolescence as a second individuation process paved the way for a new approach to the study of adolescent individuation and identity (or in his words, "character"). Blos (1967) built upon the groundbreaking work of Margaret Mahler and her colleagues (Mahler, Pine, & Bergman, 1975), who detailed the "psychological birth of the human infant" through intrapsychic separation and individuation processes. Blos noted that while the successful establishment of an autonomous self in life's earliest years rested upon the toddler's ability to incorporate or internalize an image of his or her primary caretaker, such intrapsychic organization hindered further development during adolescence and beyond. During the second individuation process, it was this very internalized parent that needed to be relinquished if development were to progress. Blos saw adolescence as a time of relinquishing the old intrapsychic arrangement of that which has been considered self (the parental introjects) and creating a new psychological structure, distinct from the old introjects and individuated in the expression of an adolescent's own genuine interests and desires. Blos found regressive thoughts and actions to be necessary for further development and to be common phenomena accompanying this loss of the childhood sense of self. A feeling of heightened distinctiveness from others as well as a new form of connection to them are the subjective experiences following successful adolescent individuation. Now others can be recognized and appreciated as agents in their own right rather than merely as internalized orchestrators of one's responses to life.

Narrative approaches to adolescent identity also draw many ideas from Erikson's original writings. Although somewhat varied in their emphases, narrative writers commonly underscore the process of autobiographical reasoning and how people make sense of their past experiences to create a coherent identity in the present that is projected and reevaluated in the future. The stories that one tells about one's life in an attempt to create a coherent identity are not intended to be an accurate portrayal of every life experience; rather, one chooses what is meaningful at a particular point in time and tries to make sense of the experience (McAdams, 2015). Whether or not one has an audience, a person works and reworks their life experiences through a narrative in an attempt to make some sense of things and to create an identity. Narratives generally aim to integrate questions about who I am now with how I came to be this way and where my life might be going next (McAdams, 2015). McLean (2008) and Fivush, Habermas, Waters, and Zaman (2011) noted that an optimal narrative identity helps individuals find purpose and meaning in life and a sense of coherence and unity within themselves; at the same time, an optimal narrative should be flexible and enable one to incorporate new insights, life lessons, and experiences over time. Coherence in one's narrative likely reflects a sense of identity continuity over time, while "irreconcilable differences between the me-that-was and the me-that-is can be understood as incoherence in identity" (Pasupathi, 2014, p. 21).

Adolescent identity in the context of life-span development

While various schools of thought place different emphases on the role of the individual and the social and/or cultural setting in the identity formation process of adolescence and young adulthood, most conceptualize identity formation as a lifelong enterprise. Thus, this volume also emphasizes adolescent and emerging adult identity development in a manner reflecting this understanding. Just as the significance of a painting cannot be fully grasped without knowledge of its contextual origins and resulting influences on later art, so identity and its development and eventual consolidation during adolescence and young adulthood cannot be fully appreciated without knowledge of its childhood antecedents and consequent adult possibilities.

Identity as the balance between self and other

Despite usages of different identity-related concepts in contemporary theories of adolescent and young adult identity development, a basic commonality is present as one looks across the general theoretical approaches to the essence of identity. In some way, shape or form, identity is commonly defined as a balance or interaction between that considered to be self and that considered to be other. The means by which we differentiate ourselves from other people in our lives as we become aware of our own organic functions constitutes the very core of our experience of personal identity. American novelist Thomas Wolfe struggled through his life to differentiate his own identity from that internalized image of his primary caretaker. This intrapsychic battle was replayed in many of his adolescent and adult relationships: "His popularity [as a writer] is partially due to his being a chronicler of the human aspirations for individuation, for the establishment of a real self, as well as of the feelings of loss associated with this search" (Masterson, 1986). Though using differing terms and concepts, Erikson, Blos, McAdams, Pasupathi, Côté, Rogoff, Rivas-Drake and others all provide descriptions of how the balancing and rebalancing of boundaries between self and other produce more differentiated experiences of identity as well as new forms of relationship with other people and social groups at various life stages. Adolescence encompasses one phase of heightened activity for most in this intrapsychic and interpersonal juggling act.

The structure of this volume and its chapters

In the preparation for a new edition of any volume, there is a temptation in updating information to delete "older" material, leaving the reader with a clear sense of what research is currently being undertaken but with little or no appreciation for the foundations upon which that current research has been built. In this volume, we certainly have updated new trends in identity theory and research from a variety of perspectives and present the most current information on key topics of contemporary interest in the field, but we have also retained a focus on the origins of these concepts and their development through their conceptions to the present time. In this way, we hope that readers will have a deeper appreciation of the origins of identity concepts and how they have been modified and adapted through the years to arrive at current understandings and research trends, along with the implications that current work holds for social response.

With this long-range, overview goal in mind, the initial four chapters of this volume begin with theory and view identity development during adolescence and young adulthood with varying emphases placed on the role of the individual and the role of the environment in this process. The following two chapters deal with special identity issues particularly impacting the current generation of youths – those of intersectionality as it relates to gender and sexuality as well as technology and how each affects and is affected by the identity formation process of adolescence. The concluding chapter places the identity formation process of adolescence and young adulthood within the context of life-span identity development, focusing, in particular, on the how the resolutions to identity issues of adolescence may have long-term implications for ongoing developments during adulthood.

The four theoretical chapters (Chapters 2–5) follow a similar pattern of presentation. One major theorist and/or researcher, who has played a key role in the development of the particular approach to identity, is introduced at the chapter's beginning. A brief biographical statement is presented as a way of illustrating the historical context of important ideas in the field, as well as to provide the reader with a sense of the excitement of discovery and striving after innovation that comes from the study of identity development as viewed by that scholar. Key components of identity from this theoretical perspective are presented, followed by a statement of what constitutes an optimal identity from this particular orientation. Criticisms of the construct are detailed as well as an overview of the historical backdrop to key ideas. The focus then turns to research measures that have been developed to assess key dimensions of the adolescent identity formation process within this framework, as well as major research findings that have appeared over time. A section on current trends in identity research follows, and a discussion of the implications that each theory holds for social response in the promotion of optimal identity development for adolescents and young adults concludes each theoretical chapter presented in this volume.

Two subsequent chapters (Chapters 6 and 7) then turn to explore the concept of intersectionality and identity integration with reference to gender and sexuality as well as technology and social media use as a catalyst for adolescent identity formation. Intersectionality and the concept of identity integration emphasize the importance of understanding identity in its totality and complexity. In Chapter 6, attention is placed on the particular intersection of adolescent gender and sexuality, as an illustration of research that crosses boundaries and offers guidelines for advances in future research practice (Cole, 2009). In Chapter 7, there is an exploration of the relatively new research field on adolescent identity development in digital landscapes. Even though this is a new field, exciting studies are being launched and several future directions for research are already evident.

A concluding chapter focuses on the role that identity resolutions of adolescence and young adulthood have for ongoing facets of identity development over the course of adulthood. The chapter examines available theory and research across the models examined in this volume to focus on some of the normative changes in identity that are likely to occur through ongoing phases of adult life. The chapter considers dimensions of one's identity formed during adolescence and young adulthood that are likely both to remain stable and to change over time. It also questions whether or not there are different types of contexts that may be associated with different patterns of identity stability and change during adult life. And in conclusion, it considers how adolescent resolutions to identity are likely to impact one's capacity for intimacy, generativity, and integrity during adult life.

Summary

The general aim of this volume is to understand how adolescents and young adults navigate through life, more or less successfully, to develop a sense of who they are and how they can best find personal satisfaction in the adult worlds of love and work. The volume also highlights the ways in which context interacts with individual factors to shape individual identity pathways. Four models of adolescent identity formation are presented, accompanied by critical comment, reviews of related research, and a discussion of the implications that each theory holds for social response to promote optimal development. Each model is based on particular assumptions, focuses on specific understandings of identity, adopts particular research methods, holds particular views about the role of context in development, and describes differing mechanisms for change in addition to differing implications for social response. Contemporary meanings of gender and sexuality as well as technology and social media use may play a particular role in the identity formation experience of many adolescents, and the roles of these changing social forces on adolescent identity development are reviewed. A discussion of the place that adolescent identity formation holds in ongoing identity development during adulthood and the role that adolescent identity resolutions have for addressing issues of intimacy, generativity, and integrity during adult life conclude this volume. Einstein once noted it is the theory that decides what we can observe. It is hoped that the theoretical approaches and special identity topics presented in this volume, however, will in no way set limits to future ways of understanding, researching, and responding to the identity formation process of adolescence.

Note

1 Emerging adulthood (18 to 29 years old) is posited to be descriptive of people who delay some aspects of the transition to adulthood, either in terms of their own view of themselves as an adult and/or in terms of individuals delaying some objective social markers of adulthood (Arnett, 2015). In Arnett's view, young adulthood refers to chronologically younger individuals who are adults in their cultures, in relation to subjective and objective indicators (Arnett, 2015). However, others writing about identity have used

the term young adulthood to refer to those in the decade of the twenties or to working or unemployed youths who have completed their years of formal education (e.g., Luyckx and colleagues in some of their identity studies, such as Luyckx & Robitschek, 2014). We have thus opted to use the terms emerging and young adulthood interchangeably in this book.

References

Arnett, J. J. (2015). *Emerging adulthood: The winding road from the late teens through the twenties* (2nd ed.). New York, NY: Oxford University Press.

Baumeister, R. F. (1986). *Identity: Cultural change and the struggle for self.* New York, NY: Oxford University Press.

Baumeister, R. F. (1987). How the self became a problem: A psychological review. *Journal of Personality and Social Psychology, 52,* 163–176.

Blos, P. (1967). The second individuation process of adolescence. *Psychoanalytic Study of the Child, 22,* 162–186.

Burkitt, I. (2011). Identity construction in sociohistorical context. In S. J. Schwartz, K. Luyckx, & V. L. Vignoles (Eds.), *Handbook of identity theory and research, Vol. 1* (pp. 267–283). New York, NY: Springer.

Cole, E. R. (2009). Intersectionality and research in psychology. *American Psychologist, 64,* 170–180.

Côté, J. E. (2006). Identity studies: How close are we to developing a social science of identity? An Appraisal of the field. *Identity: An International Journal of Theory and Research, 6,* 3–25.

Côté, J. E. (2015). Identity formation research from a critical perspective: Is a social science developing? In K. C. McLean & M. Syed (Eds.), *Oxford handbook of identity development* (pp. 527–538). New York, NY: Oxford University Press.

Côté, J. E., & Levine, C. (2002). *Identity formation, agency, and culture: A social psychological synthesis.* Mahwah, NJ: Lawrence Erlbaum Associates.

Cushman, P. (1990). Why the self is empty. *American Psychologist, 45,* 599–611.

Damon, W. (2008). *The path to purpose: Helping our children find their purpose in life.* New York, NY: Simon & Schuster.

Douvan, E., & Adelson, J. (1966). *The adolescent experience.* New York, NY: Wiley.

Eichas, K., Montgomery, M. J., Meca, A., & Kurtines, W. M. (2017). Empowering marginalized youth: A self-transformative intervention for promoting positive youth development. *Child Development, 88,* 1115–1124.

Erikson, E. H. (1968). *Identity youth and crisis.* New York, NY: W. W. Norton.

Erikson, E. H. (1975). *Life history and the historical moment.* New York, NY: W. W. Norton.

Ferrer-Wreder, L. A., Montgomery, M. J., Lorente, C. C., & Habibi, M. (2014). Promoting optimal identity development in adolescents. In T. P. Gullotta & M. Bloom (Eds.), *Encyclopedia for primary prevention intervention for adolescents* (pp.1278–1287). New York, NY: Springer Science + Business Media.

Fivush, R., Habermas, T., Waters, T. E. A., & Zaman, W. (2011). The making of autobiographical memory: Intersections of culture, narratives and identity. *International Journal of Psychology, 46,* 321–345.

Galliher, R. V., McLean, K. C., & Syed, M. (2017). An integrated developmental model for studying identity content in context. *Developmental Psychology, 53,* 2011–2022.

Gergen, K. J. (1991). *The saturated self: Dilemmas of identity in contemporary life.* New York, NY: Basic Books.

Goren, E. (2017). The analyst as witness, historian, and activist: A conversation with Robert J. Lifton. In E. R. Goren, & J. L. Alpert (Eds.) *Psychoanalysis, trauma, and community: History and contemporary reappraisals* (p. 165). New York, NY: Routledge.

Hammack, P. L. (2014). Theoretical foundations of identity. In K. C. McLean, & M. Syed (Eds.), *The Oxford handbook of identity development* [E-reader version] (pp. 1–37). New York, NY: Oxford University Press. doi: 10.1093/oxfordhb/9780199936564.013.027

Josselson, R. (1980). Ego development in adolescence. In J. Adelson (Ed.), *Handbook of adolescent psychology* (pp. 186–199). New York, NY: Wiley.

Luyckx, K., & Robitschek, C. (2014). Personal growth initiative and identity formation in adolescence through young adulthood: Mediating processes on the pathway to well-being. *Journal of Adolescence, 37,* 973–981.

Mahler, M. S., Pine, F., & Bergman, A. (1975). *The psychological birth of the human infant.* New York, NY: Basic Books.

Masterson, J. F. (1986). Creativity as a vehicle to establish a real self: Jean Paul Sartre, Edvard Munch, Thomas Wolfe. In J. F. Masterson (Ed.), *The real self: A developmental and object relations approach* (cassette recording 4). New York, NY: Masterson Group.

McAdams, D. P. (2015). Three lines of personality development: A conceptual itinerary. *European Psychologist, 20,* 252–264.

McCullers, C. (1946). *Member of the wedding.* New York, NY: Houghton Mifflin Company.

McLean, K. C. (2008). Stories of the young and the old: Personal continuity and narrative identity. *Developmental Psychology, 44,* 254–264.

Offer, D., & Offer, J. (1974). Normal adolescent males: The high school and college years. *Journal of the American College Health Association, 22,* 209–215.

Pasupathi, M. (2014). Autobiographical reasoning and my discontent: Alternative paths from narrative to identity. In K. C. McLean, & M. Syed (Eds.), *The Oxford handbook of identity development* [E-reader version] (pp. 1–30). New York, NY: Oxford University Press. doi: 10.1093/oxfordhb/9780199936564.013.002

Pew Research Center (2010). *Millennials: Confident, connected, and open to change.* Washington, DC: Pew Research Center.

Rattansi, A., & Phoenix, A. (1997). Rethinking youth identities: modernist and postmodernist frameworks. In J. Bynner, L. Chisholm & A. Furlong (Eds.), *Youth, citizenship and social change in a European context* (pp. 121–150). Aldershot: Ashgate.

Rogoff, B. (2016). Culture and participation: A paradigm shift. *Current Opinion in Psychology, 8,* 182–189.

Slugoski, B. R., & Ginsburg, G. P (1989). Ego identity and explanatory speech. In J. Shotter & K. J. Gergen (Eds.), *Texts of identity* (pp. 36–55). London: Sage.

Tolan, P., Ross, K., Arkin, N., Godine, N., & Clark, E. (2016). Toward an integrated approach to positive development: Implications for intervention. *Applied Developmental Science, 20,* 214–236.

Triandis, H. C. (1989). The self and social behavior in differing cultural contexts. *Psychological Review, 96,* 506–520.

Tupuola, A. M. (1993). Critical analysis of adolescent development – a Samoan women's perspective. Unpublished master's thesis, Victoria University of Wellington, New Zealand.

Twenge, J. M. (2006). *Generation me: Why today's young Americans are more confident, assertive, entitled – and more miserable than ever before.* New York, NY: Free Press.

Umaña-Taylor, A. J., Kornienko, O., Douglass Bayless, S., & Updegraff, K. A. (2018). A universal intervention program increases ethnic-racial identity exploration and resolution to predict adolescent psychosocial functioning one year later. *Journal of Youth and Adolescence*, *47*, 1–15.

Wainryb, C., & Recchia, H. (2014). Youths' constructions of meanings about experiences with political conflict: Implications for processes of identity development. In K. C. McLean, & Syed, M. (Ed.), *The Oxford handbook of identity development* [E-reader version] (pp. 1–33). New York, NY: Oxford University Press. doi: 10.1093/oxfordhb/9780199936564.013.008

2 Adolescence as identity synthesis

Erikson's psychosocial approach

> Siddhartha reflected deeply as he went on his way. He realized that he was no longer a youth; he was now a man. He realized that something had left him, like the old skin that a snake sheds. Something was no longer in him, something that had accompanied him right through his youth and was part of him: this was the desire to have teachers and to listen to their teachings. He had left the last teacher he had met, even he, the greatest and wisest teacher, the holiest, the Buddha. He had to leave him; he could not accept his teachings.
>
> (Hermann Hesse, *Siddhartha*, 1951, p. 30)

In his novel *Siddhartha*, Hermann Hesse movingly recounted the journey of a man in search of his own identity. The story opened in an idyllic communal setting along a sunny and tranquil river bank (complete with fig tree), as Siddhartha sensed the first nuances of inner discontent. Family and friends alike loved and admired the handsome and supple Siddhartha, and his destiny as a prince among Brahmins was the fate envisaged by all for this great Brahmin's son. For Siddhartha, however, knowledge of such a future brought no satisfaction or peace of mind. After a final meditation, the young man announced his intention of joining the Samanas, a wandering group of ascetics who practiced a lifestyle in all ways contrary to the values held dear by childhood friends and mentors. Through such action, Siddhartha's single goal was to let the self die, to become empty, to become something other than himself. Despite all efforts of self-denial through pain, hunger, thirst, and fatigue, however, Siddhartha could not escape his own existence. After several unsatisfying years with the Samanas, Siddhartha once more sought new hope for peace by testing the way of the Buddha in conquering the self. After a short time it became clear, however, that such efforts would also fail to bring salvation, and it is at this point that we met Siddhartha ruminating on his newfound learnings in the opening quotation, as he left the grove of the Buddha. It seemed that neither complete identification with childhood's teachers nor their complete banishment from his existence could help Siddhartha to solve the riddle of the self and so structure an identity that would see him through (or at least into) adult life. Perhaps no piece of literature so adequately and accurately anticipates the themes central to Erikson's writings on identity formation during adolescence, and it is to Siddhartha we later return for illumination of Erikson's concepts.

Erik Erikson was the first psychoanalytic writer to enquire seriously into the phenomenon of identity formation during adolescence. His approach was based upon, but diverged in important ways from, Freud's biologically based psychosexual orientation to personality development. Erikson moved beyond classic psychoanalysis with its focus on the id and libidinal drivers of development to emphasize the ego and its adaptive capacities in the environment. Rather than viewing others as objects of cathexis important to intrapsychic functioning as did Freud, Erikson saw others as interacting with and regulating the ego to provide a context in which the self could find meaning and coherence. Moving beyond Freud's goal of raising human misery to mere unhappiness, Erikson painted not only a more optimistic picture of human capabilities, but also shifted the emphasis of psychoanalysis from pathology to healthy functioning. Finally, Erikson recognized that personality development did not end in adolescence but rather continued to evolve throughout the life-span.

Erikson the person

Erikson was born in Germany in 1902 to Danish parents. His birth was the result of an affair his mother had following the break-up of her first marriage. Erikson was raised by his mother and German pediatrician stepfather, whom his mother had met when Erik was three years old. Erikson did not learn of the circumstances of his biological parentage until adolescence. However, a sense of being "different" both as a stepson in a reconstituted family and as a blond, blue-eyed Dane growing up in a German Jewish community pervaded much of Erikson's childhood. Questions regarding his biological father preoccupied Erikson's attentions throughout much of his life (Friedman, 1999). Upon graduating from high school and with no particular career plans, young Erikson was drawn to the role of an artist, a "passing" identity providing some income while still allowing the young man a much needed psychosocial moratorium before choosing his life's work. Additionally, sketching gave training in the recording of impressions, a skill vital to his later profession. The artist's vocational choice also made a definitive statement to his stepfather about the role in medicine the elder physician had envisaged for his stepson. From late adolescence, Erikson traveled throughout Europe until his mid-twenties (Hopkins, 1995). He later responded to Robert Coles's questioning about his youth: "Yes, if ever an identity crisis was central and drawn out in somebody's life, it was so in mine" (Coles, 1970, p. 180).

It was eventually the invitation of childhood friend Peter Blos to join the staff of a small school in Vienna that placed Erikson in a position to meet Freud's inner circle (Friedman, 1999). In Vienna, he was invited by Anna Freud to train and prepare to become a child psychoanalyst. Again, not quite belonging to Freud's community of medical rebels, Erikson's stepson relationship to the psychoanalytic profession did not furnish him with a more settled sense of vocational identity until much later, when his own artistic talents could be integrated with his psychoanalytic practice through theoretical writing – the sketching of impressions through linguistic rather than visual form. It was there in Vienna that Erikson also married Canadian Joan Serson, who became his intellectual partner and editor for the rest of his life (Hopkins, 1995).

Erikson and Joan left Vienna with their two young sons as Hitler came to power in Germany, and they eventually migrated to Boston where a psycho-analytic association had recently been formed. It was in this social context that Erikson, one of the society's few non-medical members, found a professional niche as one of the area's first practicing child analysts (Friedman, 1999). Throughout his impressive career, Erikson accepted appointments at Yale, the University of California, Berkeley, the Austin Riggs Center, and Harvard, all without accruing a single earned academic degree beyond high school. It was in 1950 that Erikson's theoretical framework was adopted in total by the White House Conference on Children that provided a national charter for child and adolescent development in the United States. In 1978, Harvard University awarded Erikson an honorary doctorate and later established the Erik H. and Joan M. Erikson Center to provide a forum for interdisciplinary studies of the life cycle. Erikson died in 1994 following a brief illness, just prior to his ninety-second birthday.

It is not surprising that the theme of identity so central to Erikson's own life became central in his writings on life-cycle development. Now, with at least ten books and a collection of individual papers dedicated to examining the nature of identity formation during adolescence and the life cycle, Erikson's contributions are an appropriate starting point for enquiries into adolescent identity development.

The nature of ego identity

What then is identity and how does it develop during adolescence? Erikson first used the term "ego identity" to describe a central disturbance among some return-ing Second World War veterans who were experiencing a loss of sameness and continuity in their lives:

> What impressed me most was the loss in these men of a sense of identity. They knew who they were; they had a personal identity. But it was as if sub-jectively, their lives no longer hung together – and never would again. There was a central disturbance in what I then started to call ego identity.
>
> (Erikson, 1968, p. 42)

He continued by noting that it was often a decisive yet innocent moment in the lives of these soldiers wherein the needs of a man's social group, those of his biological organism, and those idiosyncratic to his own development and family history met in irreconcilable conflict, heralding the breakdown of personal mean-ing and life continuity.

Several concepts basic to Erikson's later work emerged from the observation of these veterans. First, identity seemed to be most easily definable through its absence or loss; it was only when one could no longer take for granted the fabric of one's unique existence that identity's foundational threads became exposed and more clearly apparent. It was through such loss of ego identity or its developmental failure that opportunity existed for understanding more normative modes of identity formation and the means by which society could foster optimal development. Erikson's clinical experience also sensitized him to questions of how identity formed and developed for the wider non-patient population.

Furthermore, the soldiers' tales brought the tripartite nature of identity into view. Freud had left psychoanalysis focused on the role played by biology in personality development. However, a somewhat dissatisfied Erikson believed that traditional psychoanalysis could not capture the real meaning of identity, for it did not have a means to understand the impact of the environment on individual personality development (Erikson, 1968). While biology was important to individual biography, so too were an individual's life history as well as the presiding cultural and historical context, argued the analyst. For one medical officer veteran who came to Erikson's attention, it was the combination of lowered group morale in his unit followed by group panic over loss of leadership (social and historical context), physical fatigue and illness (biological state), and his lifelong denial of anger following a traumatic childhood incident (individual life history) that culminated in his loss of ego identity and eventual treatment. Erikson conceptualized and defined identity in an interdisciplinary way; he believed that biological endowment, personal organization of experience, and cultural milieu all interact to give meaning, form and continuity to one's unique existence.

Following his initial statements on identity, Erikson was persuaded to expand and elaborate the construct. As a psychosocial phenomenon, he saw identity rooted both within the individual as well as within the communal culture (Erikson, 1970). Subjectively, the theorist suggested what it feels like to have a sense of identity by citing a letter from William James to his wife:

> A man's character is discernible in the mental or moral attitude in which, when it came upon him, he felt himself most deeply and intensely active and alive. At such moments there is a voice inside which speaks and says: "*This* is the real me!"
>
> (James, cited in Erikson, 1968, p. 199)

One knows when identity is present, in greater or lesser degree. For the individual, identity is partly conscious and partly unconscious. It gives one's life a feeling of sameness and continuity, purpose and direction, yet also a "quality of unselfconscious living"; it is also taken for granted by those in possession of it. Identity involves conflict. During adolescence, identity development involves a time when biological endowment and intellectual processes must eventually meet societal expectations for a suitable display of adult functioning. Identity depends upon the past and determines the future; rooted in childhood, it serves as a base from which to meet later life tasks (Erikson, 1970). Erikson (1968) did not elaborate in similar detail on the "social" side of the psychosocial partnership, though he did stress the importance of the social context in providing the child with something to value and adhere to. Erikson also viewed identity as a generational issue, pointing to the responsibility of adults to provide an ideological framework for its youth (if only for the purpose of giving adolescents a structure against which to rebel and forge their own values).

Identity: development and resolutions

Perhaps Erikson's most concise account of how identity develops is to be found in *Toys and Reasons*: "[T]he process of identity formation depends on the interplay of what young persons at the end of childhood have come to mean to themselves and what they now appear to mean to those who become significant to them" (Erikson, 1977, p. 106). This deceptively simple statement is based upon a number of developmental principles basic to Erikson's concept of identity. The theorist distinguished identity formation, which generally occurs during adolescence, from the childhood processes of introjection and identification. That first sense of "I," he suggested, emerged only through the trustful interplay with a parental figure during infancy (Erikson, 1968). It was in the experience of a safe relationship that the child comes to know itself as distinct from its beloved developmental partner. At this point, *introjection*, or the incorporation of another's image, operated and prepared the way for more mature forms of identity resolution. During childhood "being like" admired others and assuming their roles and values reflects the mechanism of *identification* as the primary means by which the self is structured. It is only when the adolescent is able to select some and discard other childhood identifications in accordance with his or her interests, talents and values that *identity formation* occurs. Identity formation involves a synthesis of these earlier identifications into a new configuration, based upon but different from the sum of its individual parts. It is a process also dependent on social response; identity formation relies on the way society "identifies the young individual, recognizing him as somebody who had to become the way he[1] is and who, being the way he is, is taken for granted" (Erikson, 1968, p. 159). Thus, identity does not first emerge during adolescence, but rather evolves through earlier stages of development and continues to be reshaped throughout the life cycle.

Erikson used the term *epigenesis* to describe this property of identity development as well as broader aspects of personality change. Meaning literally "upon" (*epi*) "emergence" (*genesis*), epigenesis implies that "one item develops on top of another in space and time" (Evans, 1967, pp. 21–22). Suffice it to say at this point that identity formation during adolescence emerges from what young people (through their introjections and identifications) at the end of childhood come to know as their selves. Yet it also transcends these earlier forms in the individual's realization and society's recognition of personal interests and talents.

To return now to Siddhartha and his beleaguered quest: in his journey, this Brahmin's son tried many means by which Erikson suggested identity resolution was possible. Through his childhood years, Siddhartha appeared successfully to have internalized and identified with his father and the later vocational, ideological, and sexual roles he was expected to play as an up-and-coming Brahmin priest. We are told of his father's happiness in watching the son grow up to become a great priest among Brahmins. A psychosocial *foreclosure* appeared well on the way, whereby Siddhartha seemed prepared to step into predetermined roles in his family and culture. While Erikson did not detail this identity solution, it has been elaborated through empirical research which will be presented in a later section of this chapter.

Soon, however, shadows passed across Siddhartha's eyes and a restlessness made its presence known as he began to feel the beginnings of discontentment within. The late adolescent's decision to join a group of wandering ascetics whose values presented a diametric contrast to all those of his own heritage seemed to be a choice of *negative identity*. Such a solution for Siddhartha illustrates the ego's attempt to adhere to something distinctly other than its past, to go beyond the bounds of given experience and to begin anew. Here, there was no synthesis of previous identifications to give some foundation to later identity, but rather an effort to jettison all identifications and start the task of creating a self completely different from its origins. Siddhartha attempted to cancel his previous self through denial of physical needs and the self-destructive infliction of pain. Erikson commented on such a form of negative identity resolution:

> Such vindictive choices of a negative identity represent, of course, a desperate attempt at regaining some mastery in a situation in which the available positive identity elements cancel each other out. The history of such a choice reveals a set of conditions in which it is easier for the patient to derive a sense of identity out of a total identification with that which he is least supposed to be than to struggle for a feeling of reality in acceptable roles which are unattainable with his inner means.
>
> (Erikson, 1968, p. 176)

For some troubled adolescents, it is better to be somebody totally other than what existed during childhood rather than struggle to reintegrate the past into a present and future having some continuity with one's previous existence. There is often much relief following the choice of a negative identity, however destructive that solution may ultimately be.

For Siddhartha, however, that relief did not come. His realization came that complete immersion in the "contra-culture" of the Samanas' community and later Buddhist collective failed to solve the riddle of his existence. He departed, and it is at this point that the young man continued his ruminations that opened this chapter:

> The reason why I do not know anything about myself, the reason why Siddhartha has remained alien and unknown to myself is due to one thing, to one single thing – I was afraid of myself, I was fleeing from myself. . . . I wished to destroy myself . . . in order to find in the unknown innermost, the

> nucleus of all things. . . . But by doing so, I lost myself on the way. . . . [Now]
> I will learn from myself, be my own pupil; I will learn from myself the secret
> of Siddhartha.
>
> (Hesse, 1951, pp. 30–31)

At this point Siddhartha entered a *moratorium* that carried him in search of different roles that allowed greater possibilities for synthesizing and integrating all that had gone before. Anxiety, however, soon became his companion:

> [A]n icy chill stole over him. . . . Previously when in deepest meditation, he
> was still his father's son, he was still a Brahmin of high standing, a religious
> man. Now he was only Siddhartha . . .
>
> (Hesse, 1951, p. 33)

Siddhartha's realization brought with it a new challenge for development: to *achieve* an identity, a sense of self that synthesized earlier identifications into a new whole that was now uniquely his own.

Siddhartha's life is a case study of the evolution of identity from adolescence into old age. After experiencing many roles and building various lifestyles that fit his innermost needs at the time, Siddhartha returned in his old age to the river over which many of his earlier life journeys had crossed and beside which he eventually found peace. Through many inward and external travels in adult life, Siddhartha demonstrated how the achievement of an identity does not remain fixed, resolved once and for all, but rather is constantly open to change through shifting needs and circumstances:

> Such a sense of identity is never gained nor maintained once and for all. Like
> a good conscience, it is constantly lost and regained, although more lasting
> and more economical methods of maintenance and restoration are evolved
> and fortified in late adolescence.
>
> (Erikson, 1956, p. 74)

An optimal sense of identity

If soma, ego, and society have done their jobs, what should be present by the end of adolescence and the beginnings of early adulthood? Subjectively, there should be a sense of well-being: "Its most obvious concomitants are a feeling of being at home in one's body, a sense of 'knowing where one is going' and an inner assuredness of anticipated recognition from those who count" (Erikson, 1968, p. 165). With its psychosocial connotation, optimal identity formation should show itself through commitment to those work roles, values, and sexual orientations that best fit one's own unique combination of needs and talents within a context that both recognizes and supports these choices. It is this more directly observable commitment feature of ego identity that has been at the heart of most empirical attempts to address some of identity's many properties.

Identity as a stage in the life-cycle scheme

As hinted previously, identity has a past. Erikson portrayed identity as the fifth stage in an eight-act sequence of life conflicts one encounters along the road from birth to death in old age. While the primary focus in this chapter is on identity, it nevertheless is important to appreciate the contribution that both earlier and later acts make to the complete life drama.

Erikson conceptualized the life cycle as a series of stages, critical periods of development which involved bipolar conflict that must be addressed and resolved before one can proceed unhindered. According to the epigenetic principle, each stage had a critical time of emergence, which contributed, in turn, to the functional whole. There is a proper rate and sequence of development; the child must crawl before she can walk.

The polarity of each stage presented a crisis, a crucial turning point where development must make a move for better or for worse as one oriented to the physical environment as well as social and historical context: "Each successive stage and crisis has a special relation to one of the basic elements of society, and this for the simple reason that the human life cycle and man's institutions have evolved together" (Erikson, 1963, p. 250). The developmental possibilities of each stage do not demand "either/or" resolutions, but rather some dynamic balance of "more or less" between the poles; hopefully that balance favors the positive end. Erikson described his fifth stage, which came to the fore during adolescence, as that of *identity versus role confusion*. Here, as mentioned earlier, the young person is faced with the psychosocial dilemma of synthesizing yet transcending earlier identifications of childhood to realize aptitudes in social roles, while the community, in turn, provides its recognition and contribution to an individual's sense of self. Ironically, it may be one's willingness to undergo times of temporary uncertainty that gives the achievement resolution its ultimate strength. Stage resolutions should not be regarded as achievement scales based only on the more positive pole; they represent a balance between positive and negative poles that determine an individual's characteristic mode of adapting to the environment. One does not, however, enter the life drama during the fifth identity formation act. Identity versus role confusion has been preceded by four earlier stages, each having a necessary place in the unfolding chain of life-cycle tasks. All of Erikson's eight stages are now briefly reviewed to illustrate their relationships to the identity crisis of adolescence.

Trust versus mistrust/hope

As the opening scene in the life-cycle production, *trust versus mistrust* sets the stage for all that is to follow. It is during infancy that the developmental crisis of trust is met, based in part on Freud's biological concern with early oral experience. Through the mutual regulation and interaction between caretaker and infant, a rudimentary sense of ego identity is born. The child comes to know itself in relation to another and gains a sense of inner continuity, sameness, and trust in itself and its developmental partner.

In her short story "The door of life," Enid Bagnold (1972) described the inter-actions between a mother and her 4-day-old infant that reflected the building blocks of basic trust. The mother was finely attuned to the child's movements, as she worked to set some kind of order and rhythm into the baby's life. Mother tried to keep too much stimulation from the child at bay, so that her baby became able to enjoy her gaze and respond to expected routines. This heightened sensitivity of both players to the nuances of each other's movements illustrates the importance of mutuality to development. The quality of the caretaker's messages gives the infant a sense that it is all right to be, to be oneself, and to become "what other people trust one will become" (Erikson, 1963, p. 249).

Somewhere between the polar extremes of trust and mistrust, most of us find an adaptive balance; neither complete trust nor complete mistrust of the world are ultimately beneficial. An optimal resolution to this infant crisis has scales tipped more firmly toward the trusting pole, leading to *hope*, which in turn is the basic ingredient for later survival. It is also through this dynamic balance that a sense of "I," as one who can hope emerges to serve as the very rudimentary foundation for identity in adolescence.

Autonomy versus shame and doubt/will

Following the sense of basic trust, life's next developmental hurdle during the second and third years is that of developing autonomy. Again, finding a biologi-cal base in Freud's anal stage of development, Erikson's sense of autonomy is characterized by the child's increasing awareness of its self through control of bodily functions and expression of other motor and linguistic skills (performing in concert with the expectations of important others in the social milieu).

Holding on or letting go of body wastes is one of the child's earliest oppor-tunities to exercise complete control over the outcome of events, regardless of parental desire. Such auspicious occasions as toilet-training episodes provide tod-dlers with an experience of *will*, something that originates from within in response to social conditions and highlights the issue that wills of developmental partners can differ. With *trust* in order, it is now possible to risk one's own *will* against the response that such self-expression might bring. This "counterpointing of identi-ties" again carries the rudiments of later adolescent identity.

Newfound linguistic and locomotor skills conspire to aid the development of autonomy during toddlerhood. By the age of two and a half years, the child is using the personal pronoun "I" (as well as the declarative "no") to give further evidence of will. Now possessing the motoric status of "one who can walk," one is also in a position to encounter social response, for better or worse. The account of sociali-zation experiences of a young Papago Indian girl cited by Erikson illustrate again the role of the social environment in aiding and abetting this developmental task:

[T]he man of the house turned to his three-year-old granddaughter and asked her to close the door. The door was heavy and hard to shut. The child tried, but it did not move. Several times the grandfather repeated: "Yes, close the door." No one jumped to the child's assistance. No one took the responsibility away from her. On the other hand, there was no impatience, for after all the child was small. They sat gravely waiting until the child succeeded and her grandfather gravely thanked her. It was assumed the task would not be asked of her unless she could perform it, and having been asked, the responsibility was hers alone just as if she were a grown woman.

(Erikson, 1963, p. 236)

Such an experience of personal autonomy in completing a difficult task was met with a social response that could only convey a sense of respect for and recognition of the child's developing sense of self.

Like all of Erikson's stages, an adaptive balance between the two extremes is necessary for optimal development. When the scale is weighted towards shame and doubt, one retains a sense of inferiority, of being "not good enough" through all of life's later stages. As a corollary, however, it is knowledge that one is fallible and capable of evoking a less than favorable social response that tempers absolute autonomy and serves to regulate the self in a social order.

Initiative versus guilt/purpose

The third act of Erikson's life drama is met during the preschool years and coincides with Freud's phallic stage of development; pleasure in infantile genitality gives rise to Erikson's social as well as sexual sense of being "on the make" in the stage of *initiative versus guilt*. Now adept at mastering such skills as playing batman on a tricycle and more complicated gender roles, the preschooler possesses the ability to imagine. This capacity, so central to early childhood play, carries with it the seeds for *initiative* in the translating of thoughts to action. Only from an autonomous position is it possible to initiate; in knowing *that* one is, it is then possible to learn *what* one is. Issues such as what kind of person to become and what kinds of gender roles to adopt now become critical questions. From initiative grows a sense of purpose and ambition that are vital to tasks of adolescence and adulthood. It is initiative that "sets the direction toward the possible and the tangible which permits the dreams of early childhood to be attached to the goals of an active adult life" (Erikson, 1963, p. 258).

Locomotor skills and language continue to develop. One is now able to move and expend energy finding out what this status of one who walks means and of how moving can be used for purposes other than pleasure alone to accomplish more far-reaching goals. Language becomes a tool for communication with others in sorting out the often complex and confusing state of world affairs, or at least those of the preschool playground. The following conversations, recorded by Welker (1971), illustrated not only this new linguistic function but also the young child's fascination with gender differences and roles in later life:

Laura got her hair cut very short. She and Tony were on the swings.
Laura: "Tony, do I look like a boy?"
Tony: "No."
Laura: "Look at the back of my head where my hair is so short."
Tony: "No, you're a girl."
Laura: "You know I'm a girl cause you saw me before I got my hair cut."
Tony: "I know you're a girl cause you have curly hair . . ."

* * *

Laurie, playing with Marian, said: "When I grow up, I'm going to be a daddy."
Marian replied, "You can't. Girls grow up into ladies."
"Yes, I can too," retorted Laurie, "Look, I've got big hands, and daddies have big hands."

(Welker, 1971, pp. 67–68)

Thus, identity in adolescence has roots in the purposeful activities of early childhood. Out of initiative comes the ability to fantasize about and experiment with social and gender roles of critical importance to adolescent and young adult life.

At this stage, however, the potential for guilt exists. A tip of the scales toward this negative end may leave the individual immobilized in taking future action through guilt or fear. An optimal balance would see boundless gender and social initiative tempered by an awareness of the possibilities for social criticism and sanctions. Such a balance can best be obtained by a social environment aware of its role in fostering curiosity within the limits of cultural convention.

Industry versus inferiority/competence

According to Freud, the primary school years were marked by a shift from libidinal energy focused on bodily zones to a time of sexual latency; attention becomes channeled outward towards the world of the school yard and neighborhood. In contrast to Freud's focus on sexual latency, Erikson viewed the primary school years as ones in which the practicing of skills and the completion of tasks, anticipating those of later adult work roles, were life's main focus. Industry was described as an apprenticeship to life; feelings of competence and achievement were the optimal results here. Thus, it is only through the *initiative* of an *autonomous* self which *trusts* the social milieu that the challenge of *Industry versus Inferiority* can be addressed. Social recognition for a job well done is the milieu's contribution to fostering development at this stage.

In her short story "Prelude," Katherine Mansfield illustrated an optimal response to industry in a brief interchange between young Kezia and her grandmother:

[S]he decided to go up to the house and ask the servant girl for an empty match-box. She wanted to make a surprise for the grandmother. . . . First she would put a leaf inside with a big violet lying on it, then she would put a very small white picotee, perhaps, on each side of the violet, and then would sprinkle some lavender on the top, but not to cover the heads. She often made these surprises for the grandmother, and they were always most successful.

"Do you want a match, my granny?"
  "Why, yes, child, I believe a match is just what I'm looking for."
  The grandmother slowly opened the box and came upon the picture inside.
  "Good gracious, child! How you astonished me!"
  "I can make her one every day here," she thought, scrambling up the grass on her slippery shoes.

(Mansfield, 1972, p. 90)

Such wisdom in social response can only serve to strengthen the sense of accomplishment of making and giving experienced by this young girl. Crucial to this sense of industry is identification with others who know how to do and make things. One special teacher in the lives of many gifted individuals has often been credited as the spark which ignited outstanding later achievements (Erikson, 1968). Finding one's special skills and talents during the phase of industry may have long-range implications for later vocational identity. Wise parents, teachers or other important identification figures play a critical role in fostering a sense of industry or inferiority.

Erikson (1968) observed a child's possible negative resolution of this stage, involving a sense of estrangement from one's self as well as one's work. A home environment insufficiently preparing the child for life outside its boundaries, or failure of the wider cultural milieu to recognize and reward real accomplishments of its younger members, may precipitate inferiority. Again, healthy resolution to the *industry versus inferiority* conflict sees a ratio favoring industry. At the same time, feelings of limitless competence must be checked by an awareness of one's genuine limitations in order for optimal development to occur.

Identity versus role confusion/fidelity

Moving away from Freud's biological orientation to personality development during puberty, Erikson saw physiological change as only one aspect of a more pervasive adolescent dilemma:

But even where a person can adjust sexually in a technical sense and may at least superficially develop what Freud called genital maturity, he may still be weakened by the identity problems of our era . . . fully developed genitality is not a goal to be pursued in isolation.

(Erikson, cited in Evans, 1967, p. 29)

Identity, to Erikson, incorporated yet transcended the endocrinological revolution of puberty to include psychosocial issues. It was finding a "feeling of reality" in socially approved roles.

Drawing upon resolutions to earlier stages, one now approaches the task of identity formation. Erikson suggested fidelity to be the essence of identity. To become faithful and committed to some ideological world view was the task of this stage; to find a cause worthy of one's vocational energies and reflecting one's basic values was the stuff of which identity crises are made. It is ultimately to affirm and be affirmed by a social order to which identity aspires.

Some possible ways of negotiating life's identity conflicts during the fifth act were described through Siddhartha's quest. Suffice it to say here that the stage of *identity versus role confusion* is one of life's critical crossroads in the transition to adult life; not only must this stage incorporate a *trustworthy* "I" who has evolved as an *autonomous* individual capable of *initiating* and completing (through *industry*) satisfying tasks modeled by significant others, but it must also transcend such identifications to produce an "I" sensitive to its own needs and talents and capable of finding its own niche in the surrounding social landscape.

In contrast to Freud, the curtain on development for Erikson did not fall at this point. With a favorable resolution to the identity crisis of adolescence, it is now and only now possible to proceed to the stage of *intimacy* – that meeting of an "I" with an "I," each firm in his or her own unique identity foundations. The remaining three acts of the life-cycle production, however, involve a shift of developmental focus from "I" to "we."

Intimacy versus isolation/love

For Erikson, intimacy in young adulthood encompasses far more than sexual fulfillment; in fact, sexual activity might be used in the service of an identity conflict rather than as a reflection of *love*. "Intimacy is the ability to fuse your identity with somebody else's without fear that you're going to lose something yourself" (Erikson, cited in Evans, 1967, p. 48). Intimacy involves the desire to commit oneself to a relationship, even when such commitment might call for personal sacrifice or compromise. Intimacy involves communion and can occur in a variety of forms – in same and opposite sex friendships, in love, in sexual union, and even in relationship with oneself or one's life commitments (Evans, 1967).

To Erikson, genuine intimacy was not possible until issues of identity were reasonably well resolved. Relationships of earlier adolescence often served only the purpose of self-definition rather than intimacy; another person might be used merely as a mirror to reflect a form less visible to its owner. Relationships might also involve attempts to find one's own identity through merger with another – efforts which similarly preclude intimacy. Indeed, some marriages serve such a function for those in whom identity issues remain unresolved: "Many young people marry in order to find their identity in and through another person, but this is difficult where the very choice of partner was made to resolve severe unconscious conflict" (Erikson, cited in Evans, 1967, p. 49). Ultimately, there is only enough identity for one.

Drawing upon Martin Buber's concepts of "I" and "Thou," Moustakas captured the character of genuine intimacy in the following passage:

Growth of the self requires meetings between I and Thou, in which each person recognizes the other as he is; each says what he means and means what he says; each values and contributes to the unfolding of the other without imposing or manipulating. And this always means some degree of distance and independence. It does not depend on one revealing to another everything that exists within, but requires only that the person be who he is, genuinely present.

(Moustakas, 1974, p. 92)

Here the identities of "I" and "Thou" must be assured in order for such a relationship of mature, unselfish love to occur.

Isolation is the psychosocial alternative creating conflict at this stage. If true "engagement" with another is elusive, one might "isolate . . . and enter, at best, only stereotyped and formalized interpersonal relations; or one may, in repeated hectic attempts and dismal failures, seek intimacy with the most improbable partners" (Erikson, 1968, p. 167). Isolation can occur in the context of a relationship just as intimacy can exist in the physical absence of a partner. "[T]here are partnerships which amount to an isolation *à deux*, protecting both partners from the necessity to face the next critical development – that of generativity" (Erikson, 1963, p. 266). An ideal balance between intimacy and isolation results in a relationship which allows time for both withdrawal and communion between partners. It is the recognition of one's ultimate aloneness that gives intimacy its base, and it is one's capacity for security in that aloneness that makes genuine intimacy possible.

Generativity versus stagnation/care

The next task for that "we" to meet during adulthood is taking a place in society at large and *caring* – for one's offspring, productions, social contributions, and future generations. Erikson again noted the limitations of Freud's psychosexual scheme with its emphasis on genital maturity as the epitome of development:

I would go even further than that and say that Freud, by paying so much attention to the prepubertal impediments of the genital encounter itself, underemphasized the procreative drive as also important to man. I think this is a significant omission, because it can lead to the assumption that a person graduates from psychoanalytic treatment when he has been restored to full genitality. As in many movies, where the story ends when lovers finally find one another, our therapies often end when the person can consummate sexuality in a satisfactory, mutually enriching way. This is an essential stage but I would consider generativity a further psychosexual stage, and would postulate that its frustration results in symptoms of self-absorption.

(Erikson, cited in Evans, 1967, p. 52)

Erikson's concept here does not imply that generativity could be met only in parenting; it resides also in the desire of an *autonomous* "I" as part of an *intimate* "we" to contribute to the present and future well-being of other life cycles. Such generative individuals provide the figures necessary for introjection and identification by younger members of a society.

The counterpart to generativity is stagnation or self-absorption, whereby personal comfort becomes the primary motivator for action. When this resolution occurs, individuals "often begin to indulge themselves as if they were their own – or one another's – one and only child; and where conditions favor it, early invalidism, physical or psychological, becomes the vehicle of self-concern" (Erikson, 1963, p. 267). Alternatively, procreation or other forms of production are not necessarily the expression of generativity; true care must take root for generativity to flourish.

Again, an optimal balance between generativity and self-absorption is necessary. One needs to be selective of those people and projects to nurture in the interests of self-preservation; unlimited energy and resources are not available to one through life's passages, and some attention to self-interest is crucial in perpetuating a generative life attitude. As in all previous life stages, the ratio needs to favor the more positive pole for healthy development to proceed.

Integrity versus despair/wisdom

The final act of the life drama requires facing the developmental task of balancing *integrity* with *despair*. More difficult to define than preceding stages, integrity "is the acceptance of one's one and only life cycle as something that had to be and that, by necessity, permitted of no substitutions. . . . In such final consolidation, death loses its sting" (Erikson, 1963, p. 268). One gauge of integrity is the ability to accept one's own mortality. A life lived in contributing one's guidance, gifts, and talents to future generations is not regretted, and death is not feared as time shortens before the last curtain call. An old age favoring integrity is characterized by the *wisdom* of mature judgment and a reflective understanding of one's own "accidental" place in the historical scheme of things.

On the other hand, the potential for despair in old age exists to counterpoint integrity. In a life culminating in despair, one is unable to identify a different path toward a more comfortable and satisfying conclusion. Erikson (1976) illustrated the conflict of this final stage of development through a character study of Dr. Borg, the leading figure in Ingmar Bergman's film *Wild Strawberries*. In a car journey to Lund to receive the highest honor of his medical profession, an aged and retired Dr. Borg also departed on a psychological journey back in time through his own development. Borg's precarious psychosocial balance as the scene opens is tipped toward despair. At the age of seventy-six he has begun to realize that it was actually he who had turned away from others and life, rather others turning away from him. And he had, in fact, begun to feel really quite isolated and alone in his old age. One of the car's passengers, Borg's daughter-in-law Marianne, took it upon herself to drive the old man's despair to the surface. Through her efforts, Borg was offered some opportunity for salvation through the journey by rebalancing solutions to earlier psychosocial stages that enabled him to find a more fulfilling old age. Identity themes were carried forward for Borg as he reworked his sense of self to become more intimate with and caring about what he would soon leave behind.

Identity themes are thus met again in old age, where the sense of the "I" that has developed and established itself in social contexts through earlier stages of development must rest content (or not) on what it *is*. Unlike Dr. Borg in Bergman's film fantasy, such opportunities for change are, however, in real life limited for most:

> [A] sense of "I" becomes a most sensitive matter again in old age, as an individual's uniqueness gradually and often suddenly seems to have lost any leeway for further variations such as those which seemed to open themselves with each previous stage. Now, non-Being must be faced "as is."
>
> (Erikson, 1984, p. 102)

The favorable balance of integrity with despair again gives wisdom its ultimate strength. Remaining open to existential issues of being and non-being as well as Kierkegaard's sense of dread, presents very real opportunities for despair. Willingness to address sobering questions such as the meaning of one's existence and the inevitability of one's own death make deeper the tranquility that integrity brings.

Identity is thus an ingredient of all stages of the human life cycle. Having roots in infant trust, identity is also present in the *integrity versus despair* conflict of old age. Identity formation during adolescence reflects developmental resolutions to all preceding stages and serves as base for personality developments that lie ahead. In adolescence, however, identity assumes a change in form. Through a process different from the internalizations and identifications during earlier psychosocial stages, identity's configuration now evolves into a new structure, different from (but related to) the sum of its parts. Through the synthesis of all earlier childhood identifications, the "I," like Siddhartha's sense of self, is now ready to move forward, no longer looking backwards.

Criticism of Erikson's identity concept

Erikson's definition of identity has been criticized on a number of grounds. Unclear or imprecise formulations of identity have been the source of numerous difficulties for many readers of Erikson. The analyst himself suggested that the concept should be defined from different angles, and he proceeded to use the term for emphasizing different issues at different points. At times, identity referred to a structure or a configuration; at other times, it referred to a process. Still on other occasions, identity was viewed as both a conscious subjective experience as well as an unconscious entity. Roazen (2000, p. 438) noted that despite Erikson's capacity for insight, his writing could also be "subtle, elusive, and sometimes hard to follow." In a rather candid comment given during a radio interview, Erikson himself stated, "I think one could be more precise than I am, or than I am able to be. I very much feel that scientific training and logic would have helped a lot"

(Erikson, cited in Stevens, 1983, p. 112). Yet it is this very breadth of phenomena captured through Erikson's formulations of identity that many social scientists have suggested makes the construct more amenable to research than much of psychodynamic theory. Wallerstein (2014) also argued that Erikson's life-cycle stage scheme should regard optimal stage resolutions as aspirational endpoints, rather than essential steps toward optimal functioning; varying degrees of success in this process, he suggested, give rise to our uniquely individual characters.

Empirical validation of the psychosocial issues addressed at different stages that were described by Erikson has been questioned by some critics. Ciaccio (1971) was one of the first investigators to test whether or not conflicts purported by Erikson to be inherent in some of the early developmental stages were actually at issue for groups of boys aged 5, 8, and 11 years old. Although psychosocial strengths or attitudes did seem to progress with age in the sequence described by Erikson, the negative aspects (or crises) of the stages did not find such confirmation. Additional research raised questions regarding Erikson's proposed timing of development; issues of focal concern at specific ages have varied across samples, possibly reflecting the influence of different cultural and/or historical factors (Schwartz, Adamson, Ferrer-Wreder, Dillon, & Berman, 2015). While finding empirical support for central propositions of Erikson's theory, Côté (2015) suggested that identity formation is a much more gradual process for most than Erikson's concept of "identity crisis" implies.

Erikson's views on womanhood and the inner space have drawn equally sharp responses from critics. To Erikson, anatomy was destiny as behavior reflected sexual morphology; boys emphasized outer space in their predominantly aggressive and intrusive play, while girls focused on the inner space in their more peaceful, passive activities. The scientific validity of this observation was questioned shortly after its publication by Caplan (1979), who failed to replicate results from Erikson's single experiment in any findings from a series of studies. Furthermore, many in the following decades attacked the idea that women could not attain their identity until a suitable partner was found and "welcomed to the inner space." Now, however, Erikson's comments on women's identity are recognized as a likely product of the cultural attitudes toward women in the United States at the time of his writing.

Additionally, Erikson's epigenetic scheme of identity formation, many have argued, reflects cultural bias. It would seem that conditions for identity crises could only be ripe in cultural contexts that allow choice as to social, ideological, and vocational roles. Schwartz (2015) noted that in societies with few economic resources, where a majority of teens live in poverty, and/or where governments are corrupt or ineffectual, the possibility of identity exploration is an issue that youths could ill afford. Additionally, the continuity and sameness important to basic trust between parent and child takes on a different slant in the communal child rearing experiences of the kibbutz infant (Scharf, 2001). Despite such criticisms, however, Erikson's theory continues to offer important insights and has sparked an array of empirical inquiries into identity formation during and beyond adolescence.

Measuring ego identity

Erikson's vivid descriptions of the adolescent identity formation process have presented a challenge to researchers attempting to examine and understand the phenomenon empirically. In a frequently cited definition of ego identity, Erikson (1959, p. 116) described many different dimensions of identity's structure and functions: "[Ego identity is] an evolving configuration of constitutional givens, idiosyncratic libidinal needs, favored capacities, significant identifications, effective defenses, successful sublimations, and consistent roles." It is not surprising, then, that different research approaches have emerged to examine various dimensions of the identity formation experience. Erikson himself never wished to undertake empirical studies to validate his theory of personality development and hence devised no measures of ego identity to enable researchers to explore its many properties.

Later investigators have focused on specific dimensions of Erikson's identity concept. The bulk of research attention over the past decades has elaborated exploration and commitment processes in the identity formation task of adolescence, though a growing body of research also has examined such issues as resolutions to "identity versus role confusion" in relation to other life-cycle stages (e.g., Hearn et al., 2012), the role that identity distress may play in life-cycle development (e.g., Berman et al., 2014), narrative approaches to identity development (e.g., McLean & Syed, 2016), micro-level processes of identity development (e.g., Van der Gaag, De Ruiter, & Kunnen, 2016), identity control theory (e.g., Kerpelman, Pittman, & Lamke, 1997), cognitive styles associated with various identity statuses (e.g., Berzonsky & Papini, 2015), and quality of identity commitments (Waterman et al., 2013) to name a few areas of investigation. Narrative approaches to identity drawn from Erikson's writings have now attracted sufficient research interest so that they will be elaborated in Chapter 4 of this volume.

Erikson's virtue of fidelity, however, has drawn the greatest research attention, and it has been through studies initiated by James Marcia (1966, 1967; Marcia, Waterman, Matteson, Archer, & Orlofsky, 1993, 2011) that the process of identity exploration and commitment have been most fully examined. Investigators are currently working to detail the exploration and commitment processes. Marcia's model of the identity statuses has now generated over 900 studies of the identity formation process over the past five decades. This approach will be overviewed in the next section of this chapter, while recent, more nuanced expansions of Marcia's exploration and commitment processes will be presented in the "Current directions in identity research" section of this chapter.

Marcia's identity statuses

On the basis of Erikson's writings on identity, Marcia (1966, 1967) developed the Identity Status Interview (ISI). This interview has been revised and expanded over several decades, and early, mid-, and late adolescent versions, as well as an adult version, are available with interview guidelines and scoring instructions

(Marcia et al., 1993, 2011). The interview consists of domains deemed to be salient to the adolescent in question. For the late adolescent, areas commonly examined are vocational plans, religious and political values, sexual expression and sex role values. Semi-structured questions are designed to assess any current identity-defining commitments the individual might hold, how stable those are, and how any commitments have been or are being undertaken. If commitments are not present, the interview questions also probe whether or not the respondent is attempting to make any such decisions or not. Interviews generally last 30 to 45 minutes and are recorded for later assessment. Interrater reliability has generally been about 80–85% agreement between two raters. Among studies that have corrected for chance agreements, this percentage far exceeds agreements expected by chance. Expected patterns of relationships with other variables have helped to establish construct validity of the ISI (see Kroger & Marcia, 2011, for a review).

Marcia reasoned that fidelity or commitment to a vocation, a set of meaningful values (religious and political beliefs), and a sexual identity (sexual expression and sex role values) that Erikson had described are the observable cues indicative of a more or less successful identity resolution for those in many Western contexts. From Marcia's observations, however, commitment or fidelity comes in several forms. While Erikson saw identity as a balance between commitment and confusion about one's values and roles in society, Marcia identified two distinct types of commitment and two of non-commitment. Individuals adopting an achievement or foreclosure orientation have both made commitments to various social roles and values. However, *identity achieved* individuals have done so following a decision-making period, while *foreclosures* have bypassed the identity formation process to simply adopt roles and values of childhood identification figures. Similarly, moratoriums and diffusions both lack commitment to a place in the social context. However, *moratoriums* are undergoing an evaluative process (ego synthesis) in search of suitable social roles and values for themselves, while *diffusions* are not. These commitment types or identity statuses were empirically validated as four distinct modes of dealing with identity defining issues during adolescence, and expected patterns of relationships with other variables helped to establish construct validity of the ISI (see Marcia et al., 1993, 2011 for a review).

A paper and pencil measure of identity status was developed by Adams and colleagues (Adams, 1999). The Objective Measure of Ego Identity Status II (EOM-EIS-II) was composed of 64 items presented in a Likert-scale format that assess the degree of identity achievement, moratorium, foreclosure and diffusion an individual demonstrated within eight identity defining domains. Occupational, political, religious, and philosophy of life values constituted the general ideological domain, while friendship, dating, sex role, and recreational values comprised a general interpersonal domain. Reliability was established over a number of studies via measures of internal consistency. Cronbach alphas were generally around 0.66. Test–retest reliability studies showed an average correlation of 0.76. Efforts to establish construct, predictive, and concurrent validity generally produced moderate to high relationships between the EOM-EIS-II and associated measures (Adams, 1999). Recently, Schwartz, Adamson,

Ferrer-Wreder, Dillon, and Berman (2015) examined the utility of the EOM-EIS-II across several cultural contexts. While finding the internal structure of the instrument to be consistent across settings, their results also suggested that identity content areas and item wording may need to be altered to be more culturally meaningful in particular contexts.

Two currently popular, additional paper and pencil measures were developed to extend Marcia's concepts of the exploration and commitment processes: the Dimensions of Identity Development Scale (DIDS; Luyckx, Goossens, Soenens, & Beyers, 2006; Luyckx, Schwartz, Goossens, Soenens, & Beyers, 2008) and the Utrecht-Management of Identity Commitments Scale (U-MICS; Crocetti, Rubini, & Meeus, 2008). The DIDS is a 25-item instrument presented in a 5-point Likert scale format, with three scales reflecting different forms of identity exploration (*exploration in breadth, exploration in depth*, and *ruminative exploration*) and two scales reflecting different forms of identity commitment (*commitment making* and *identification with commitment*). *Exploration in breadth* corresponds to Marcia's exploration concept, whereby the degree to which adolescents have explored alternative roles and values is assessed, while *exploration in depth* looks at the extent to which existing commitments have been re-examined and refined against the respondent's internal interests and values. *Ruminative exploration* refers to the possibility of a "perpetual moratorium" process, whereby the individual remains "stuck" in ongoing identity exploration, unable to make meaningful identity choices; this process is most likely to be dysfunctional. *Commitment making* is similar to Marcia's commitment concept, referring to the degree to which adolescents adopt meaningful identity-defining roles and values. *Identification with commitment* reflects the degree to which individuals feel certain about or identify with the identity commitments they have made. Each of the five scales is composed of five items. Cronbach alphas for the five scales ranged from 0.79 to 0.86 for two initial samples, while internal construct validity for the five scales and external construct validity for the three exploration scales were in line with predictions (Luyckx et al., 2006).

The 13-item U-MICS (Crocetti et al., 2008) is composed of three scales (*commitment, in-depth exploration*, and *reconsideration of commitment*) using a Likert format. The *commitment* (5 items) and *exploration in-depth* (5 items) scales correspond to the same dimensions of identity described above for the DIDS instrument. The *reconsideration of commitment* scale (3 items) refers to abandoning initial identity choices and evaluating possible alternatives. Two domains were examined in initial studies – education and friendship; each of these two domains contain the 13 items noted above and are presented in a Likert scale format. "My education/best friend gives me certainty in life" is found on the *commitment* scale, while "I often reflect on my education/best friend" is found on the *exploration in-depth* scale. Internal construct validity was supported by a three factor solution, while external validity was established in predicted directions with various personality and relational variables. Later research has indicated moderate to good internal reliabilities (0.63 to 0.82) for each scale across seven different national contexts (Dimitrova et al., 2015).

These elaborations of exploration and commitment processes have brought valuable insights into the process of identity development and produced a wealth of studies on the types of and steps in identity exploration and commitment processes. Clusters from both the DIDS and U-MICS have been extracted, also purporting to reflect Marcia's identity statuses. However, this procedure may be problematic for a number of reasons that Waterman (2015) has detailed, and he indicates caution when trying to interpret results from studies utilizing identity status clusters derived from these more recent instruments. For example, in contrast to the Identity Status Interview (Marcia et al., 1993, 2011) and the EOM-EIS-II (Adams, 1999) that assessed identity exploration and commitment through past and present circumstances across a number of identity-defining domains, both the DIDS and U-MICS phrase items in the present tense only. This present tense wording makes evaluation of previous exploration impossible to assess; knowledge of any past identity exploration is necessary to accurately differentiate Marcia's foreclosure and achievement statuses. Additionally, neither the DIDS nor the U-MICS enables the researcher to assess the quality of the commitment in terms of its match with an individual's own interests and values, and both instruments assess only a small selection of identity domains. As Waterman (2015) noted, these types of problems make findings from identity status clusters derived from these latter instruments difficult to compare with the identity statuses derived from more direct measures. These latter instruments have, however, made a more nuanced examination of identity exploration and commitment processes possible and have stimulated much research. Further, from an intervention perspective, these present-oriented indicators of identity commitment and exploration (e.g., mean level or continuous changes in the *amount* of exploration and/or commitment) could be useful for capturing incremental changes in identity development and thereby inform the structuring of identity-related interventions.

Historical backdrop to Erikson's and Marcia's psychosocial models

Erikson's theoretical writings on identity and personality development emerged from origins in psychoanalysis. Erikson (1959), however, was among the early psychoanalysts to focus on ego rather than id processes in personality development. Classic psychoanalysts had also focused primarily upon the Oedipal phase of development, when the superego (conscience) was formed, and balances among the personality structures of id, ego, and superego were established (Marcia, 1994). Interest in pre-Oedipal development and the structuralization of the self had received little attention until Erikson's writings. Freud had used the concept of identity only once to refer to his Jewish heritage (Erikson, 1959). However, as a student of Anna Freud, Erikson was undoubtedly influenced by the adaptive processes of the ego and its mechanisms of defense. Hartmann (1958) had also focused upon the ego and formulated concepts of primary and secondary autonomy and ego epigenesis, while Rapaport (1960) and White (1959), respectively, had contributed work on the role of the ego in development and in the drive toward competence. However, it was Erikson (1959) who focused attention on the adaptive processes of ego development across the entire life cycle. Erikson's writings, however, were never well integrated into the psychoanalytic mainstream, nor was he adequately credited with his early influence on the field of psychoanalytic ego psychology (Wallerstein, 1998). Indeed, it was only Rappaport (cited in Erikson, 1959) who delineated the contributions of but two men, Hartmann and Erikson, and pointed out the profound influences each had on the field of ego psychoanalytic psychology (Wallerstein, 1998).

A number of contemporary object relations approaches emerged from Erikson's writings, laying varied emphases on the role of relationships in the development of the self and on elements of the surrounding milieu in individual identity development. Jacobson (1964), Bowlby (1969) and Mahler (Mahler, Pine, & Bergman, 1975) all examined the role of internal representations of relationships during infancy and early childhood in the development of an autonomous sense of self and other, while Winnicott (1953) described the role of transitional objects in this process. Blos (1967) examined further changes to these internal representations during the course of adolescence. However, it was Jacobsen (1964) who unfortunately set the rather dismissive tone for Erikson's writings on the development of the self. Thus, Erikson's influence as a forerunner to later object relations and ego psychoanalytic theory has only rarely been acknowledged (Wallerstein, 1998).

Marcia (2004) described how his interest in Erikson's (1959) concept of identity arose during his clinical internship. Marcia, under the supervision of David Gutmann (Erikson's former teaching assistant at Harvard) was assigned to undertake a psychodiagnostic review of a 16-year-old boy, a new admission to the hospital. The boy's psychological tests indicated a severe thought disorder, indicative of schizophrenia. However, six months later, the youth was released from the hospital with no signs of this illness; it was likely that this young man had undergone a severe identity crisis. Marcia reflected on this experience as he selected a dissertation topic: the construct validation of Erikson's identity construct. With many false starts and amused skepticism from peers and professors, Marcia constructed the identity statuses. Over the years of his career, Marcia wished to make Erikson more accessible to the social science community. With his construct now reviewed in most major textbooks on adolescent development, Marcia has certainly succeeded in accomplishing that goal.

Research findings on adolescent identity exploration and commitment processes

While identity and its development during adolescence have been examined from many angles, Marcia's (1966; Marcia et al., 1993, 2011) identity status approach has either generated or served as a springboard for the largest body of investigations to date, and the brief review below will focus on studies using this approach; the "Current directions in identity research" section will focus on recent efforts that examine exploration and commitment processes in greater detail. Early research with the identity statuses through the 1970s, 1980s, and 1990s focused on individual personality, cognitive, and relational differences associated with the different identity statuses, while subsequent work has examined developmental patterns of change over time, as well as gender, ethnic/cultural/contextual factors associated with the identity statuses. Identity status clusters derived from more recent instruments have also examined a number of these issues, though some problems with this approach have been noted by Waterman (2015) that were described earlier in this chapter. Because the identity statuses remain a focus of many past as well as current approaches to adolescent identity, the profiles of each identity status, based upon findings from nearly five decades of research, are described briefly below.

Identity achieved adolescents have been through a thoughtful, decision-making process of searching for and finding meaningful psychosocial roles and values that "fit" with their own interests and needs. From meta-analytic studies, identity achieved youths are less reliant on the opinions of others to make their decisions and score consistently higher on measures of "internal locus of control" compared with other identity status groups (Lillevoll, Kroger, & Martinussen, 2013a). Identity achieved individuals function well under stress and use more planful, rational and logical decision-making strategies compared to people described by other identity statuses (Boyes & Chandler, 1992; Marcia et al., 1993, 2011). No significant differences in intelligence, however, have appeared across the identity statuses as assessed in various studies by at least six different measures (Marcia et al., 1993, 2011). The identity achieved, along with foreclosed individuals, have shown the highest levels of self-esteem compared with other statuses from meta-analytic results, and are satisfied with the way they are (Makros & McCabe, 2001; Ryeng, Kroger, & Martinussen, 2013a; Schwartz et al., 2011). Meta-analyses also indicated that the identity achieved individuals are most likely to be at post-conformist levels of ego development as well as post-conventional levels of moral reasoning (Jespersen, Kroger, & Martinussen, 2013a, 2013b). Identity achievements have tended to be intimate in their close relationships and more secure in their attachment patterns (Beyers & Seiffge-Krenke, 2010; Årseth, Kroger, Martinussen, & Marcia, 2009). Achievements are also able to perceive parental strengths and weaknesses and come from families in which parents support their autonomy (Grotevant & Cooper, 1985; Willemsen & Waterman, 1991). In general, more positive mental health outcomes have been found among those identity achieved individuals who explored and synthesized identity possibilities into an identity configuration that is uniquely their own (see Kroger & Marcia, 2011, for a review).

Moratorium adolescents and young adults are in the throes of trying to make decisions about important identity questions, and they are anxious, changeable, and intense in their personal relationships. While possessing the capacity for intimacy, they have tended to shy away from the commitments demanded by it (Dyk & Adams, 1990; Josselson, 2017; Orlofsky, Marcia, & Lesser, 1973). In many ways, moratoriums resemble identity achievements in their cognitive complexity, higher levels of moral reasoning, and ego development (Jespersen et al., 2013a, 2013b; Slugoski, Marcia, & Koopman, 1984). Moratoriums also have demonstrated greater degrees of skepticism than other identity statuses (Boyes & Chandler, 1992), as well as greater openness to experience and experiential orientation (Stephen, Fraser, & Marcia., 1992; Tesch & Cameron, 1987). Parents of moratorium youths have tended to foster independence in their child-rearing practices (Frank, Pirsh, & Wright, 1990; Grotevant & Cooper, 1985).

Foreclosure adolescents have adopted strong, identity-defining commitments based on identifications with important others rather than their own identity explorations. Meta-analytic studies have found foreclosures of both sexes to be more authoritarian in attitude compared with other identity statuses (Ryeng et al., 2013b). These individuals have tended to seek the approval of others and have based their actions on what others think. Perhaps as a result of their rigid adherence to authoritarian values, studies have found foreclosures to be less anxious compared with other identity status groups (Lillevoll et al., 2013a) and least open to new experiences (Stephen et al., 1992; Tesch & Cameron, 1987). If there is no openness or willingness to question life commitments, there is little room for anxiety to enter. Foreclosures also have used less complex cognitive styles (Slugoski et al., 1984), though meta-analytic studies have those in the fore-closed identity status to be more mixed in their levels of moral reasoning and ego development compared to achievement and moratorium individuals (Jespersen et al., 2013a, 2013b). In interpersonal relationships, foreclosures have tended to be "well-behaved" and engaged in stereotypic or merger styles of relationships with significant others (Dyk & Adams, 1990; Levitz-Jones & Orlofsky, 1985). Youths who have remained foreclosed over the course of late adolescence are more non-secure (anxious or detached) in attachment profiles than youths of any other identity status group (Kroger & Haslett, 1988; Papini, Micka, & Barnett, 1989). Foreclosures have reported very close relationships with parents, while their parents, in turn, have encouraged conformity and adherence to family values (Frank et al., 1990; Grotevant & Cooper, 1985; Willemsen & Waterman, 1991).

Diffusion adolescents and young adults are less homogeneous as a group than the other identity statuses. The inability to make identity commitments may have resulted from cultural conditions (producing few viable identity options) as well as developmental deficits. Diffusions have been unlikely to be involved in intimate relationships and lacking any real sense of self to contribute to others (Josselson, 2017). Meta-analytic studies have shown lower levels of self-esteem to be associated with the uncommitted moratorium and diffusion statuses (Ryeng et al., 2013a). Furthermore, diffusions have shown high levels of an "external locus of control" and low levels of an "internal locus of control" in comparison with other identity statuses (Lillevoll et al., 2013b). The diffusions have used less complex cognitive styles than moratoriums and achievements (Slugoski et al., 1984). In terms of interpersonal relationships, diffusions have tended to be distant and withdrawn, most likely to be stereotyped or isolated in their relationships with others (Orlofsky et al., 1973). Their reports of parents' childrearing practices have indicated caretakers who were distant and rejecting (Josselson, 2017); dif-fusions furthermore have shown a lack of awareness of family issues (Gfellner & Bartoszuk, 2015). In general, diffusions have exhibited more troubled or risky behaviors in comparison with those of other identity statuses (Josselson, 2017; Schwartz et al., 2011).

Developmental patterns of change

Marcia et al. (1993, 2011) intended the identity statuses to reflect "snapshots" at a particular point in time of how individuals were attempting (or not) to make key, identity-defining decisions. Questions thus arose regarding the length of time one was likely to remain in any given identity status and the course of the most common trajectories of both identity status change and stability, as well as events that were most likely associated with identity status change and stability over time.

Investigations of identity status change during adolescence and young adulthood have identified common patterns of progressive movement from foreclosure and diffusion positions to moratorium and achievement statuses among those individuals who do change over this time frame. Meta-analyses of a number of both longitudinal and cross-sectional studies of identity status change during adolescence and young adulthood have been undertaken (Kroger, Martinussen, & Marcia, 2010). Among results from meta-analyses of longitudinal studies, a little over one-third of individuals (36%) showed some type of progressive identity status change (defined as diffusion to foreclosure, moratorium, or achievement; foreclosure to moratorium or achievement; and moratorium to achievement) over an average range of three years. Some 15% of participants showed regressive identity status change, while, surprisingly, almost half (49%) of individuals were found to be in the same identity status over this same period of time. Among results from cross-sectional studies across the years of late adolescence and young adulthood, the mean proportion of identity achievements increased steadily over time, though only about one-third of the sample (34%) had reached identity achievement by age 22 years. Foreclosure and diffusion statuses declined across high school years, but fluctuated throughout late adolescence and young adulthood. It appears that identity achievement remains elusive for many individuals during the time frame in which Erikson suggested identity formation is a key developmental task, leaving considerable scope for identity development through the adult years of life.

Subsequent developmental studies of identity status change have produced similar findings. During the late adolescent and young adult years, diffusion and foreclosure statuses have generally decreased or remained stable, while the identity achieved status has either increased or remained stable (e.g., in Belgium: Luyckx, Klimstra, Duriez, Van Petegem, Beyers, 2013; Verschueren, Rassart, Claes, Moons, & Luyckx, 2017; in Japan: Hatano & Sugimura, 2017). In a cross-sectional study in Trinidad, the achieved identity status was most commonly found in middle age, compared with adolescence, emerging, and young adulthood years (Arneaud, Alea, & Espinet, 2016). In a longitudinal study of Swedish young adults, Carlsson, Wängkvist, and Frisén (2015) found about half of their participants were coded in the same identity status from ages 25 to 29 years, except for those in the moratorium status, which decreased. In the United States,

Cramer (2017) found a modest increase in identity achievement scores between ages 18 and 35, as well as a decrease in moratorium and foreclosure scores; little change in diffusion scores was found over this interval. Josselson (2017) found similar stability in the diffusion status from late adolescence through mid-adulthood. In general, identity appears to be a long, slowly developing process that occurs throughout adolescent and at least young adult life; at the same time, there also may be considerable identity status stability, particularly in diffusion and fore-closure statuses from late adolescence through early and middle adulthood years. More comments will be made about ongoing identity development from adolescence through adulthood in Chapter 8.

Where identity change has occurred, perceived conflict and/or stressful life events, both positive and negative emotional experiences, readiness for change, planfulness, using resources, and intentional behavior appear to be key elements associated with an identity exploration process (Anthis, 2011; Bosma & Kunnen, 2001; Luyckx & Robitschek, 2014; Van der Gaag, Albers, & Kunnen, 2017). The use of narrative methods to gain new insights into identity development over time have recently begun (i.e., Carlsson et al., 2015).

Gender and ethnicity in identity status research

Questions have been frequently asked about the possibility of gender and ethnic differences in the adolescent identity formation process, and these issues will be examined in greater detail in Chapters 5 and 6 of this volume. The focus here will be on investigations that have emerged through studies of identity exploration and commitment processes.

A number of studies have examined the possibility of gender differences in identity status within particular identity domains as well as in overall identity assessments. In a narrative analysis, Kroger (1997) found few gender differences in identity status distributions for general or domain ratings of identity status as well as in the timing of the developmental process itself. The studies reviewed were primarily from North American contexts. More recent studies from a diversity of cultural settings, however, produced somewhat more diverse findings in response to identity-defining domains as well as developmental timing of identity status changes (e.g., in Sweden: Carlsson et al., 2015; in South Africa: Alberts & Bennett, 2017). It may be that different cultural norms for the two genders in more diverse settings can at least partially account for the more mixed findings.

A further question that has been of great interest to identity researchers has been potential gender differences in the sequential ordering of Erikson's identity and intimacy tasks of adolescence and young adulthood. Through past decades, many writers have suggested that the Eriksonian tasks of *identity versus role confusion* and *intimacy versus isolation* may co-develop for women, rather than following a sequential order, as Erikson proposed. Meta-analytic research does indicate that this pattern of co-development may exist for some, but not all, women and few men (Årseth et al., 2009). Details of this research will be discussed in Chapter 8 of this volume,

One's *ethnicity* is an aspect of identity that involves both membership in an ethnic group and the assumption of the values and attitudes of that group (Phinney, 2006). Over past decades, research on ethnicity and cultural context in the identity formation task of adolescence and young adulthood has increased exponentially. Identity, ethnic, and cultural context are interdependent, and greater contact among people of various cultural backgrounds has led to the need for many to develop a bicultural identity (Vedder & Phinney, 2014). As Schwartz, Zamboanga, Meca, and Ritchie (2012) have noted, though, many youths in cultural majority groups take their ethnicities for granted and do not consider ethnicity as a key, identity defining element. However, the same cannot be said for ethnic minority youths.

Through the 1990s, much research on ethnic identity confirmed a model of ethnic identity development proposed by Phinney (1989) that was based on Marcia's identity status model. Phinney's work suggested three stages in ethnic identity development:

1   an initial stage with little or no questioning of ethnic identity and its meaning (foreclosure/diffusion);
2   a moratorium stage which questioned preexisting ethnic attitudes and the place of one's ethnicity in present life circumstances; and
3   an achieved ethnic identity, in which one attained a secure, positive sense of one's identity as a member of an ethnic group, with an acceptance of other groups.

Subsequent longitudinal work has indicated a significant change to more complex levels of ethnic identity development over time for late adolescents and young adults of various ethnic minority groups (e.g., Syed & Azmitia, 2009; Vedder & Phinney, 2014).

Further research regarding adolescent ethnic identity development over the past two decades has focused on a number of issues, including cultural and subcultural variations in the ethnic identity formation process, the question of how a bi-cultural identity develops, dimensions of social contexts that facilitate and impede positive ethnic identity development, and immigration and acculturation in the ethnic identity formation process. These issues will be elaborated more fully in Chapter 5.

Current directions in identity research

Within the past decade, identity research based on Erikson's writings have seen developments in a number of new directions. Perhaps the largest area of expansion has come through efforts to elaborate and refine identity exploration and commitment processes (Crocetti et al., 2008; Luyckx et al., 2006, 2008). For example, through use of the DIDS (Luyckx et al., 2006, 2008), Luyckx and his colleagues reasoned that ongoing identity development involved re-examining one's commitments over time. They differentiated an additional type of moratorium process that they termed, "ruminative exploration" to describe individuals that appeared stuck in their identity development due to overwhelming choices and/or fears of making the "wrong one," having unrealistic expectations, or perfectionism. Those showing ruminative exploration were characterized as ready for change but lacking the ability to make realistic plans or show intentional behaviors (Luyckx & Robitschek, 2014). Additionally, Luyckx and colleagues differentiated both the "classical" or troubled diffusion found by Marcia from a "carefree diffusion" status. When examining adolescent identity status trajectories over three points in time during a one-year period, Luyckx, Klimstra, Schwartz, and Duriez (2013) found troubled diffusions attempted some exploration of identity issues over time, albeit in a haphazard and unsystematic way, while carefree diffusions were not motivated to undertake any identity exploration at all. Troubled diffusions also evidenced far lower levels of self-esteem and community integration over time than other identity status groups. The identity achieved developed a clear set of goals for themselves and were able to shut down the exploration process when commitments were decided, while foreclosures appeared not personally to endorse nor be as identified with their commitments as were the achievements.

Further use of both the DIDS (Luyckx et al., 2006) and U-MICS (Crocetti et al., 2008) have generated some interesting findings regarding identity exploration and commitment processes. Longitudinal studies using these instruments have pointed to some interesting patterns of change. For example, Becht et al. (2017) examined exploration and commitment dynamics across five years of adolescence for individual participants. For the educational identity domain, their findings showed that increasing identity commitment level and decreasing commitment fluctuations were predictive of less identity reconsideration over time. Research on additional identity domains is necessary in order to explore this finding further. A further longitudinal study by Klimstra, Hale, Raaijmakers, Branje, & Meeus (2010) of adolescents aged 12–20 years found that levels of identity commitment did not change much over this time, while reconsideration of commitments changed substantially (as one would expect). Additionally, exploration in breadth increased in the 16–20 years age range. Increases in exploration in depth during late adolescence from this study were also replicated by Luyckx & Robitschek (2014), alongside exploration in breadth. These identity process-oriented studies showed that forming an initial sense of identity stability through commitment is an important phenomenon for younger adolescents, while more reflective identity explorations and subsequent commitments are the purview of older adolescents. Among college students 18–22 years, commitment making, exploration in breadth, and exploration in depth increased, while identification with commitment first decreased but increased again toward the end of the study (Luyckx et al., 2008). Studies of older adolescents and young adults have shown a general pattern of progressive identity development, though there may be regressive changes, as well as large individual differences in developmental trends (Klimstra & van Doeselaar, 2017). The study of exploration and commitment dimensions over time allows many insights into the complexities of identity commitment, blockages, and revision processes during adolescence and young adulthood.

A very recent avenue of promising research links identity exploration and commitment processes to their neurological underpinnings. Becht and colleagues (Becht et al., 2018) were interested in the question of how changes in brain areas associated with certain behaviors during adolescence might actually facilitate elements of the identity formation process. The researchers wished to test whether individual differences in initial levels of and structural changes in the brain's grey matter volume might be linked with certain identity-related behaviors during adolescence. Specifically, the researchers addressed whether NAcc (nucleus accumbens in the limbic regions that have been linked to pursuit of valued and long term goals) and PFC (pre-frontal cortex grey matter that has been linked with cognitive control and information seeking behaviors) might be linked with goal directedness and information seeking behaviors in the identity formation process. Decreasing grey matter volume in the brain is normal in brain maturation, though there are large individual differences in initial levels of grey matter and in the extent of changes over time. The researchers combined self-reported questionnaire and brain imaging data to test whether individual differences in initial level and structural changes of NAcc and PFC grey matter volume predicted later identity commitments, in-depth exploration, and reconsideration of commitments. They hypothesized that a more prolonged developmental trajectory of both NAcc and PFC grey matter volume would allow more time for identity exploration and predict a more mature adolescent identity over time. Findings confirmed that adolescents with higher goal pursuit self-reports and higher NAcc volume showed stronger identity commitments with less uncertainty about them over time. Adolescents with higher PFC volume and more prolonged PFC volume development indicated more reflection on their identity commitments in the service of strengthening and maintaining them over time. This research offers a new and very important step toward understanding the neurological underpinnings of adolescent identity formation processes that will hopefully stimulate future studies of the brain-behavior relationship.

A number of issues related to the contexts of identity development are also being examined in greater detail. The role of contexts, generally, in the identity formation process has been described at both theoretical and empirical levels. Côté (1996) attempted theoretically to describe ways in which culture and identity are interrelated. Furthermore, he tested the relationship between agency and identity formation, inspiring more interdisciplinary approaches to understanding the identity formation process across diverse settings (e.g., Côté, 2015; Côté & Schwartz, 2002). Galliher, McLean, and Syed (2017) carried this interdisciplinary notion further by proposing a general framework for the study of identity and identity domains within historical, cultural, and political contexts and described ways to evaluate identity development in circumstances of shifting cultural norms, values, and attitudes.

Criticism of the identity status construct

Schwartz, Luyckx, and Crocetti (2015) have argued for newer models and newer methods to study identity development during adolescence. The increasing volume of studies employing the DIDS (Luyckx et al., 2006, 2008) and the U-MICS (Crocetti et al., 2008) have generated considerable discussion in the identity literature as to whether it may be most beneficial to focus on identity exploration and commitment as independent processes or to retain a "person-centered approach" by focusing on identity status clusters derived from the paper and pencil instruments described above (see, for example, the debate on this issue in McLean & Syed, 2015). It has also been argued that recent, "process" oriented models of identity development overcome the difficulty of the "static" outcomes that some have ascribed to Marcia's identity statuses. However, these more recent process models have also been used to extract identity status clusters, and, despite the problems of measurement identified by Waterman (2015) that were described earlier, these clusters have also captured some dimensions of ongoing identity development during and beyond the years of adolescence as Marcia's identity statuses have done (e.g., Carlsson et al., 2015; Fadjukoff, Pulkkinen, & Kokko, 2016; Verschueren et al., 2017).

Crocetti and Meeus (2015) argued for the use of both person and variable centered approaches, although particular research questions should ultimately determine the choice of method; person-centered approaches may be best suited for capturing identity development through various identity status pathways, for example, as researchers try to find predictors and consequences of various identity status transitions. A focus on exploration and commitment measures alone, however, can provide useful information about how incremental exploration and commitment dynamics may impact long-term identity goals.

Syed and McLean (2016) noted that the idea of identity integration is understudied in identity research, particularly with its theoretical and practical importance to Erikson's (1968) theory of lifespan development. Marcia's identity status construct, they observed, placed heavy emphasis on personal agency rather than fully appreciating the restrictions that context and opportunity may impose on an individual. Furthermore, in the identity status approach, they pointed out, there has been little research undertaken to understand the relations among identity domains and how they become integrated into one's general sense of identity. Syed and McLean observed that some research focused exclusively on individual identity domains (e.g., ethnicity, vocation, religion) and how they developed, rather than on how these domains developed in relation to each other, which they believed would be a more productive approach (research through the 1980s and 1990s, however, did examine the congruence of identity status ratings across all domains and in relation to an integrated assessment in an attempt to partially address this question). Yet, it is clear that more research attention to the issue of the interplay between identity processes and contents within varied contexts will advance the field.

Identity status research and the focus on identity exploration and commitment have been essential to advancing what is known about identity development more generally. As the field of identity studies moves forward, such progress is likely to be accelerated by greater consideration of how context and life conditions are important to identity development (these issues are explored in Chapters 5–7), by learning about identity development through using diverse research methods (e.g., interviews, surveys, diaries, and physiological measurement), and by further theoretical work that maps out the intersections between essential processes of identity development including but also reaching beyond exploration and commitment variables (e.g., memory and autobiographical reasoning, see Chapter 4).

Implications for social response

Social response is intimately linked to identity development through all eight of Erikson's life-cycle stages. From the mutual recognition and regulation of infant and caretaker behavior to the definition of identity through social roles and supportive contexts in adolescence to reflection over one's engagements and social participation in the integrity tasks of old age, recognition from both a developmental partner and a larger social group has been critical to resolving the conflict of each stage in a favorable direction. Assuming more or less favorable solutions have been found to the conflicts of preceding eras, parents, close associates, and the educational, employment, recreational, religious, health, political, and legal systems of one's cultural context have a vital role to play in the formation of identity during adolescence. All such contexts help to regulate attitudes and behaviors of their younger members, and all are capable of becoming too cooperative in the provision of labels that may not ultimately serve the best interests of youths seeking identity definition. It is through social willingness *not* to predetermine roles and to allow youths a moratorium period that identity formation is best facilitated; it is social tolerance for role experimentation without labeling that eventually benefits all concerned (Erikson, 1968).

Erikson himself cited numerous examples of ways in which the psychiatric profession and legal system could provide youths with labels that offered a ready identity to troubled adolescents but did not allow optimal resolution to the conflicts of this stage. Just as an adolescent psychiatric patient may "choose the very role of patient as the most meaningful basis for an identity formation" (Erikson, 1968, p. 179), others might gratefully adopt the role of "criminal" or "delinquent" that courts and psychiatric agencies could so easily and cooperatively confer. Society's *refusal* to provide ready role definitions for such adolescents and *not* to treat their experimentations as the final identity are in the best interests of the entire community.

In social response to the formation of identity, the importance of the community's recognition has been emphasized. Such recognition, however, must extend beyond a mere response to accomplishment alone. Social lip service to adolescent achievement cannot replace genuine opportunities provided by a society for individual talents to be both realized and recognized. How might educational and therapeutic interventions best serve adolescents in each of Marcia's four identity statuses? Each identity status reflects a time of special need and would seem to require differential social responses.

Resolution of identity issues for the identity achieved makes need for psychotherapeutic intervention unlikely. Self-definition has been constructed through the identity formation process and resolutions to the conflicts of preceding stages have been successful in order for identity achievement to occur. The need for counseling might arise for such an individual only in situations of crisis and would involve short-term intervention techniques (Marcia, 1986, 1993). Educational settings must continue to provide new opportunities for insight and exploration, meet genuine needs and allow opportunity for individual talent to be expressed and channeled into real social roles. Experimental schools that encourage individual exploration and the pursuit of curricula relevant to a student's own interests and talents would initially appear to offer ideal educational opportunities for identity development. However, Erikson (1968) advocated a less radical solution to the curriculum dilemma, at least during the stage of industry. He considered a teacher's guidance and encouragement for children's explorations of new areas of learning in the world of reality rather than fantasy to be an important step toward a child's eventual participation in the world of adult accomplishment. Schools with flexible curricula designed both to address changing student and social needs and also to provide challenges and conflict situations were best suited to enhancing later identity development, according to Erikson (1968). It is the job of the school and other social institutions to provide avenues for enhancing the identity achieved individual's way of influencing others, both in their immediate contexts and larger social surrounds.

Moratoriums, very much in the throes of the identity formation process, often appear in psychotherapeutic or counseling settings. Ironically, they probably need direct intervention less than some foreclosure or diffusion youths, who are less likely to request assistance (Marcia, 1986). A sympathetic "other" who does not become aligned with various aspects of the moratorium's struggle, but rather acts in a Rogerian way to reflect prospective identity elements in the interests of identity synthesis, would seem the best form of assistance here. It is important that therapist or counselor not be allied with any one side of the moratorium's conflict. Such a therapeutic attitude merely externalizes the conflict into the therapeutic relationship rather than keeping the conflict within the individual, hence delaying its resolution (Marcia, 1986). Educational environments similar to those proposed for the identity achieved individual are likely to best help the moratorium to explore vocational, ideological, and sexual values available in his or her society and find a social niche that matches individual interests and talents. A curriculum relevant to the genuine needs of adolescents (for example, human sexuality, peace education, education for parenting, vocational skills training, international relations) are the focus for many programs of psychological education (Blustein, Ellis, & Devenis, 1989). Opportunities for adolescents to become exposed to and "try out" a variety of work roles through work–study programs at high school or college, as well as having interested and sympathetic adults available for listening, also facilitate resolution to a psychosocial moratorium period.

For the foreclosed individual, identity is reached through identification with significant others rather than ego synthesis of one's own identity elements. Much has been vested in "being loved and cared for" by identification figures at the expense of self-definition and identity development. Appearing to proceed smoothly along the track toward occupational goals and steadfast in their ideological beliefs, these youths have avoided any form of serious exploration. As a consequence, rigid identity structures are formed which become impervious to challenges from new life situations. Confidence and security have been the foreclosure's reward for adhering to prescribed role expectations. These youths rarely come for counseling or psychotherapy except when such beliefs have been threatened or otherwise disrupted. Foreclosures would seem to be the most neglected status for psychotherapeutic, counseling, or educational intervention in cultural contexts where identity formation is adaptive (Marcia, 1986).

Counseling or psychotherapy with foreclosed adolescents must recognize the rigidity of this identity structure and the security it provides, while striving slowly to provide new models for identification and introducing greater alternatives for choice. It should be noted that direct challenge to foreclosure commitments are likely to result in a further solidifying of defenses and closure to new possibilities (Marcia, 1986). Vocational or personal counseling should proceed very slowly, with gradual encouragement to consider new options and identify with potentially new role models. Marcia (1994) pointed out that people cannot be "taught" to explore alternatives; the process of considering alternatives for many foreclosures becomes laden with fears of rejection from significant others. Adults, instead, should provide safety, structure, facilitation, and some direction. An educational environment which supports open exploration of occupational and ideological alternatives rather than rewarding premature commitment could do much to foster identity development among the adolescent foreclosed. However, it must be recognized that a safe context is essential for those who might begin to question internalized roles and standards and move toward a more self-determined choice.

The diffusion status captures the greatest range of individuals having difficulty in finding a social niche. Here, failure to resolve favorably conflicts of preceding psychosocial stages may be primarily responsible for adolescent identity difficulties. For some diffusions, early massive ego failure makes "being something" beyond the realm of the possible; just being, and developing some feeling of coherence, is their main developmental task. Intervention efforts with such individuals would occur primarily in a psychotherapy setting. Difficult though it may be, therapeutic aims would address issues of basic trust in relationships and ultimately in oneself (Erikson, 1968). It is only through a return to this basic developmental conflict that any possibility exists for the emergence of an autonomous sense of self. If a diffusion's difficulties begin no earlier than the stage of industry, a facilitative psychotherapeutic or educational response might assist the individual in finding or reconnecting with interests and talents that have lain dormant through childhood (Marcia, 1986). Efforts should be made to help the diffusion become aware of his or her own unique attributes and experiences. Some forms of structured choice in the therapeutic or educational arenas might eventually be presented to diffusions in the interests of providing an experience of self through choosing an alternative best suited to personal preferences and competencies. Jones (1994) noted that many school-based prevention and intervention efforts for adolescents have focused on specific, isolated problem behaviors (such as substance abuse). He pointed out that if intervention programs were designed to address specific underlying developmental deficits at an individual level, then reduction of problem behaviors would be a side effect of a generally more effective developmental intervention.

Systematic research on identity intervention programs has expanded greatly over past decades. Markstrom-Adams, Ascione, Braegger, and Adams (1993) was one of the first studies to provide evidence that short-term intervention training strategies in social perspective taking might facilitate ideological identity achievement. More recently, Kurtines and his colleagues (e.g., Berman, Kennerly, & Kennerly, 2008; Eichas, Meca, Montgomery, & Kurtines, 2015) have been particularly active in developing identity intervention programs to facilitate positive identity development based on Erikson's (1968) identity concepts.

One example of such an intervention is by Berman et al. (2008), who administered the Daytona Adult Identity Development Program to university students enrolled in an elective personal growth psychology course. The program facilitated small group discussions each week for an hour and a half over a 15-week semester on identity issues important to group members, following readings on identity issues and homework "self-tests" on identity related themes. After participation in this program, students' identity exploration scores increased significantly, while identity distress scores decreased significantly. In addition, there was a significant decrease in those rated as foreclosed in identity status, with a concomitant increase in identity achievement.

A recent review of this and other programs by Ferrer-Wreder, Montgomery, Lorente, and Habibi (2014) concluded that it is possible to influence the process of identity development among adolescents, and that the most promising identity intervention strategies appear to have the following three key elements:

1   expanding self-understanding through identity exploration;
2   teaching critical thinking and problem-solving skills; and
3   helping youth learn to take control and accept responsibility for their own life decisions.

Ferrer-Wreder and colleagues (2014) also addressed the issue of whether or not concerned adults should try to influence the identity development process. From studies to date, they concluded an unequivocal "yes." Their review showed that positive youth identity development interventions promoted healthy psychosocial functioning and reduced or protected against adjustment difficulties. They also found that such identity intervention programs might be particularly valuable for ethnic minority youth. Future research can fruitfully examine factors that facilitate identity development outcomes as well as address why certain targeted interventions work for particular groups of youth (Ferrer-Wreder et al., 2014). Future research should also aim to identify youth at risk of problematic identity development for purposes of early interventions (Josselson, 2017).

Summary

Ego identity as conceptualized by Erik Erikson is a psychosocial construct which can be understood only through the interaction of biological foundations, ego organization, and social context. During adolescence, features of identity which have formed through more or less favorable resolutions to earlier stages of developmental conflict, must now evolve into a new configuration, different from yet based upon the earlier introjections and identifications of childhood. Furthermore, the balance achieved during the identity versus role confusion conflict of adolescence will affect all developmental stages encountered during adult life. Marcia has empirically elaborated Erikson's identity versus role confusion conflict, describing four identity resolutions based on attitudes of exploration of and commitment to particular social roles and values. Subsequent research has elaborated these exploration and commitment processes. The identity statuses and various types of exploration and commitment processes have implications for effective educational, counseling, and psychotherapeutic interventions.

Note

1 In this chapter, the use of "he" is retained from original writings when quoted but should be understood in the sense of "people" more generally.

References

Adams, G. G. (1999). The objective measure of ego identity status: A manual on theory and test construction. Unpublished manuscript, University of Guelph, Ontario, Canada.

Alberts, C., & Bennett, M. J. (2017). Identity formation among isiXhosa-speaking adolescents in a rural Eastern Cape community in South Africa: A brief report. *Journal of Psychology in Africa, 27*, 198–202.

Anthis, K. (2011). The role of conflict in continuity and change: Life events associated with identity development in racially and ethnically diverse women. *Identity: An International Journal of Theory and Research, 11*, 333–347.

Arneaud, M. J., Alea, N., & Espinet, M. (2016). Identity development in Trinidad: Status differences by age, adulthood transitions, and culture. *Identity: An International Journal of Theory and Research, 16*, 59–71.

Årseth, A. K., Kroger, J., Martinussen, M., & Marcia, J. E. (2009). Meta-analytic studies of identity status and the relational issues of attachment and intimacy. *Identity: An International Journal of Theory and Research, 9*, 1–32.

Bagnold, E. (1972). The door of life. In E. D. Landau, S. L. Epstein and A. P. Stone (Eds.), *Child development through literature* (pp. 6–14). Upper Saddle River, NJ: Prentice-Hall (originally published 1938).

Becht, A. I., Nelemans, S. A., Branje, S. J. T., Vollebergh, W. A. M., Koot, H. M., & Meeus, W. (2017). Identity uncertainty and commitment making across adolescence: Five-year within-person associations using daily identity reports. *Developmental Psychology, 53*, 2103–2112.

Becht, A. I., Bos, M. G. N., Marieke, G. N., Nelemans, S. A., Peters, S., Vollebergh, W. A. M., ... Crone, E. A. (2018). 'Goal-directed correlates and neurobiological underpinnings of adolescent identity: A multi-method multi-sample longitudinal approach.' *Child Development, 89*, 823–836.

Berman, S. L., Kennerley, R. J., & Kennerley, M. A. (2008). Promoting adult identity development: A feasibility study of a university-based identity intervention program. *Identity: An International Journal of Theory and Research, 8*, 139–150.

Berman, S. L., Ratner, K., Cheng M., Li, S., Jhingon, G., & Sukumaron, N. (2014). Identity distress during the era of globalization: A cross-national comparative study of India, China, and the United States. *Identity: An International Journal of Theory and Research, 14*, 286–296.

Berzonsky, M. D., & Adams, G. R. (1999). Reevaluating the identity status paradigm: Still useful after 35 years. *Developmental Review, 19*, 557–590.

Berzonsky, M. D., & Papini, D. R. (2015). Cognitive reasoning, identity components, and identity processing styles. *Identity: An International Journal of Theory and Research, 15*, 74–88.

Beyers, W., & Seiffge-Krenke, I. (2010). Does identity precede intimacy? Testing Erikson's theory on romantic development in emerging adults of the 21st century. *Journal of Adolescent Research, 25*, 387–415.

Blos, P. (1967). The second individuation process of adolescence. *Psychoanalytic Study of the Child, 22*, 162–186.

Blustein, D. L., Ellis, M. V., & Devenis, L. E. (1989). The development and validation of a two-dimensional model of the commitment to career choices process. *Journal of Vocational Behavior, 35*, 342–378.

Bosma, H. A., & Kunnen, E. S. (2001). Determinants and mechanisms in ego identity development: A review and synthesis. *Developmental Review, 21*, 39–66.

Bowlby, J. (1969). *Attachment.* New York, NY: Basic Books.

Boyes, M. C., & Chandler, M. (1992). Cognitive development, epistemic doubt, and identity formation in adolescence. *Journal of Youth and Adolescence, 21*, 277–304.

Caplan, P. J. (1979). Erikson's concept of inner space: a data-based reevaluation. *American Journal of Orthopsychiatry, 49*, 100–108.

Carlsson, J., Wängkvist, M., & Frisén, A. (2015). Identity development in the late twenties: A never ending story. *Developmental Psychology, 51*, 334–345.

Ciaccio, N. V. (1971). A test of Erikson's theory of ego epigenesis. *Developmental Psychology, 4*, 306–311.

Coles, R. (1970). *Erik H. Erikson: The growth of his work.* Boston, MA: Little Brown.

Côté, J. E. (1996). Identity: a multidimensional analysis. In G. R. Adams, R. Montemayor, & T. Gullotta (Eds.), *Psychological development during adolescence: Progress in developmental contextualism* (pp. 130–180). Newbury Park, CA: Sage.

Côté, J. E. (2015). Identity formation research from a critical perspective: Is a social science developing? In K. C. McLean & M. Syed (Eds.), *Oxford handbook of identity development* (pp. 527–538). New York, NY: Oxford University Press.

Côté, J. E., & Schwartz, S. J. (2002). Comparing psychological and sociological approaches to identity: Identity status, identity capital, and the individualization process. *Journal of Adolescence, 25*, 571–586.

Cramer, P. (2017). Identity change between late adolescence and adulthood. *Personality and Individual Differences, 104*, 538–543.

Crocetti, E., & Meeus, W. (2015). The identity statuses: Strengths of a person-centered approach. In K. C. McLean & M. Syed (Eds.), *The Oxford handbook of identity development* (pp. 97–114). New York, NY: Oxford University Press.

Crocetti, E., Rubini, M., & Meeus, W. H. J. (2008). Capturing the dynamics of identity formation in various ethnic groups. Development and validation of a three-dimensional model. *Journal of Adolescence, 31*, 207–222.

Dimitrova, R., Crocetti, E., Kosic, R., Buzia, C., Tair, E., Tausova, J., . . . Jordanov, V. (2015). The Utrecht-Management of Identity Commitments Scale (U-MICS): Measurement invariance and cross-national comparisons of youth from six European countries. *European Journal of Psychological Assessment, 12*, 727–743.

Dyk, P. H., & Adams, G. R. (1990). Identity and intimacy: An initial investigation of three theoretical models using cross-lag panel correlations. *Journal of Youth and Adolescence 19*, 91–109.

Eichas, K., Meca, A., Montgomery, M. J., & Kurtines, W. M. (2015). Identity and positive youth development: Advances in developmental intervention science. In McLean, K. C., & Syed, M. (Eds.), *Oxford handbook of identity development* (pp. 337–354). New York, NY: Oxford University Press.

Erikson, E. H. (1956). The problem of ego identity. *Journal of the American Psychoanalytic Association, 4*, 56–121.

Erikson, E. H. (1959). *Identity and the life cycle.* Psychological Issues Monograph 1. New York, NY: International Universities Press.

Erikson, E. H. (1963). *Childhood and society,* 2nd ed. New York, NY: Norton.

Erikson, E. H. (1968). *Identity, youth, and crisis.* New York, NY: Norton.

Erikson, E. H. (1970). Autobiographic notes on the identity crisis. *Daedalus, 99*, 730–759.

Erikson, E. H. (1976). Reflections on Dr. Borg's life cycle. *Daedalus, 105*, 1–28.

Erikson, E. H. (1977). *Toys and reasons: Stages in the ritualization of experience.* New York, NY: Norton.

Erikson, E. H. (1984). Reflections on the last stage – and the first. *Psychoanalytic Study of the Child, 39*, 155–165.

Evans, R. I. (1967). *Dialogue with Erik Erikson.* New York, NY: Harper & Row.

Fadjukoff, P., Pulkkinen, L., & Kokko, K. (2016). Identity formation: A longitudinal study from age 27 to 50. *Identity: An International Journal of Theory and Research, 16*, 8–23.

Ferrer-Wreder, L. A., Montgomery, M. J., Lorente, C. C., & Habibi, M. (2014). Promoting optimal identity development in adolescents. In Gullotta, T. P., & Bloom (Eds.), *Encyclopedia for primary prevention intervention for adolescents* (pp. 1278–1287). New York, NY: Springer Science + Business Media.

Frank, S. J., Pirsh, L.A., & Wright, V. C. (1990). Late adolescents' perceptions of their relationships with their parents: Relationships among de-idealization, autonomy, relatedness, and insecurity and implications for adolescent adjustment and ego identity status. *Journal of Youth and Adolescence, 19*, 571–588.

Friedman, L. J. (1999). *Identity's architect: A biography of Erik H. Erikson.* New York, NY: Scribner.

Galliher, R. V., McLean, K. C., & Syed, M. (2017). An integrated developmental model for studying identity content in context. *Developmental Psychology, 53*, 2011–2022.

Gfellner, B. M., & Bartoszuk, K. (2015). Emerging adulthood in North America: Identity status and perceptions of adulthood among college students in Canada and the United States. *Emerging Adulthood, 3*, 368–372.

Grotevant, H. D., & Cooper, C. R. (1985). Patterns of interaction in family relationships and the development of identity exploration in adolescence. *Child Development, 56*, 415–428.

Hartmann, H. (1958). *Ego psychology and the problem of adaptation,* New York, NY: International Universities Press.

Hatano, K., & Sugimura, K. (2017). Is adolescence a period of identity development for all youth? Insights from a longitudinal study of identity dynamics in Japan. *Developmental Psychology*, *53*, 2113–2126.

Hearn, S., Saulnier, G., Strayer, J., Glenham, M., Koopman, R., Marcia, M. (2012). Between integrity and despair: Toward construct validation of Erikson's eighth stage. *Journal of Adult Development*, *19*, 1–20.

Hesse, H. (1951). *Siddhartha*. New York, NY: New Directions Publishing Corp.

Hopkins, J. R. (1995). Erik Homburger Erikson (1902–1994). *American Psychologist*, *50*, 796–797.

Jacobsen, E. (1964). *The self and the object world*. New York, NY: International Universities Press.

Jespersen, K., Kroger, J., & Martinussen, M. (2013a). Identity status and ego development: A meta-analysis. *Identity: An International Journal of Theory and Research*, *13*, 228–241.

Jespersen, K., Kroger, J., & Martinussen, M. (2013b). Identity status and moral reasoning: A meta-analysis. *Identity: An International Journal of Theory and Research*, *13*, 266–280.

Jones, R. M. (1994). Curricula focused on behavioral deviance. In S. L. Archer (Ed.), *Interventions for adolescent identity development* (pp 174–190). Newbury Park, CA: Sage.

Josselson, R. (2017). *Paths to fulfillment: Women's search for meaning and identity*. New York, NY: Oxford University Press.

Kerpelman, J., Pittman, J., & Lamke, L. K. (1997). Toward a microprocess perspective on adolescent identity development. *Journal of Adolescent Research*, *12*, 325–346.

Klimstra, T., Hale, Raaijmakers, Branje, & Meeus (2010). Identity formation in adolescence: Change or stability? *Journal of Youth and Adolescence*, *39*, 150–162.

Klimstra, T., & van Doeselaar, L., (2017). Identity formation in adolescence and young adulthood. In J. Specht (Ed.), *Personality development across the lifespan* (pp. 293–308). San Diego, CA: Elsevier Academic Press.

Kroger, J. (1997). Gender and identity: The intersection of structure, content, and context. *Sex Roles*, *36*, 747–770.

Kroger, J., & Haslett, S. J. (1988). Separation–individuation and ego identity status in late adolescence: A two-year longitudinal study. *Journal of Youth and Adolescence*, *17*, 59–81.

Kroger, J., & Marcia, J. E. (2011). The identity statuses: Origins, meanings, and interpretations. In S. J. Schwartz, Luyckx, K., & Vignoles, V. (Eds.) *Handbook of identity theory and research* (pp. 31–53). New York, NY: Springer-Verlag.

Kroger, J., Martinussen, M., & Marcia, J. E. (2010). Identity status change during adolescence and young adulthood: A meta-analysis. *Journal of Adolescence*, *33*, 683–698.

Levitz-Jones, E. M., & Orlofsky, J. L. (1985). Separation–individuation and intimacy capacity in college women. *Journal of Personality and Social Psychology*, *49*, 156–169.

Lillevoll, K. R., Kroger, J., & Martinussen, M. (2013a). Identity status and anxiety: A meta-analysis. *Identity: An International Journal of Theory and Research*, *13*, 214–227.

Lillevoll, K. R., Kroger, J., & Martinussen, M. (2013b). Identity status and locus of control: A meta-analysis. *Identity: An International Journal of Theory and Research*, *13*, 253–265.

Luyckx, K., Goossens, L., Soenens, B., & Beyers, W. (2006). Unpacking commitment and exploration: Preliminary validation of an integrative model of late adolescent identity formation. *Journal of Adolescence*, *29*, 361–378.

Luyckx, K., Klimstra, T. A., Duriez, B., Van Petegem, S. Beyers, W. (2013). Personal identity processes from adolescence through the late twenties: Age differences, functionality, and depressive symptoms. *Social Development, 22,* 701–721.

Luyckx, K., Klimstra, T. A., Schwartz, S. J., & Duriez, B. (2013). Personal identity in college and the work context: Developmental trajectories and psychosocial functioning. *European Journal of Personality, 27,* 222–237.

Luyckx, K., & Robitschek, C. (2014). Personal growth initiative and identity formation in adolescence through young adulthood: Mediating processes on the pathway to wellbeing. *Journal of Adolescence, 37,* 973–981.

Luyckx, K., Schwartz, S. J., Berzonsky, M. D., Soenens, B., Vansteenkiste, M., . . . Goossens, L. (2008). Capturing ruminative exploration: Extending the four-dimensional model of identity formation in late adolescence. *Journal of Research in Personality, 42,* 58–82.

Luyckx, K., Schwartz, S. J., Goossens, L, Soenens, B., & Beyers, W. (2008). Developmental typologies of identity formation and adjustment in female emerging adults: A latent class growth analysis approach. *Journal of Research on Adolescence, 18,* 595–619.

Mahler, M. S., Pine, F., & Bergman, A. (1975). *The psychological birth of the human infant.* New York, NY: Basic Books.

Makros, J., & McCabe, M. P. (2001). Relationships between identity and self-representations during adolescence. *Journal of Youth and Adolescence, 30,* 623–639.

Mansfield, K. (1972). Prelude. In E. Bowen (Ed.), *34 short stories* (pp. 85–97). London: Collins (originally published 1918).

Marcia, J. E. (1966). Development and validation of ego identity status. *Journal of Personality and Social Psychology, 3,* 551–558.

Marcia, J. E. (1967). Ego identity status: relationship to change in self-esteem, "general maladjustment," and authoritarianism. *Journal of Personality, 35,* 118–133.

Marcia, J. E. (1986). Clinical implications of the identity status approach within psychosocial developmental theory. *Cadernos de Consulta Psicologica, 2,* 23–34.

Marcia, J. E. (1993). Relational roots of identity. In J. Kroger (Ed.), *Discussions on ego identity* (pp. 101–120). Hillsdale, NJ: Lawrence Erlbaum Associates.

Marcia, J. E. (1994). Ego identity and object relations. In J. Masling & R. F. Bornstein (Eds.), *Empirical perspectives on object relations theory* (pp. 59–103). Washington, DC: American Psychological Association.

Marcia, J. E. (2004). Why Erikson? In K. R. Hoover (Ed.), *The future of identity: Centennial reflections on the legacy of Erik Erikson* (pp. 43–59). Lanham, MD: Lexington Books.

Marcia, J. E., Waterman, A. S., Matteson, D. R., Archer, S. L. and Orlofsky, J. L. (1993, 2011). *Ego identity: A Handbook for psychosocial research,* New York, NY: Springer-Verlag.

Markstrom-Adams, C., Ascione, F. R., Braegger, D. & Adams, G. R. (1993). Promotion of ego identity development: Can short-term intervention facilitate growth? *Journal of Adolescence, 16,* 217–224.

McLean, K. C., & Syed, M. (Eds.) (2015). *The Oxford handbook of identity development.* New York, NY: Oxford University Press.

McLean, K. C., & Syed, M. (2016). Personal, master, and alternative narratives: An integrative framework for understand identity development in context. *Human Development, 58,* 318–349.

Moustakas, C. E. (1974). *Portraits of loneliness and love.* Englewood Cliffs, NJ: Prentice-Hall.

Orlofsky, J. L., Marcia, J. E. & Lesser, I. M. (1973). Ego identity status and the intimacy versus isolation crisis of young adulthood. *Journal of Personality and Social Psychology, 27,* 211–219.

Papini, D. R., Micka, J. C., & Barnett, J. K. (1989). Perceptions of intrapsychic and extra-psychic functioning as bases of adolescent ego identity status. *Journal of Adolescent Research, 4*, 462–482.

Phinney, J. S. (1989). Stages of ethnic identity development in minority group adolescents. *Journal of Early Adolescence, 9*, 34–49.

Phinney, J. S. (2006). Ethnic identity exploration in emerging adulthood. In J. Arnett & J. L. Tanner, (Eds). (2006). *Emerging adults in America: Coming of age in the 21st century.* (pp. 117–134). Washington, DC: American Psychological Association.

Rapaport, D. (1960). *The structure of psychoanalytic theory: A systematizing attempt.* Psychological Issues Monograph 6. New York, NY: International Universities Press.

Roazen, P. (2000). Review of "Ideas and identities: The life and work of Erik Erikson." *Psychoanalytic Psychology, 17*, 437–442.

Ryeng, M. S., Kroger, J., & Martinussen, M. (2013a). Identity status and self-esteem: A meta-analysis. *Identity: An International Journal of Theory and Research, 13*, 201–213.

Ryeng, M. S., Kroger, J., & Martinussen, M. (2013b). Identity status and authoritarian-ism: A meta-analysis. *Identity: An International Journal of Theory and Research, 13*, 242–252.

Scharf, M. (2001). A "natural experiment" in childrearing ecologies and adolescents' attachment and separation representations. *Child Development, 72*, 236–251.

Schwartz, S. J. (2015). Turning point for a turning point: Advancing emerging adulthood theory and research. *Emerging Adulthood, 4*, 1–11.

Schwartz, S. J., Adamson, L., Ferrer-Wreder, L. A., Dillon, F., & Berman, S. L. (2015). Identity status measurement across contexts: Variations in measurement structure and mean levels among White American, Hispanic American, and Swedish emerging adults. *Journal of Personality Assessment, 86*, 61–76.

Schwartz, S. J., Beyers, W., Luyckx, K., Soenens, B., Zamboanga, B. L., Forthun, L. F., . . . Waterman, A. S. (2011). Examining the light and dark sides of emerging adults' identity: A Study of identity status differences in positive and negative psychosocial functioning. *Journal of Youth Adolescence, 40*, 839–859.

Schwartz, S. J., Luyckx, K., & Crocetti, E. (2015). What have we learned since Schwartz (2001)?: A reappraisal of the field of identity development. In K. C. McLean, & M. Syed (Eds.), *The Oxford handbook of identity development* (pp. 539–561). New York, NY: Oxford University Press.

Schwartz, S. J., Zamboanga, B. I., Meca, A., & Ritchie, R. A. (2012). Identity around the world: An Overview. *New Directions in Child and Adolescent Development, 138*, 1–18.

Slugoski, B. R., Marcia, J. E., & Koopman, R. F. (1984). Cognitive and social interactional characteristics of ego identity statuses in college males. *Journal of Personality and Social Psychology, 47*, 646–661.

Stephen, J., Fraser, E., & Marcia, J. E. (1992). Moratorium–achievement (Mama) cycles in lifespan identity development: Value orientations and reasoning system correlates. *Journal of Adolescence, 15*, 283–300.

Stevens, R. (1983). *Erik Erikson: An introduction.* Maidenhead: Open University Press.

Syed, M., & Azmitia, M. (2009). Longitudinal trajectories of ethnic identity during the college years. *Journal of Research on Adolescence, 19*, 601–624.

Syed, M., & McLean, K. C. (2016). Understanding identity integration: Theoretical, meth-odological and applied issues. *Journal of Adolescence, 47*, 109–118.

Tesch, S. A., & Cameron, K. A. (1987). Openness to experience and development of adult identity. *Journal of Personality, 55*, 615–630.

Van der Gaag, M. A. E., Albers, C. J., & Kunnen, E. S. (2017). Micro-level mechanisms of identity development: The role of emotional experiences in commitment development. *Developmental Psychology, 53,* 2205–2217.

Van der Gaag, M. A. E., de Ruiter, N. M. P., & Kunnen, E. S. (2016). Micro-level processes of identity development: Intra-individual relations between commitment and exploration. *Journal of Adolescence, 47,* 38–47.

Vedder, P. & Phinney, J. S. (2014). Identity formation in bi-cultural youth: A developmental perspective. In V. Benet-Martinez, & Hong, Y. Y. (Eds), *The Oxford handbook of multicultural identity* (pp. 335–354). New York, NY: Oxford University Press.

Verschueren, M., Rassart, J., Claes, L., Moons, P., & Luyckx, K. (2017). Identity statuses throughout adolescence and emerging adulthood: A large scale study into gender, age, and contextual differences. *Psychologica Belgica, 57,* 32–42.

Wallerstein, R. S. (1998). Erikson's concept of ego identity reconsidered. *Journal of the American Psychoanalytic Association, 46,* 229–247.

Wallerstein, R. S. (2014). Erik Erikson and his problematic identity. *Journal of the American Psychoanalytic Association, 62,* 657–674.

Waterman, A. S. (2015). What does it mean to engage in identity exploration and to hold identity commitments? A methodological critique of multidimensional measures for the study of identity processes. *Identity: An International Journal of Theory and Research, 15,* 309–349.

Waterman, A. S., Schwartz, S. J., Hardy, S. A., Kim, S. Y., Lee, R. M., Armenta, B. E. . . .Agocha, V. B. (2013). 'Good choices, poor choices: Relationship between the quality of identity commitments and psychosocial functioning.' *Emerging Adulthood, 13,* 163–174.

Waterman, A. S., & Whitbourne, S. K. (1981). The inventory of psychosocial development: A review and evaluation. *JSAS Catalog of Selected Documents in Psychology, 11* (ms. no. 2179).

Welker, J. N. (1971). Observations and comments concerning young children in a preschool. Unpublished Manuscript, Department of Applied Behavioral Sciences, University of California, Davis.

White, R. (1959). Motivation reconsidered: The concept of competence. *Psychological Review, 66,* 297–333.

Willemsen, E. W., & Waterman, K. K. (1991). Ego identity status and family environment: A correlational study. *Psychological Reports, 69,* 1203–1212.

Winnicott, D. W. (1953). Transitional objects and transitional phenomena: A study of the first not-me possession. *International Journal of Psychoanalysis, 34,* 89–97.

3 Adolescence as a second individuation process

Blos's psychoanalytic perspective and an object relations view

I remember several years ago when I first came to the university I was so relieved to be out of the house and so angry with my parents for wanting to "control" my life. But looking back now, I realize just how much I wanted them to tell me what to do, even though I got so irritated with every idea that they had. Sometimes, I think I just really wanted my parents to *be* me, and I could just sit back and watch it all happen. . . . Now, I realize that they just couldn't tell me what was right for me – that was something that I had to find for myself. The past few years have been a really scary time. But now I couldn't imagine doing anything other than what I'm doing now, music school and performance work that I love so much.

(Sarah, aged 22, a conservatory of music student)

I (JK) remember clearly that first meeting with Sarah as she sat in my office having just arrived at the university. I was to be her student advisor during her time of study, and she appeared so lost as to which direction to take in her coursework, floundering between wanting to do things just to distance herself from her parents' wishes and then wanting to pursue numerous different possibilities that might make her feel like she was really "in charge" of herself. Sarah came back each semester over her first two years for me to sign her schedule of classes, unable to really settle on any clear directions for the future and beginning to fear that finding her way in life was a totally hopeless project. The question arose of whether or not she really wanted to be at the university at all. In the meantime, Sarah had begun picking up her old violin, which she said always brought her feelings of such peace and satisfaction, and it seemed to help her now, as she enviously watched her friends find partners and begin working toward some life goals. At the end of two and a half years, Sarah decided to leave the university until she could really decide what she wanted to do. Two more years passed. One day, a knock came on my door, and there was Sarah. She had wanted to stop by just to let me know what she was doing now. Her words that opened this chapter testify to the psychological changes that seem to have taken place as Sarah made peace with both her internalized and external parents to pursue life goals that *she* now found deeply satisfying. Sarah's experiences illustrate the gradually unfolding second individuation process elaborated by Peter Blos, in his psychoanalytic account of character formation (identity development) during adolescence.

Through a complex labyrinth of psychoanalytic routes, Blos's work emerged and marked an interesting crossroads in the evolution of psychodynamic theory itself. While retaining many contours of classic psychoanalytic maps that stress the resolution of Oedipal conflict for healthy personality development, Blos also appreciated the significance of pre-Oedipal experiences in determining modes of later interpersonal relatedness. An awareness of the potentially productive rather than unconditionally maladaptive role played by regression in adolescent character formation was also critical to Blos's modification of orthodox psychoanalytic theory. Although retaining an appreciation of the place of adolescence on the road to genital maturity, Blos was one of the few psychodynamic theorists to focus almost exclusively on developments taking place during this youthful transition.

In line with most psychodynamic contributions, Blos's notions came to us via the experiences of troubled individuals seeking relief from distress. While developmental difficulty is of enormous value in highlighting normative psychodynamic processes, the non-normative foundations of Blos's theoretical architecture must be remembered. In this chapter, particular effort will be made to select and describe psychodynamic processes central to Blos's conceptualization of *normative* character formation during adolescence. Later in the chapter, Blos's contributions will be elaborated with recent insights from object relations theory and research on the second individuation process of adolescence, derived primarily from non-clinical populations.

Blos the person

Peter Blos was born in 1903 in Karlsruhe, Germany, and was a lifelong friend of Erik Erikson. Blos undertook his initial training in biology, a field in which he was awarded a PhD from the University of Vienna in 1934. In the very early years of his career, he was greatly stimulated by his associations with Anna Freud and August Aichhorn at the Vienna Psychoanalytic Institute. There, he began his psychoanalytic studies and directed the now famous Experimental School in association with Anna Freud, August Aichhorn, Dorothy Burlingham, and Erik Erikson. From these early experiences arose Blos's lifelong professional commitment to the welfare of youth (Esman, 1997).

Blos (like Erikson) migrated to the United States with Hitler's rise to power. He settled in New York to further a career that eventually spanned six decades. A gifted teacher and clinician, Blos held several faculty and supervisory positions at the New York Psychoanalytic Institute and the Columbia University Center for Psychoanalytic Training and Research prior to his retirement from active teaching in 1977. Among his later professional honors was receipt of the Heinz Hartmann Award from the New York Psychoanalytic Institute. Blos's lifelong interests in psychodynamic processes of adolescence were reflected in some of his book titles: *On Adolescence* (1962); *The Young Adolescent: Clinical Studies* (1970); and *The Adolescent Passage* (1979). His last volume, *Son and Father: Before and Beyond the Oedipus Complex* (1985), traced the reciprocity of the son–father relationship over the course of the generations, as the son becomes a father in turn. Peter Blos died in 1997 at the age of 93 years. He was regarded by many as one of the last in a great generation of clinical scholars who helped form the foundations of contemporary psychoanalysis (Esman, 1997) as well as providing the critical link to contemporary separation individuation theory of adolescent and adult development (Usher, 2017).

The nature of character formation

Where Erikson used the term "ego identity," Blos preferred the use of "character" to denote that entity which restructured and consolidated during adolescence. However, the nature of that entity, which formed at the end of adolescence, differed for the two psychoanalysts. Character, to Blos, was that aspect of personality which patterned one's responses to stimuli originating both within the environment as well as within the self. Unlike Erikson, Blos did not focus primarily on ego processes in the formation of character but rather on the dynamic balance between id, ego, and superego structures.

Blos (1968) posited four challenges which are related to the formation of character; without addressing and favorably resolving each of these issues, adolescents would retain a character deficient in the structure necessary for healthy functioning during adult life. Failure to resolve adolescent challenges may or may not be based on earlier developmental arrest. Blos's four character challenges of adolescence, detailed in the next section, were as follows:

- the second individuation process
- reworking and mastering childhood trauma
- ego continuity
- sexual identity

The second individuation process of adolescence involved the relinquishing of those very intrapsychic parental representations, internalized during toddlerhood, and forming the foundation of childhood identity. Blos found regression to be a normative feature of adolescent character development, as teens disengaged from early ties to their internalized parental representations. In reworking childhood trauma, adolescents must return to, rather than avoid, the scene of early organismic insult and re-experience the injury so that it could be mastered rather than defended against throughout adult life. Similar to Erikson's suggestion of the need for a sense of inner continuity and sameness as an indication of healthy identity formation, Blos's notion of ego continuity referred to the need for a sense of personal history; one could not have a future without a past. In line with orthodox psychoanalytic theory, Blos saw the reactivation of childhood Oedipal issues and the formation of a sexual identity as the final critical challenge to adolescent character formation. It was the young person's ability to seek romantic relationships outside of the original family constellation that indicated the successful resolution of this challenge.

These four challenges, central to adolescent character formation, rested on a history of individual antecedents – from constitutional givens to infant interpersonal experience to resolution of early childhood Oedipal conflicts. Like ego identity, character can be conceptualized only in developmental terms; its origins begin in infancy and its stabilization appears at the end of adolescence. Blos did not trace the development of character through adulthood, however. Character formation involved progressively higher levels of differentiation and independence from the environment. Subjectively, one's character was one's sense of self: "Psychic life cannot be conceived without it [character], just as physical life is inconceivable without one's body. One feels at home in one's character. . . . If must be, one dies for it before letting it die" (Blos, 1968, p. 260). The four character formation challenges should be regarded as components of a total process; their integrated resolution marks the end of adolescence (Blos, 1976). Blos's four cornerstones of character formation are described in the following section.

The challenges detailed

Crucial to the psychoanalyst's portrayal of adolescent character is a basic understanding of object relations theory. This approach, broadly defined, rested on the assumption that in our relationships we react according to the internal representations we hold of people important to us in the past as well as to the person actually before us now. Greenberg and Mitchell put it succinctly:

> People react to and interact with not only an actual other but also an internal other, a psychic representation of a person which in itself has the power to influence both the individual's affective states and . . . overt behavioral reactions.
>
> (Greenberg & Mitchell, 1983, p. 10)

Thus, our responses to those before us now may have only the vaguest of associations with present-tense external reality. Rather, interactions may be governed equally by internal representations of past important others who, in turn, define the present limits of our autonomous functioning.

Within psychoanalysis, a number of object relations theorists have made important contributions by exploring the implications of this last statement (e.g., Fairburn, Guntrip, Jacobson, Kernberg, Klein, Kohut, and Mahler). Blos's writings on the restructuring of internal representations during adolescence drew particularly upon the work of Margaret Mahler. Though Mahler's work was based on development in early life, Blos found great parallels in the processes by which adolescents must deal with issues of self-differentiation. Blos's second individuation process will be discussed more fully than the remaining challenges, for it is this issue that has stimulated the greatest theoretical and empirical interest among those attempting to understand the normative adolescent experience. The past 40 years have seen a burgeoning of both theoretical and empirical efforts to elucidate intrapsychic and interpersonal ramifications of this internal, differentiation process.

The second individuation process

In groundbreaking work conducted in the 1960s, Margaret Mahler[1] made extensive observations of healthy mother–infant and mother–toddler dyads in a naturalistic setting to delineate the process by which the child differentiates itself from its primary caretaker and becomes an autonomous human being. While mothers and infants were the main focus of Mahler's initial observational work and theory construction, "mother" should be understood here as "primary caretaker" in the child's early development. Separation and individuation referred to two parallel tracks that develop in tandem in the sequence by which the infant moves from an undifferentiated experience of self to a toddler with a sense of separateness from yet relatedness to the physical world of reality. By separation, Mahler, Pine, and Bergman (1975, p. 4) alluded to the child's "emergence from a symbiotic fusion with the mother," while individuation denoted "those achievements marking the child's assumption of his own individual characteristics." In short, Mahler and her colleagues attempted to chart "the psychological birth of the human infant."

Mahler followed these developmental tracks through a sequence of specific stages. One's resolution to these phases determined the health or pathology of character during the course of later life. Successful navigation of these stages was to Mahler what resolution of the Oedipal crisis was to Freud in setting the foundation for adult character structure. The hyphenated term "separation–individuation" refers specifically to four subphases of development experienced during infancy and toddlerhood; separation–individuation subphases follow neonatal stages of autism[2] and symbiosis.

At the beginning of life, according to Mahler, newborns are unable to differentiate themselves from their surroundings. There are not internal representations of the external world, for there is little awareness of external objects. Maintaining physiological homeostasis was the main task for the infant in this *autistic* phase of life, and it was only the gradual awareness of a caretaker (the mother, in Mahler's observations) that propelled the child into the next stage of normal *symbiosis* at about three to four weeks of age. Now there was dim recognition of mother, but she was perceived only as an extension of the infant's self. In the observations of Mahler et al. (1975, p. 44), "the infant behaves and functions as though he and his mother were an omnipotent system – a dual unity within one common boundary." It was from this base that the four subphases of separation–individuation proceeded, encompassing a growing intrapsychic differentiation between self and other.

More recent research on infant development has challenged Mahler's descriptions of autistic and symbiotic stage capacities by demonstrating that infants are born with perceptual and cognitive capacities too sophisticated to suggest their inability to differentiate self from other in their earliest weeks of life (Blum, 2004; Stern, 1985). This research also cast doubt on the whole existence of a symbiotic phase and the *raison d'être* for the stages of separation–individuation proposed by Mahler that lay ahead. Pine (1990, 1992) responded with the proposition that infants experience *moments* of merger or non-differentiation which have an affective significance sufficiently strong to account for the merger wishes observed in later life. While young infants may not spend all of their time in states of merger, such experiences, along with the caretaker's responses, would affect the subsequent course of separation–individuation subphases to follow. In response to Pine, Blum (2004) argued that a symbiotic phase should not be considered the same as symbiotic "moments." Rather, Blum suggested that Mahler's description of a "feeling of oneness" or "dual unity" (with the emphasis on the dyad or pair) to be more in keeping with newer research evidence during the stage of symbiosis, rather than a notion of fusion (of having a single boundary between two psychologically fused people). Most critics have acknowledged, however, the validity of the way in which the differentiation of the self from the non-self proceeded throughout infancy during the separation–individuation process.

Beginning awareness of mother's existence as a separate person heralded the first subphase of the separation–individuation process, according to Mahler. She used the term *hatching* to capture development during this time of *differentiation*, when the 5- to 10-month-old infant achieved the physical and intrapsychic capacities to check out what the external world had to offer. Tentative explorations began as infant slid from lap to floor and became a veteran of the not-too-far-from-mother's-feet environment. With increased locomotion, a new subphase ensued; *practicing* made its developmental entrance between about 10 and 15 months and marked an interval of increased exploration, escalating into an exhilarating "love affair with the world." As long as mother remained available, a "home base" for emotional "refueling" through the day's new adventures, all was well. It was not until about 15 to 22 months during the *rapprochement* subphase that mother was experienced as a separate person, a self in her own right. Such recognition brought a sense of great loss to the toddler and called for new strategies (seemingly regressive) in response. Attempts at "wooing" mother, at re-engaging her in external activity as a hoped for filler to an intrapsychic vacuum, lay at the heart of the *rapprochement crisis*. The realization ultimately dawned, however, that there was no return to the self–object fusion of earlier times. The toddler's conflict between the need for maternal (primary caretaker) incorporation on the one hand and separation and individuation on the other was at its height. The father (or additional caretaker) played a vital role here in supporting the child against the backward symbiotic pull.

Bergman and Harpaz-Rotem (2004) revisited Mahler's understanding of this rapprochement crisis in light of more recent developmental research. They suggested the concept of "co-construction" to describe how primary caretakers and toddlers worked to repair misunderstandings and conflicts through the rapprochement subphase of the separation–individuation process in infancy. It was not until the final, open-ended subphase of *libidinal object constancy* during the third year that life became less painful for both primary caretaker and child. Two accomplishments occurred at this time: "(1) the achievement of a definite, in certain aspects lifelong, individuality, and (2) the attainment of a certain degree of object constancy" (Mahler et al., 1975, p. 109). Object constancy implied the child's intrapsychic incorporation of both the "good and bad" parts of the maternal image to allow the child some physical distance from the mother of reality. Such accomplishment set the foundation for an intrapsychic structure that would be the basis of identity, at least until adolescence. While Mahler noted that clinical outcomes to the infant *rapprochement* crisis would be mediated by developmental crises of adolescence, she did not comment specifically on the implications of optimal infant separation–individuation subphase resolutions for adolescent development (Mahler et al., 1975).

Blos was quick to appreciate the applications of Mahler's work to the intrapsychic restructuring that occurred during adolescence:

> I propose to view adolescence in its totality as the second individuation process, the first one having been completed toward the end of the third year of life with the attainment of object constancy. Both periods have in common a heightened vulnerability of personality organization. Both periods have in common the urgency for changes in psychic structure in consonance with the maturational forward surge. Last but not least, both periods – should they miscarry – are followed by a specific deviant development (psychopathology) that embodies the respective failures of individuation.
>
> (Blos, 1967, p. 163)

Blos likened the infant's "hatching from the symbiotic membrane" described by Mahler to the adolescent process of "shedding family dependencies," that loosening of ties with the internalized parent that sustained the child though phallic and latency periods. Adolescent disengagement from this internalized parental representation allowed the establishment of new, extra-familial romantic attachments. Where such adolescent intrapsychic restructuring did not occur, the young person, at best, might merely substitute the original infantile attachment with a new love object, leaving the *quality* of the attachment unaltered.

Blos (1967) noted further accomplishments contingent upon successful resolution to the second individuation process:

- the acquisition of stable and firm self and object boundaries;
- the loss of some rigidity and power by the Oedipal superego; and
- greater constancy of mood and self-esteem, resulting from less dependence on external sources of support.

Up until adolescence, the child could make legitimate demands upon the parental ego, which had often served as an extension of the child's own less developed structure. Maturation of the child's own ego went hand in hand with disengagement from the internalized representations of caretakers: "[D]isengagement from the infantile object is always paralleled by ego maturation" (Blos, 1967, p. 165). It is through ego maturation that a firm sense of self, different from that of parents, not overwhelmed by internalized superego demands and more capable of self-support, emerged to mark the end of the second individuation process:

Individuation implies that the growing person takes increasing responsibility for what he[3] does and what he is, rather than depositing this responsibility
onto the shoulders of those under whose influence and tutelage he has
grown up.

(Blos, 1967, p. 168)

As Anna Freud has indicated, a mother's (or primary caretaker's) job is to be
there to be (intrapsychically) left. Or, in the more recent words of Usher (2017,
p. 104), "You can go home again (if you resolve your rapprochement crisis)."
Only in this way are adolescents able to disengage from parental internalizations and seek their own vocational and romantic fortunes in the world beyond
the family doorstep without guilt, while still maintaining altered external bonds
with caretakers and enjoying new forms of both intra- and interpersonal relationships with parents.

Central to successful resolution of adolescent individuation is regression. It is
only through the young person's ability to renew contact with infantile drives that
the psychic restructuring of adolescence can occur:

Just as Hamlet who longs for the comforts of sleep but fears the dreams that
sleep might bring, so the adolescent longs for the comforts of drive gratification but fears the reinvolvements in infantile object relations. Paradoxically,
only through regression, drive and ego regression, can the adolescent task be
fulfilled.

(Blos, 1967, p. 171)

In the words of one wall poster I observed in a university bookshop, "The best
way out is always through." Though not drawing any direct comparisons with
the intrapsychic conflicts and regressive behavior of Mahler's *rapprochement*
toddlers, Blos found the parallels between adolescent and toddler regressive functions to be striking. In Blos's view of the years post-infancy, it was only during
adolescence that regression could serve a normative developmental function.

Common adolescent regressive behaviors are phenomena such as a return to
"action" rather than "verbal" language (for example, passivity in response to situations best addressed by verbal expression of need), idolization of pop stars and
famous characters (reminiscent of the young child's idealization of parents), emotional states similar to merger (such as with religious or political groups), and
constant frenetic activity to fill the sense of internal object loss. Blos hastened to
add that it takes a relatively intact ego to survive the test of non-defensive regression during adolescence. Where ego organization has been deficient through
infant separation–individuation subphases, such deficiencies are laid bare with
the removal of parental props during adolescence: "The degree of early ego inad-
equacy often does not become apparent until adolescence, when regression fails
to serve progressive development, precludes individuation, and closes the door
to drive and ego maturation" (Blos, 1967, p. 175). It is the adolescent peer group
that, under optimal conditions, supplies support during the loss of childhood's

psychic structure. Just as *rapprochement* children try to re-engage the primary caretaker in their activities to cope with the pain of internal object loss, so too do adolescents seek solace from peers while relinquishing intrapsychic object ties. Mourning accompanies the loss of childhood's self.

Blos illustrated, with clinical example, the second individuation process in need of outside assistance for resolution. Let us, however, move from the clinical to the commonplace and view, by way of example, a more normative adolescent experience in terms of Blos's first character challenge:

> To pass from the romantic to the commonplace, imagine if you will the father of an adolescent boy settling into his chair in front of the television set after a grueling day with the conviction that he has earned his preprandial drink and a half hour's peace. His son, with whom he has been on surprisingly good terms for several days, slouches into the room and in response to his father's greeting mutters something that might equally well be understood as either "Hello" or "Hell, no!" Ten minutes or so go by in silence, until, in response to the news commentator's remarks on the energy crisis, the son begins to mutter angrily. The father, thinking the boy's vocalizations are an invitation to conversation, says something viciously provocative such as, "It looks as if we'll be facing some pretty tough problems in the next few years." In response the boy launches into a condemnation of his father's entire generation. As he warms to the task, he becomes more pointed and specific, reminding his father that if he were only willing to walk or bicycle the seven or eight miles to work instead of driving that gas-guzzling Volkswagen, the energy shortage would soon be resolved. But no! The hedonistic, materialistic, and self-indulgent orientation displayed by his father and all his contemporaries is robbing the boy's generation of any hope of physical warmth, mobility, and perhaps even survival.
>
> To emphasize his disgust with the situation, the boy announces he is going to find his mother. If dinner isn't ready, he plans to raise hell. If it is ready, he won't eat. His father once more is left feeling that whenever he interacts with his son, he misses some crucial point that would explain the whole interchange.
>
> (Coppolillo, 1984, pp. 125–126)

The saga continued as the son returned within several hours to greet his father cheerfully and request use of the family car to drive his girl across town for pizza. To the father's suggestion of a stroll to the nearby pizza parlor to save gas for posterity, he received an emphatic, "No! That just won't do! The pizza across town is just what he has a taste for at the moment. All other considerations are unimportant" (Coppolillo, 1984, p. 126). The father concluded that adolescence was indeed a period of "normal psychosis" (and the son that his father merely wished to deprive him of use of the family car).

In considering the above scenario, the young man's argumentative efforts with his father over the energy crisis appeared as a possible intrapsychic distancing technique designed to combat fears of infantile re-engulfment. In attacking the lifestyle of the parental generation, the youth pressed an ideological stand of "his own" – a stand that was quickly abandoned, however, when inconvenient. Forceful opposition to an innocuous reality might reflect fighting an other-than-external battle. Additionally, regression to infantile demands for immediate drive satisfaction (in both the Freudian and automotive senses here), coupled with rapid mood swings, are common to adolescence, indicating the fluidity of self and object representations: "The unavailability of the accustomed and dependable internal stabilizers of childhood seems to be responsible for many of the typical and transient personality characteristics of this age" (Blos, 1983, p. 582). Only when this labile young man is firm in his own sense of identity will such fluidity disappear, along with the need to push anything other than his own genuinely felt ideological concerns.

Before leaving Blos's second individuation challenge, brief mention must be made of resolutions that are less than optimal. Certainly, the tragic lives of many great artists and writers have been traced to both severe infant and adolescent separation and individuation difficulties. In chilling visual form, Norwegian painter Edvard Munch has dramatically communicated the separation anxiety plaguing his own existence in his well-known painting *The Scream*. Terrified, despairing eyes and an open mouth forming an unbridled scream are primitive features of the artist's central character, who appeared against the background of a sky ablaze. Munch's multiple and severe early childhood losses resulted in his own incomplete adolescent separation and individuation processes; this theme of profound separation anxiety was reflected in many of his works (Masterson, 1986). The life of Jean-Paul Sartre was also dulled by separation and individuation arrest (Masterson, 1986). In his autobiography, *Words*, Sartre says of his own life, "I had no true self" (1964, p. 75). "My mother and I were the same age and we never left each other's side. She used to call me her attendant knight and her little man; I told her everything" (Sartre, 1964, p. 148).

Among means of avoiding the adolescent individuation challenge are efforts at distancing from parents in ways other than through intrapsychic separation. Blos (1967) noted that attempts by adolescents to create physical or ideological space from their families do little to address the underlying intrapsychic task. Such abortive resolutions are reminiscent of Erikson's negative identity:

> By forcing a physical, geographical, moral, and ideational distance from the family or locale of childhood, this type of adolescent renders an internal separation dispensable. . . . The incapacity to separate from internal objects except by detachment, rejection, and debasement is subjectively experienced as a sense of alienation.
>
> (Blos, 1967, pp. 167–168)

It is noteworthy that Blos here also made use of the term *separation* in association with the second individuation process, though he did not detail either the separation or individuation tracks outlined by Mahler.

Reworking and mastering childhood trauma

Blos suggested that even those exposed to the kindest of childhood fates have innumerable opportunities for emotional injury. Furthermore, childhood trauma is a relative term; its impact depends both on the magnitude of the danger itself as well as the child's own vulnerability to such assault (Blos, 1962). Mastering childhood trauma is a lifelong task. One often sets up life situations that, in effect, recreate the original injury and thereby provide opportunities for mastery and resolution. Adolescence, because of its role in the consolidation of character, is a time when "a considerable portion of this task is being accomplished" (Blos, 1962, p. 132). At the close of adolescence, infantile traumas are not removed but rather (optimally) integrated into the ego and experienced as life tasks. In cases of optimal character formation, the individual is able to find satisfying ways to cope with what was originally an unmanageable childhood ordeal. Each effort at mastery of residual trauma results in heightened self-esteem. Reworking childhood's Oedipus complex is one specific example of this more generic adolescent task.

Blos (1968) drew upon Freud's writings to conclude that childhood trauma could have both positive and negative effects on character formation. Individuals may attempt to reactivate trauma, remembering and reliving it for integration into character as described above, or they may avoid the entire process, "a reaction that leads to the reactive character formation via avoidances, phobias, compulsions, and inhibitions" (Blos, 1968, p. 255). Adolescents who choose this latter option do not allow themselves the opportunity to come to terms with trauma, but rather remain under its directive in defensive maneuvers during the years that follow.

Because of the anxiety generated by residual trauma, there is often an urgency, a strong push toward expression in character: "Due to its origin character always contains a compulsive quality; it lies beyond choice and contemplation, is self-evident and compelling: 'Here I stand, I cannot do otherwise' (Luther)" (Blos, 1968, p. 255). The lives of many highly creative individuals such as Martin Luther have been presented as psychoanalytic evidence of attempts to remold childhood trauma into a mature ego organization at the close of adolescence.

Ego continuity

The third precondition for optimal character formation is that of ego continuity. Blos regarded this phenomenon as critical to character formation: "[A]dolescent development can be carried forward only if the adolescent ego succeeds in establishing a historical continuity in its realm. If this is prevented, a partial restructuring of adolescence remains incomplete" (Blos, 1968, pp. 256–257). Particularly apparent in situations where a child must accept a distorted reality to survive, lack of ego continuity results from a denial of one's own experience.

Ego continuity during adolescence served a purpose beyond that of conflict resolution; rather, it had an integrative and growth-stimulating function as the internalized parental representation became no longer needed and was cast by the wayside. Ego maturation gives rise to a "sense of wholeness and inviolability" during adolescence. It was only during late adolescence that the capacity to form one's own view of the past, present, and future emerged (Blos, 1976). Character formation at the close of adolescence is dependent upon the framework provided by ego continuity.

Sexual identity

The formation of character also involves establishment of a sexual identity. Sexual identity differs from gender identity, which is formed in early life. In traditional psychoanalytic form, Blos viewed adolescence as a necessary regressive return for completion of phallic stage Oedipal issues in order to establish, ultimately, a sexual identity.[4] Just as Blos stressed the necessity of an adolescent return to pre-Oedipal periods for restructuring intrapsychic parental bonds, he indicated that mature sexual interest could emerge only upon a return and final resolution to conflicts of childhood's Oedipal years:

> I venture to say that not until adolescence has the developmental moment arrived for the oedipal drama to be completed and the realization of mature object relations to be initiated. This step must be taken in adolescence or it never will, certainly not without circumstantial good fortunes and therapeutic intervention – in any case, not without much suffering which not every human adult is capable to endure.
>
> (Blos, 1989, p. 17)

With ego consolidation through the time of latency, however, the adolescent experiences such renewed Oedipal strivings at a different level. The Oedipus complex revived during adolescence is not the same as the childhood conflict:

> From my work with adolescents – male and female – I have gained the impression that the decline of the Oedipus complex at the end of the phallic phase represents a suspension of a conflictual constellation rather than a definitive resolution, because we can ascertain its continuation on the adolescent level. In other words, the resolution of the Oedipus complex is completed – not just repeated – during adolescence.
>
> (Blos, 1979, pp. 476–477)

Resolution during adolescence involves addressing both positive and negative Oedipal components (sexual love for both the opposite and same sex parent, respectively).

Character formation through adolescence

Whereas Freud saw adolescence as one general stage of psychosexual development, Blos felt the need for further detail here also. In tracing the formation of character through the adolescent passage, Blos (1962, 1971) described four phases of development during which the challenges are addressed. Each phase forms part of an orderly sequence which has its own time and place of ascendance; phases are not linked to specific chronological ages but rather to the intrapsychic issues they address. While Blos did not attend to all life-cycle phases in charting the evolution of identity, he did detail phases preceding and following adolescence; they too encapsulated important times in the building and consolidation of character.

The period of *latency*, which precedes adolescence, provides a time in which the ego and superego gain growing control over instincts. While the early Freudians saw latency as a time of sexual quiescence, Blos acknowledged that sexual interests and activities remained alive and well during this phase (as do many neo-Freudian psychoanalysts). In sum, the key function of latency is to provide a time for consolidation after the upheaval of the Oedipus complex.

Pre-adolescence heralds an increase in both sexual and aggressive drives with a concomitant decrease in ego control; stimuli which trigger impulse arousal often seem to have little direct relationship to the drive itself. Those working with young adolescents are aware how quickly any experience can become the source of sexual excitement. Direct gratification of instinctual impulse ordinarily meets strong superego resistance. Solution, for the mediating ego, rests with defenses such as repression, reaction formation and displacement. Compulsive interests and activities also function to contain pre-adolescent anxiety within manageable limits.

Early adolescence is distinguished by pubertal maturation alongside the young person's genuine beginnings of separation from early object ties. Additionally, sexual energy previously attached to the Oedipal triangle now begins to seek an extrafamilial outlet. Superego codes are diminished as the old internalized ties with parents loosen, and the ego is left to fumble in its regulatory function. Same-sex friendships of early adolescence are idealized; that is, young people search for friends who possess qualities that they do not have. In this way, desired characteristics can be obtained vicariously. One's ego ideal is often represented by such a friend. Not surprisingly, these early adolescent relationships are generally doomed to sudden demise because the demands placed on such friendships are too burdensome to bear for long.

It is only during the emergence of *adolescence proper* that one's interests turn to the sexual arena. Now there is no return to old Oedipal and pre-Oedipal object ties, and such finality shakes intrapsychic organization to its core. Life at this time, according to Blos, is generally in turmoil, yet at the same time new doors to development begin to open. The consolidation of sexual love involves the ability to shift from the early adolescent overvaluation of the self (as evidenced by the self-serving function of the same-sex chum) to a genuine interest in the identity of another. Before this can happen, however, one must experience the intrapsychic vacuum between "old" and "new" loves, the time of transitory nothingness. Coping mechanisms often involve states of heightened affect or frenzied activity, ways to "feel alive" and thus fill the intrapsychic void with an overdose of reality. In this way, boundaries of the self are protected from feared dissolution, accompanied frequently by poor judgment. Resolutions to both positive and negative Oedipal strivings are gradual and extend into adolescence's final phase.

Late adolescence sees a continued interest in the search for sexual love. Additionally, "the individual registers gains in purposeful action, social integration, predictability, constancy of emotions, and stability of self-esteem" (Blos, 1962, p. 128). Late adolescence is primarily a time of consolidation – a stabilizing of sexual identity into what is posited to be an irreversible pattern, establishing firm representations of self and others, and developing a greater sense of autonomy. Character has thus been formed.

Blos termed the final transition phase from adolescence to adulthood *post-adolescence*. It is marked by further structural integration: "In terms of ego development and drive organization, the psychic structure has acquired by the end of late adolescence a fixity which allows the postadolescent to turn to the problem of harmonizing the component parts of the personality" (Blos, 1962, p. 149). The work of postadolescence is to find outlets in a social reality through which sexual drive and "life tasks" (those resolutions to early trauma) can be expressed. With the decline of instinctual conflict, the ego is free to attend to this job.

A healthy character structure

What then is optimal psychological functioning at the close of adolescence? Blos (1983) has suggested that it involves the capacity to tolerate some degree of anxiety and depression, inevitable concomitants of the human condition. While the beginnings of adolescence go hand in hand with pubertal change, no such physiological delimiters mark its end:

> In summary fashion, I might say that puberty is an act of nature and adolescence is an act of man. This statement emphasizes the fact that neither the completion of physical growth, nor the attainment of sexual functioning, nor the social role of economic self-support are, by and in themselves, reliable indices for the termination of the adolescent process.
>
> (Blos, 1979, pp. 405–406)

What *is* a reliable index of character formation is the degree of coordination and integration among ego functions; adolescent closure occurs when character challenges become integrated and function in unison to mark an ensuing phase of greater autonomy and stability. Blos (1979, p. 410) noted this arrival "when ego autonomy, in alliance with the ego ideal, challenges partially but effectively the dominance of the superego." There is also a gradual change in the nature of relationships, both public and private, which are chosen with more discrimination and as a reflection of the individual's own needs and desires. Thus, if all goes well for our erstwhile pizza-driven, conservation-minded citizen of an earlier section, we might look several years hence to find a young man, very much in love with his marital and business partner, seated at Sunday dinner with his parents and engaged in a lively exchange of ideas on how the young couple's established fast food packaging business might make use of recycled paper. Blos concluded with a final warning, however, that "[e]ven if the consolidation of late adolescence has done its work in good faith, the framework of any personality structure can only stand up well over time if relatively benign circumstances continue to prevail" (1979, p. 411).

Criticism of Blos's construct and the second individuation process

Resting on limited clinical observations, Blos's construct has evoked criticism applicable to much of psychodynamically oriented theory. Not only are empirical foundations often shaky, but normative developmental principles are inferred from observations of those appearing in clinical settings. Furthermore, Blos often failed to deliver. In Blos's discussion of regression, for example, many specific questions regarding systems affected by and circumstances associated with a return to earlier stages remained unanswered, although more recent theory and research has attempted to address some of these issues (e.g., Kroger, 1996; Marcia & Bilsker, 1991). Such lack of attention to detail also appeared in Blos's discussion of the second individuation process. While we are certainly "now eager to trace the steps of individuation during adolescence" (Blos, 1967, p. 166), such steps were not subsequently delineated; Blos failed to identify specifically how Mahler's subphases of infant separation–individuation might be found during adolescence. Blos (1967) also did not focus on the issue of separation–individuation guilt that would likely accompany the formation of a separate sense of self. Erreich (2011) noted the likely link between the fear of being abandoned by the primary object (parent) and the guilt one is likely to experience over the desire to separate from the internalized other points to the need for further efforts to understand this phenomenon.

Literature on the second separation–individuation process of adolescence has supported a number of Blos's theoretical postulates, with some modifications. While adolescence does, indeed, seem to encompass a second individuation process, research suggested, however, that it was a phenomenon generally addressed in later, rather than in middle phases as indicated by Blos (e.g., Kins, Soenens, & Beyers, 2011; Koepke & Denissen, 2012; Sugimura et al., 2018). And rather than being a state of siege when Oedipal anxieties come to the fore as Blos suggested, normative adolescence seemed to be rather a time of steady, non-tumultuous maturation. Indeed, results of studies by Offer and his colleagues (e.g., Offer & Schonert-Reichl, 1992) as well as Hadiwijaya, Klimstra, Vermunt, Branje, and Meeus (2017) showed that adolescent turmoil is typical of only a small percentage of those involved in the studies; indeed, approximately 80% of adolescents in Offer's research experienced mostly satisfying and enjoyable relationships with their parents and peers, without high levels of anxiety or turmoil.

Criticism has also been leveled at Blos's adolescent utilization of the infant separation–individuation concept itself. Both Pine (1985) and Schafer (1973) cautioned against the application of separation–individuation subphases to times of the life-span other than infancy. During adolescence, for example, Schafer argued that there is no primitive merging of self and object as in infancy, and these analysts find it misleading to refer to later developmental processes with identical terms. Blass and Blatt (1996) and Blum (2004) pointed out that symbiosis, the foundation upon which the adolescent separation–individuation process rests, needs further refinement when considered as a form of relatedness both during and beyond infancy.

Other writers have suggested that separation–individuation theory can be applicable far beyond infancy and adolescence to describe additional phases of intrapsychic fusion and differentiation across different phases of adult life. For example, Colarusso (1990, 1997, 2000) has described a third, fourth, and fifth phase of individuation during young, middle, and late adult development, respectively. He argued that while adults do not repeat the original infant process described by Mahler (i.e., representational differentiation), the ongoing demands of adult life bring new phases of joining and separation, cohesion and differentiation from a significant, internalized other. Young adults in the third individuation phase must deal with issues of fusion and separation in relationships other than with those of primary objects (parents). For example, themes of intrapsychic fusion and separation reoccur with biological extensions of the self (i.e., one's own children). The fifth separation and individuation processes in old age shift to themes of fusion and separation through contemplation of leaving behind of all human relationships as death approaches. Despite criticism of separation and individuation constructs and processes, these concepts continue to generate theoretical and research interest in their applications to intrapsychic restructuring during adolescence as well as various phases of adult life (Usher, 2017).

Theoretical elaborations of the second individuation process of adolescence: links with identity

There have been efforts to detail subphases of separation and individuation processes during adolescence as Mahler and her colleagues have done during infancy and early childhood. While Blos has drawn general attention to parallels between the infant task of self–object differentiation and the differentiation between self and internalized representations by adolescents, later writers have attempted to delineate some aspects of the adolescent process more fully. While some similarities between the *processes* of infant and adolescent differentiation may exist, it must be remembered that the intrapsychic *organizations* during these two phases of the life-span are quite different.

In extending Blos's conceptualization of adolescence as a second individuation process, several contributions from object relations theory have provided guides as to how Mahler's phases and subphases of infant differentiation might be applied to the adolescent experience (for example, Esman, 1980; Josselson, 1988; Kroger, 1998). Through several longitudinal investigations with late adolescents in a university context, colleagues and I (JK) have tried to shed light on possible subphases of adolescent intrapsychic reorganization that may parallel subphases of self–object differentiation during infancy (e.g., Kroger, 1995; Kroger & Green, 1994; Kroger & Haslett, 1988). It must be remembered, however, that while the optimal outcome of infant separation–individuation subphases is to internalize a parental image in order ultimately to function autonomously in the parent's absence, the optimal outcome of adolescent separation–individuation subphases is to differentiate from that internalized parent to enable new forms of autonomy as well as connection within both internal and external environments.

It is recognized that efforts have provided only a first step toward understanding the normative differentiation experience and that frequent and intensive interviews with diverse groups of adolescents over longer time intervals are necessary to delineate the course of life's second separation–individuation process. Since the time that these studies were conducted, additional longitudinal studies of separation–individuation processes during adolescence and young adulthood have proliferated and are reviewed in a subsequent section; however, these later research designs generally do not allow additional insights into the specific subphases proposed below.

Parallels to Mahler's stage of normal symbiosis and separation–individuation subphases (differentiation, practicing, *rapprochement*, and libidinal object constancy) likely occur in normative adolescent development (Kroger, 1998). Empirical indicators for these suggestions have come via studies of ego identity status – a psychosocial measure providing clues as to underlying intrapsychic organization. Marcia's psychosocial identity statuses (described in Chapter 2) may reflect various phases in the underlying differentiation between self and parental representations. Identity achievements are characterized by an intrapsychic organization in which self and internalized parental representations are clearly distinct. Support for this proposal has come from various studies indicating an association of greater individuation (in terms of ego development, locus of control, field independence, use of mature defenses; object representation, a clear "I" position in relationships with others) with the identity achievement position (see Kroger & Marcia, 2011, for a review).

Moratoriums, differentiating from internalized parental representations, have shown some similarities to infant subphases of differentiation, practicing, and *rapprochement*, although there are also clear differences. In work by Josselson (1982), Orlofsky and Frank (1986), and Kroger (1990), early memories of moratorium research participants found them wishing to explore the world, with or without others (reminiscent of infant differentiation and practicing). Observations of moratoriums vying for power but ambivalent once it was held are reminiscent of behaviors during the infant *rapprochement* crisis (e.g., Josselson, 1982, 2017). On a measure of self-differentiation, moratoriums have scored as more fused with and simultaneously more cut off from significant others than other identity statuses (Johnson, Buboltz, & Seemann, 2003). Moratoriums have also shown more emotional reactivity than other identity groupings (Johnson et al., 2003). The authors interpreted their findings as indicative of wishes to individuate from parents while simultaneously wishing to remain fused with their internalized parental representations.

The foreclosure status would seem to reflect an intrapsychic organization having parallels with the symbiotic phase of infancy. Research with foreclosure adolescents has shown little differentiation between the self and internalized parental representations (Kroger & Marcia, 2011; Papini, Micka, & Barnett, 1989). Foreclosures have also shown more emotional overinvolvement with others, including overidentification with parents (Johnson et al., 2003; Perosa, Perosa, & Tam, 1996, 2002). Foreclosures' perceived lack of parental support, fear of parental opposition, and a history of acquiescing to parental demands also reflect little differentiation between self and internalized other (Perosa et al., 2002).

Diffusions have, on the whole, had little opportunity for internalizing parents with the concomitant difficulty in developing a cohesive sense of self (Josselson, 1987, 2017); a highly undifferentiated and laissez-faire family system providing little support for developing a unique identity has characterized diffusions' child-rearing environments (Perosa et al., 2002). Particularly noteworthy for the identity diffusions have been high scores on an emotional cut-off scale from the Differentiation of Self Inventory (Johnson et al., 2003). Emotional distancing appears to characterize the relationships diffusions have both with family and peers.

From longitudinal work, those late adolescents remaining foreclosed over a two-year interval were very likely to evidence a non-secure attachment profile (Kroger & Haslett, 1988). Moratoriums, at the conclusion of the study, were about equally divided between secure and non-secure attachment styles, while achievements were highly likely to be secure in their attachment style, evidencing greater intrapsychic self–other differentiation. Further longitudinal work by Kroger (1995) differentiated between "firm" and "developmental" foreclosures. Late adolescents who remained foreclosed over the course of their university studies evidenced significantly higher nurturance seeking needs at the outset (and conclusion) of the study than those initial foreclosures who later proceeded to moratorium and achievement positions.

A pictorial scheme for adolescents, in the process of differentiating themselves from the internalized primary caretaker, appears in Figure 3.1.

In this scheme, the diffusion position has not been described, for diffusion (in the Eriksonian sense of having no central "core") would not reflect a normative resolution to the second separation–individuation process. Subphase representations should serve as a useful base for describing social reaction to best facilitate the adolescent individuation process. Just as the caretaker must adjust his or her response to infant action through each developmental subphase for optimal ego structuralization, so too must social reaction resonate with adolescent need in each second individuation subphase in order to provide a context for optimal development.

Measuring the adolescent separation–individuation process

A number of instruments have been developed over past decades for the measurement of the adolescent separation–individuation process. Perhaps that

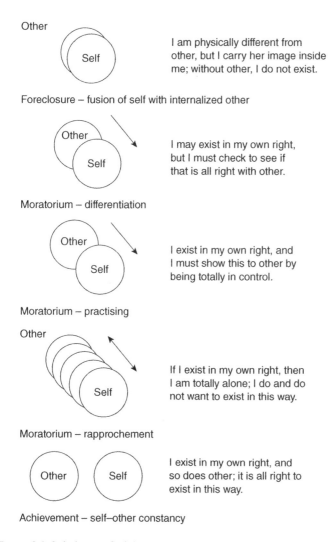

Other

I am physically different from other, but I carry her image inside me; without other, I do not exist.

Foreclosure – fusion of self with internalized other

I may exist in my own right, but I must check to see if that is all right with other.

Moratorium – differentiation

I exist in my own right, and I must show this to other by being totally in control.

Moratorium – practising

Other

If I exist in my own right, then I am totally alone; I do and do not want to exist in this way.

Moratorium – rapprochement

I exist in my own right, and so does other; it is all right to exist in this way.

Achievement – self–other constancy

Figure 3.1 Subphases of adolescent separation–individuation

most widely used has been the Separation–Individuation Test of Adolescence (Levine, 1994; Levine, Green, & Millon, 1986). The Separation–Individuation Test of Adolescence (SITA) is a 103-item, self-report inventory that presents a series of statements reflecting attitudes about relationships with parents, teachers, and peers. Items are presented in Likert Scale format on a five-point scale, ranging from "strongly agree or is always true of me" to "strongly disagree or is never true of me." The SITA's nine scales are derived from elements of the early separation–individuation process described by Mahler et al. (1975). These nine scales are as follows: Separation Anxiety (significant others experienced as abandoning), Engulfment Anxiety (close relationships feared as envelopment), Dependency Denial (denying one's need for significant others), Nurturance Seeking (strong caretaker attachment), Peer Enmeshment (strivings for intense peer intimacy), Teacher Enmeshment (strivings for intense attachments to teachers), Practicing–Mirroring (narcissistic strivings), Rejection Expectancy (significant others perceived as callous and hostile), and Healthy Separation (balance of dependence and independence strivings). The SITA was developed through a three-step validation procedure with attention to theoretical–substantive validity and internal structural validation. Cronbach's alphas for the nine scales have ranged from 0.64 to 0.88 for both clinical and non-clinical samples.

A number of additional measures of adolescent separation–individuation have been developed to assess other features of the adolescent separation–individuation process, including the following: Separation–Individuation Inventory (Bartolomucci & Taylor, 1991); Multi-Individuation Scale (Chen, Richardson, Lai, Dai, & Hays, 2018); Separation–Individuation Process Inventory (Christenson & Wilson, 1985); Adolescent Separation Anxiety Test (Hansburg, 1980a, 1980b); Psychological Separation Inventory (Hoffman, 1984); Individuation Test for Emerging Adults (Komidar, Zupančič, Sočan, & Puklek Lepušček, 2014); Munich Individuation Test of Adolescence (Kruse & Walper, 2008); Individuation Scale (Maslach, Stapp, & Santee, 1985); and the Dysfunctional Individuation Scale (Stey, Hill, & Lapsley, 2014).

Refinements have also been undertaken with some of these measures. For example, McClanahan and Holmbeck (1992), Levine and Saintonge (1993), Levine (1994), Holmbeck and McClanahan (1994), and Kruse and Walper (2008) have all suggested refinements to Levine's original Separation–Individuation Test of Adolescence. Dolan, Evans, and Norton (1992) and Lapsley and his colleagues (Lapsley, Aalsma, & Varshney, 2001; Stey et al., 2014) have made refinements to Christenson and Wilson's Separation–Individuation Inventory. Komidar, Zupančič, Puklek Lepušček & Bjornsen (2016) have developed a short version of their Individuation Test for Emerging Adults that has shown measurement invariance across two countries.

In addition, a parental separation anxiety measure (Parents of Adolescents Separation Anxiety Scale or PASAS; Hock, Eberly, Bartle-Haring, Ellwanger, & Widaman, 2001) has also been developed to assess parents' feelings about separation from their adolescent offspring. Bartle-Haring, Brucker, and Hock (2002) and Hock et al. (2001) worked to validate the measure, and it is being used now to understand specific dynamics of adolescent separation–individuation issues within families (e.g., Kins, Soenens, & Beyers, 2011). The PASAS is a 35-item instrument designed to assess parental emotions associated with adolescent separation–individuation processes. Factor analyses supported the formation of two subscales: Anxiety about adolescent distancing and Comfort with secure base role. Adolescents of parents who had high anxiety scale scores on the measure reported lower quality of attachment to both mothers and fathers.

Historical backdrop to Blos's separation–individuation challenge

Blos's early directorship of the Experimental School, run by Anna Freud and Dorothy Burlingham, and his contact with Freud and psychoanalytic circles in Vienna laid the foundations for Blos's interest in adolescents (Esman, 1997). Blos's emigration to New York when Hitler rose to power brought him into contact with the work of Margaret Mahler and inspired his consideration of adolescence as a second separation–individuation process, albeit with important distinctions from the first infant process. While Blos retained his ties to classic psychoanalytic foundations, his work, nevertheless, served as a bridge to some object relations approaches and later elaborations of the second separation–individuation process during adolescence.

From classic psychoanalysis, it was the drives that governed motivation and behavior. Relationships or interpersonal interactions were important to Freud, but only insofar as they satisfied instinctual needs (the drives). By sharp contrast, an object relations approach focused on internalized others from environmental interactions to explain motivation. Many object relations models focused on the processes of internalization (taking in the image of another and making it a part of oneself) and identification (wanting to emulate or be like an admired other) to examine the forces of environmental influences on the development of the ego. Furthermore, while classic psychoanalysis focused on conflict among id, ego and superego structures, object relations writers focused on the early structuralization of the ego itself (Greenberg & Mitchell, 1983). Blos assessed adolescents' changes in object relations through discussions of separation anxiety as well as the mourning of earlier internalized ties to parents, considerably extending Freud's notion of signal anxiety (McCarthy, 1995). By considering adolescence as a second separation–individuation process, Blos inspired many later theorists and researchers to delve more deeply into the structural reorganizations of the ego and optimal character formation upon entry into young adult life via the adolescent second separation–individuation process.

Research findings on adolescent separation–individuation

The second separation–individuation challenge entails both intrapsychic and interpersonal changes. The past four decades have witnessed a growing body of research into the adolescent intrapsychic separation–individuation process in relation to attachment and interpersonal relationships with family and peers, social adjustment, identity, and psychopathology. Here, only a selection of research that attempts *directly* to measure the second separation–individuation process of adolescence will be over-viewed in relation to other phenomena; a wealth of studies also exist that assess dimensions of adolescent separation–individuation issues less directly (by inference) in relation to other factors.

The changing nature of adolescent and young adult relationships with parents and peers has received perhaps the greatest volume of attention in the adolescent separation–individuation literature over recent decades. One focus has been on the relationship between separation–individuation and attachment patterns with parents or other significant adults. Invariably, patterns of healthy adolescent/young adult separation–individuation outcomes have been linked with secure attachment styles (see Rice, 1990, for a meta-analysis). For example, Quintana and Lapsley (1990) found a positive relationship between attachment to parents and differentiation from them, while Rice (1992) found continuity in attachment to parents over time coupled with increases in independence from them in a sample of late adolescent college students. By contrast, Delhaye et al. (2012) found non-optimal attachment and separation–individuation patterns among delinquent and (psychiatric) hospitalized adolescents, compared with controls. A meta-analysis by Mattanah, Lopez, and Govern (2011) showed the relationship between adolescent separation–individuation outcomes and parental attachment to be the strongest association across a number of possible variables in relation to adolescent separation–individuation issues. Secure attachment profiles have appeared strongly linked with optimal separation–individuation outcomes.

Another area of family focus has been on parental styles of support/communication and adolescent separation–individuation processes. Patterns of healthy adolescent separation–individuation resolutions have appeared most likely within the context of a family structure capable of supporting and encouraging both autonomy and connection (e.g., Dzukaeva, 2014; Grotevant & Cooper, 1998; Pinquart & Silbereisen, 2002; Ponappa, Bartle-Haring, & Day, 2014). Families with optimal differentiation among members, it seems, are able both to maintain emotional connections while supporting and encouraging differentiation among family members. Recent longitudinal work by Ponappa et al. (2014), for example, followed some 500 families with young adolescents at the outset over the course of four years, with three waves of data on each family. A mutual sense of connection between mothers and adolescents showed strong links with the adolescent's healthy separation–individuation outcomes over time. Meeus and his colleagues (Meeus, Iedema, Maassen, & Engels, 2005) argued that adolescent separation and individuation are two parallel, rather than sequential, processes in optimal identity and emotional adjustment during adolescence (an idea that Mahler espoused with regard to the infant separation–individuation process). It appears that the quality of adolescent–parent relationships actually provides a strong measure of intrapsychic developmental progress on the separation–individuation task for the adolescent over time.

Several researchers have examined specific family interactions that may play a role in adolescent separation–individuation. Self-disclosure in parent–adolescent communications is one indicator of relationship quality within the family, as well as the adolescent's navigation of the second separation–individuation process. In Hong Kong, Jiang, Yang, and Wang (2017) found that dysfunctional independence among young adults significantly reduced the young person's perceptions of parental responsiveness as well as relationship quality; engulfment anxiety appeared as a stronger factor than dependency denial in reducing the young adult's disclosure to parents (though the authors point out that this result may be culturally grounded). And young, dysfunctionally dependent women with high separation anxiety were likely to disclose negative aspects of themselves to their parents compared with other peers in the study. Further research into the types of disclosures both adolescents and their parents make in the family setting would be an important advance in learning more about the second separation–individuation process.

Bjornsen (2000) investigated Blos's (1985) suggestion that an important part of the second separation–individuation process is receiving a family "blessing." In his investigation of fathers and sons, Blos defined a blessing as the father's acknowledgment and acceptance of the son's adult status and, most importantly, the son's adult masculinity. Some form of blessing is needed before "childhood can be brought to a natural termination" (Blos, 1985, p. 12). Bjornsen examined the possible role of the blessing to the adolescent separation–individuation process for both genders in a sample of college students. He found that 71.5% of the 281 late adolescents sampled had received some form of blessing from a parent, and they had described the event as meaningful. Additionally, of those who had not received a blessing, about half wished that they had. Adolescents who participated in this investigation wrote powerful and sensitive accounts of the blessing they had received or wished they had received. The study did not provide details of whether or not gender of the parent was important in providing a blessing, an interesting avenue for further investigation.

Different patterns of separation–individuation have been linked to different styles of parent–adolescent communication and parental behavioral control. Premature disruption to parent–adolescent emotional ties or excessive parental intrusion have both been found to be risk factors for optimal adolescent separation–individuation outcomes. In Belgium, Kins et al. (2011) initially explored parental separation anxiety and the process of separation individuation difficulties that might be experienced by a sample of late adolescents leaving home. They found that regardless of whether or not their offspring resided with parents or lived semi-independently, both maternal and paternal separation anxiety and dependency-oriented psychological control were linked with separation–individuation difficulties among late adolescents.

Kins, Soenens, and Beyers (2012) proceeded to suggest that excessive psychological control on the part of parents might be linked with two different types of separation–individuation difficulties among adolescents: either adolescent dysfunctional dependence (where intrusive control by parents is driven by their desire for closeness to their adolescent) or dysfunctional independence (where parental control focuses on their adolescent's achievement). Kins and colleagues' research indeed showed for youth in the process of leaving home that both dysfunctional dependence as well as dysfunctional independence were associated with depression but differentially associated with attachment as follows: Late adolescents exhibiting dysfunctional dependence demonstrated attachment anxiety as they worried about not being loved by others, while those demonstrating dysfunctional independence showed high levels of attachment avoidance, feeling discomfort with closeness and dependence on another. Dysfunctional dependence has shown a strong resemblance to the Diagnostic and Statistical Manual of Mental Disorders (DSM-5) defined separation anxiety disorder; dysfunctional independence, however, has not yet been recognized by the DSM-5 as a different form of separation–individuation disorder (Kins, Soenens, & Beyers, 2012). More recently, Kavčič and Zupančič (2018) also identified similar profiles of adolescent/young adult separation–individuation resolutions through cluster analysis, and they examined these clusters with regard to each parent. The young adult profiles included the dependent type, the anxious type, the individuated type, and the individuated-independent type. Here, about half of individuals were described by the same type of separation–individuation profile in relation to both parents. Future research might well focus on each parent within a family separately, in attempting to understand their possibly unique roles in the adolescent separation–individuation process.

Kins, Soenens, and Beyers (2012) also explored specific types of psychological control on the part of parents, and found, as predicted, that dependency oriented psychological control was related to dysfunctional dependence among adolescents, and parental achievement-oriented control was linked to adolescent dysfunctional independence. Adolescents of parents high on achievement-oriented control were likely to receive the message that the pursuit of personal, independent achievement is the best route to validate self-worth, at the expense of collaboration and relationship.

Research has also suggested that it is important for adolescents to grow up in families that provide both clear and hierarchical boundaries (Minuchin, 1974). Across a number of different cultural contexts, parental boundary diffusion has been linked with difficulties in the adolescent separation–individuation process (e.g., Mayseless & Scharf, 2009; Perrin, Ehrenberg, & Hunter, 2013; Valls-Vidal, Alsina, Pérez-Testor, Guàrdia-Olmos, & Iafrate, 2016). In Spain, however, Valls-Vidal et al. (2016) found differential responses to parents by gender of adolescent across various dysfunctional family patterns. For example, feeling caught between parents has been associated with individuation difficulties for adolescents with respect to mothers but not fathers, while adolescents involved in loyalty conflicts (and scoring high on fear of love withdrawal) reported lower levels of autonomy in relation to father but not mother. Much remains to be learned about potential gender differences of both adolescents and their parents in relation to the adolescent separation–individuation process, especially in families with poor boundary definitions.

Peer relations have also been extensively examined in studies of adolescent separation–individuation. Perceptions of social support have been positively related to healthy separation–individuation during adolescence and negatively related to dependency denial and engulfment fears (McClanahan & Holmbeck, 1992). Quintana and Kerr (1993) found that participation in relationships that supported autonomy, mirroring, and nurturance needs were associated with less depression among college students and that, conversely, engulfment anxiety, separation anxiety, and denial of dependency were associated with depressive complaints. Individuated late adolescents also appeared disinclined to stereotype others (Humphreys & Davidson, 1997).

How are patterns of adolescent separation–individuation related to the capacity for intimacy with those outside the family? Rather strongly, it appears. For example, Kins, Beyers, and Soenens (2012) found that those young adults with difficulties in the second separation–individuation process also showed dysfunctional attachment patterns in relation to a romantic partner. *Dysfunctional dependence* in the adolescent separation–individuation process was strongly related to *attachment anxiety* (excessive worry about not being loved by others), while *dysfunctional independence* (discomfort with closeness and dependency on others) showed a strong relation to *attachment avoidance*. Interesting gender differences also emerged, with women more likely to express separation–individuation difficulties in a *dysfunctional dependent* manner, whereas men were more likely to express such difficulties in a dysfunctional independent manner. Furthermore, those young adults scoring high on dysfunctional independence were less likely to be involved in a partner relationship at all, perhaps because such a relationship would threaten their excessive independence.

Similar results have also come from research in Norway, Portugal, and the United States. From a Norwegian study of female university students, women identified as "Intimate" in their romantic relationships (based on interview) scored lower on separation anxiety than women who showed a "Pseudo-intimate" (superficial in their relationships) or "Merger" (overly dependent in their relationships) style of relating to a romantic partner (Årseth, Kroger, Martinussen, & Bakken, 2009). Pseudo-intimate women scored higher than Intimate women on rejection expectation and dependency denial, while Merger women were also significantly higher on dependency denial than Intimate women. Here, different styles of intimacy were strongly linked with various intrapsychic ramifications of the adolescent separation–individuation process. Saraiva and Matos (2012) also found a moderate association between adolescent separation–individuation dimensions and relationships with parents as well as a romantic partner. Earlier studies in the United States had also linked separation–individuation difficulties with non-optimal styles of intimacy during young adult life (e.g., Bellew-Smith & Korn, 1986; Levitz-Jones & Orlofsky, 1985). It thus appears that there are important links between an adolescent's resolution to the second separation–individuation process and the capacity for intimacy in a romantic relationship during late adolescent and young adult life.

Research on adolescent separation–individuation has consistently pointed to more optimal psychosocial outcomes for those who successfully navigate this intrapsychic passage (Hill, Burrow, & Summer, 2016; Holmbeck & Leake, 1999; Lapsley & Edgerton, 2002; Rice, Cole, & Lapsley, 1990). For example, young adults reporting a sense of purpose in their lives have reported fewer difficulties with the second separation–individuation process than those without a strong sense of purpose (Hill, Burrow, & Summer, 2016; Walzer & Nottis, 2013). High school students in France who scored high in separation anxiety reported significantly higher rates of cannabis use than adolescents who did not use cannabis; cannabis use was perceived to be a way of trying to reduce separation anxiety during the separation–individuation process of adolescence (Laguerre, Vavassori,

& Fernandez, 2015). Rice et al. (1990) found that late adolescent college students who reported positive separation experiences (non-anxious and unresentful reactions to a variety of separation experiences from significant others) also reported being well adjusted to university life, while those with negative, angry, or resentful responses to separation had more difficulty managing adjustment to college. Lapsley and Edgerton (2002) also found college adjustment to be positively associated with secure attachment and optimal separation–individuation outcomes. Adjustment to demands of the world at large appears intricately linked with resolution to the second separation–individuation challenge of adolescence.

The relation between separation–individuation difficulties and delinquency, loneliness, eating disorders, and depression during adolescence have been the focus of many investigations over past decades (e.g., Armstrong & Roth, 1989; Delhaye et al., 2012; Friedlander & Siegel, 1990; Marsden, Meyer, Fuller, & Waller, 2002; Mattanah, Brand, & Hancock, 2004; Milne & Lancaster, 2001; Rhodes & Kroger, 1992; Smolak & Levine, 1993; Stey et al., 2014). These works point to similar intrapsychic and familial factors that contribute to the etiology and maintenance of many non-optimal outcomes of adolescent separation–individuation and to the serious consequences for those who may fail to attain a sense of psychological separateness that enables new forms of both internal and external relationships with others.

Indirect links may exist between separation–individuation difficulties and non-optimal outcomes during adolescence. Marsden et al. (2002) showed that perceived parental control may be a mediating factor between separation–individuation resolution and eating disorders. Milne and Lancaster (2001) used path analysis to indicate that adolescent women's concerns with maternal control predicted separation–individuation difficulties, which predicted interpersonal concerns, which in turn predicted symptoms of depression. In general, adolescent difficulties in the second separation–individuation process have been linked with a number of poorer mental health outcomes relative to peers who experienced healthy separation–individuation processes. There may be a host of both intrapsychic and familial factors in the pathways to such poor mental health outcomes, and much work remains to be done to explore these potential links; understanding such links also holds important implications for effective intervention.

Current directions in adolescent separation–individuation research

A growing interest in adolescent separation–individuation research has been the question of how diverse cultural contexts may impact the separation–individuation process during adolescence. Many collectivist cultures, for example, may not encourage the development of intrapsychic separation–individuation processes during adolescence. Investigations of adolescent separation–individuation have appeared both within and across varied cultural or ethnic contexts and point to some interesting similarities and differences among adolescents (e.g., Chen et al., 2018; Choi, 2002; Kalsner & Pistole, 2003; Scharf, 2001). Scharf (2001), for example, explored variations of separation–individuation and attachment patterns among adolescents within four Israeli contexts: those living in a city; those from a kibbutz familial setting; those from a kibbutz communal setting; a transitional group raised in a communal setting as young children but who then moved into familial sleeping arrangement prior to the age of six years. The group who had lived in a communal setting (sleeping away from parents as young children) in the kibbutz evidenced less competent coping as adolescents in situations that evoked separation anxiety as well as a higher incidence of non-autonomous attachment representations.

Some studies are beginning to follow suggestions from Koepke and Denissen (2012) that a dynamic, developmental perspective be undertaken to understand how separation–individuation, identity, and parent–child relationship processes interact over time. Sugimura et al. (2018) examined the inter-relations between emotional separation, parental trust, and three dimensions of identity (synthesis, confusion, and consolidation) among young-middle adolescents in Lithuania, Italy, and Japan. In earlier research, those in living in Lithuania and Italy scored high on measures of individualism compared to those in the Japanese context (Hofstede, Hofstede, & Minkov, 2010). Sugimura and her colleagues found high consistency across Lithuanian, Italian, and Japanese contexts in terms of adolescent identity consolidation; emotional separation and parental trust were consistently linked with identity consolidation across the three national samples. However, relations between emotional separation and parental trust with identity synthesis and confusion differed across these contexts. In Lithuania and Italy (emphasizing individualism), cultural pressures were likely strong for both parents and adolescents to pursue a coherent sense of individual identity (to maximize a synthesized and minimize a confused sense of identity), and adolescents here demonstrated higher levels of identity synthesis and lower levels of identity confusion compared with those adolescents in Japan. While this study was not longitudinal in nature, its focus on the inter-relations among adolescent separation–individuation, identity, and parent–child relationship dimensions with samples living in different cultural contexts represents an important direction in adolescent research and an inspiration for future longitudinal work. In cross-cultural research involving immigrant youths, it is also important to consider possible generational differences in adolescent separation–individuation processes within any one national group. Some evidence has shown that second generation adolescent immigrants have more separation–individuation difficulties than their first generation adolescent counterparts (Oznobishin & Kurman, 2016).

Implications for social response

Though Blos did not discuss in depth the role of the social context in facilitating an adolescent's resolution to his four character challenges, parents, teachers, counselors, psychotherapists and others working closely with young people may all play critical roles in facilitating movement through the second separation–individuation process. Other adolescent character challenges are also affected by reactions from these socialization agents, as well as from the general structure of a society itself. In passing from the family to a place in the larger social order, that order must be ready to receive:

> [N]o adolescent, at any station of his journey, can develop optimally without societal structures standing ready to receive him, offering him that authentic credibility with which he can identify or polarize. . . . [T]he psychic structure of the individual is critically affected, for better or worse, by the structure of society. . . . [W]hat I try to emphasize here is the fact that the successful course of adolescence depends intrinsically on the degree of intactness and cohesion which societal institutions obtain.
>
> (Blos, 1971, p. 975)

Blos continued by noting that character formation may at times be helped not by efforts at individual remediation but rather by the rehabilitation of those very social institutions in which the adolescent is expected to find some suitable niche. Disaffected youth, though often instigators of social revolution, are seldom its cause. A society, through its institutions, must remain sensitive and responsive to youth's insights (often deadly accurate) into problems of the social structure itself (Blos, 1979).

In comments on the earlier onset of puberty, Blos cautioned against the simplistic conclusion that family and school must respond to the earlier arousal of sexual drive: "We have ample evidence to demonstrate that an acceptance of the young adolescent as a self-directing, sexually active 'young person' interferes severely with the preparatory functions of this stage" (Blos, 1971, p. 970). He continued to argue that it is critical to prolong rather than abbreviate childhood in order to allow time for intrapsychic restructuring to occur. A young person pressing toward earlier sexual activity may do so at the expense of a firmly established sexual identity in adult life.

Blos cautioned that parents and social institutions must also recognize the role they may play in adolescents' struggles for freedom from infantile dependencies. Where intrapsychic change is difficult, declarations of independence are often projected outward, in exaggerated form, onto institutions (for example, universities) which have provided youth with temporary accommodation through the adolescent passage. It is important for adults to recognize their potential for association with an internalized parental image rather than their existence merely as external agents of reality in evoking adolescent responses.

In terms of the second individuation challenge, it is informative to move beyond Blos to more recent efforts at subphase delineation, for each stage presents a time of special need which must be recognized and addressed to provide optimal conditions for development. Mahler's observations of what constitutes "ordinary devoted mothering" through each subphase of infancy is helpful in understanding ways to facilitate the second separation–individuation process. Assuming the adolescent has enjoyed the security provided by significant overlap between intrapsychic self and parental representations since childhood, the gradual elimination of that overlap is now possible. As Mahler has observed for infants, a stage of normal symbiosis is absolutely critical in order for separation–individuation subphases to proceed.

In normative adolescent development, the differentiation process is likely to begin of its own accord. It can be facilitated by adults who, despite youths' withdrawal from the closeness of earlier latency relationships, do not react in retaliation but rather with understanding of new needs for distance and independent action. Respect for adolescents as individuals in their own right rather than as extensions of one's self are crucial adult attitudes for aiding the second individuation process. The stifling effect of parental separation anxiety on adolescent separation–individuation processes has been earlier documented in work by Bartle-Haring et al. (2002) and Kins et al. (2011). As in all adolescent separation–individuation subphases, use of transitional objects may also assist adolescents' efforts in relinquishing infantile object ties (Kroger, 1998).

Counseling or psychotherapeutic intervention may be necessary when delayed or premature differentiation from the internalized parental representation takes place. Inhibited differentiation is likely to be responsible for what Erikson and Marcia have described as a foreclosed identity. Here, many of the adolescent's actions will be aimed at receiving parental approval, thereby gaining narcissistic gratification and self-esteem. With such youths, it is the therapeutic aim to promote differentiation in a manner age appropriate yet paralleling the way in which a "good enough" mother or caretaker assists the infant through the differentiation process. Following establishment of a caring relationship, therapeutic response might take the form of gentle, developmental "nudges" coupled with explorations of the youth's guilt and fear over abandoning the internalized parent (Feldberg, 1983). Additionally, over time, therapeutic work must involve the adolescent's de-idealization of the internalized parent as well as working through the mourning process (Blos, 1979).

Premature differentiation in adolescence is characterized by separation which cannot keep pace with individuation. Such misalignment may stem from fear of engulfment by the internalized parent. As a result, there is insufficient ego strength to support the push towards expression of autonomous action; poor decisions, which may result in serious injury or situations having long-term consequences, are often the result. Here, it is the therapeutic aim to harness differentiation by setting firm limits and assisting the family to do likewise. Interpretation and confrontation may also be used to work through anxieties and so bring adolescent separation and individuation tracks into closer alignment (Feldberg, 1983).

Adolescent parallels to the practicing subphase of infancy bring continued efforts to test an intrapsychic structure permitting more autonomous functioning. As the practicing toddler is assisted in further exploration by new locomotor abilities, so too may adolescents acquire the skill (and driver's license) necessary for motorized movement further into the world beyond where buses and family outings go. It is still vital, however, that significant others offer the adolescent a solid "refueling" base from which new explorations can be launched. Parental support and encouragement for such exploratory efforts during adolescence parallel the importance Mahler et al. (1975) placed on maternal reaction to the infant in all separation–individuation subphases. A balance between support and limit setting would seem to provide the optimal conditions for resolution to demands of this practicing subphase of adolescence (Feldberg, 1983).

Adolescent *rapprochement* is marked by swings between efforts at distancing and renewed efforts for closeness, as youths seek to return internalized self and parental images to the symbiotic level of earlier intrapsychic organization. The ability of adults to maintain their own ground in the face of adolescent regressive and progressive development is a difficult but necessary stance (Feldberg, 1983). A caregiver's vulnerability to adolescent assault (in defense against the latter's regressive pulls) does not enable one to remain emotionally available as youths' intrapsychic moorings become unfastened.

Libidinal object constancy represents the infant resolution to separation–individuation subphases; for the adolescent or young adult, this stage involves a consolidation of structural reorganization. Brandt nicely stated features of this final phase:

> The identity crisis of adolescence is thus caused not only because it is hard for the adolescent to find himself, but because in the process he must find himself alone. Kramer . . . sees the "experience of identity as finding oneself painfully separated from one's accustomed environment, alone, and forced to rely on one's own resources. The experience of separation from the first love object, mother, and the sensation of aloneness is one of the factors in the creation of a sense of identity." Without this separation no true autonomy or independence of the ego or superego is possible, and hence no real sense of identity can be achieved.
>
> (Brandt, 1977, pp. 517–518)

This final phase, the aim of normative parenting, counseling, and psychotherapeutic effort, would see adolescents and young adults able to meet others in a relationship of unique, autonomous individuals, each able to hold genuine interest in and connection to the identity of an other (Feldberg, 1983).

Recent research into the adolescent separation–individuation process pointed to some clinical or counseling implications for those working with youth. Lapsley and Edgerton (2002) suggested the potential counseling or clinical use of PATHSTEP, an instrument designed to detect separation–individuation difficulties. Items from the instrument may be used as initial probes in making sense of a client's difficulties (e.g., "Does the sense of who you are tend to get lost when you are in a close relationship?"). The authors also pointed to the importance of conflictual independence in normal adolescent separation–individuation. Clients with conflictual dependency problems would be at lower risk for adjustment difficulties than those with problems of self-differentiation. Holmbeck and Wandrei's (1993) research on college adjustment among first-year students suggested that adjustment may be less related to their cognitive perceptions of home-leaving and more related to object relational functioning. Intervention assistance that is directed solely to the cognitive realm for such students may be less successful than assisting development through the second separation–individuation process.

In clinical settings, a multitude of case studies exist that address issues such as working toward increased self and other differentiation within a supportive context. For example, Usher (2017) described her work with late adolescents and young adults who have "failed to launch"; her treatment in such instances involves a slow, gradual process toward overcoming resistance and working toward establishing a more equal partnership in the therapeutic context. Termination issues receive special attention for both client and therapist, as they reflect the ultimate test of "launching." Bettmann, Tucker, Behrens, and Vanderloo (2017) pointed to the success of a Wilderness Therapy program for adolescents and young adults experiencing difficulties of separation–individuation. Their program combined prolonged separation from families in conjunction with the challenges of being placed in a wilderness environment in which one needed to rely more on one's own resources. Participants, over time, received individual and group treatment from licensed practitioners and post-treatment follow-up contacts with both individuals and their families. Program outcome research found that participants reported significant changes in relationships with mothers, including less resentment, anger, guilt, and generally feeling less attachment anxiety and greater comfort with being close to others. Results for relational changes with fathers produced more mixed results. Therapists working with adolescents from collectivist cultural backgrounds in Western settings may be most effective by helping such youths to examine the personal importance of their collectivistic sense of self and strengthening their sense of ownership of collectivist attitudes (Choi, 2002).

Summary

Character formation as outlined by Blos involves the resolution of at least four challenges in order for identity to develop and stabilize at the close of adolescence: the second individuation process, reworking and mastering childhood trauma, developing a sense of ego continuity and forming a sexual identity. Object relations theorists have proposed more detailed accounts of mechanisms that may operate during the second separation–individuation process of adolescence, and a growing body of research is exploring this phenomenon in different cultural contexts. It is vital that individuals and social institutions involved with youth appreciate their potential associations with adolescents' internalized parental representations, which must be restructured if optimal resolution to the second separation–individuation process is to occur.

Notes

1 Margaret Mahler (1897–1985) was a Hungarian psychiatrist and psychoanalyst, migrating to New York City following Hitler's rise to power in Europe. In 1950, she established the Master's Chilren Center, where she undertook her work on the separation–individuation process of infancy.

2 This use of the term "autism" is not the same kind of autism that is used to denote a developmental disorder.

3 We are preserving the original language that was used by scholars in Blos's writings but recognize that "he" here refers to people in general.

4 In classic psychoanalytic tradition, Blos promoted the concept that a heterosexual relationship marked the consolidation of sexual identity during adolescence. His original concept has been modified here to reflect contemporary views.

References

Armstrong, J. G., & Roth, D. M. (1989). Attachment and separation difficulties in eating disorders: A preliminary investigation. *International Journal of Eating Disorders, 8,* 141–155.

Årseth, A., Kroger, J., & Martinussen, M, Bakken, G. (2009). Intimacy status, attachment, separation–individuation patterns, and identity status in female university students. *Journal of Personal and Social Relationships, 26,* 697–712.

Bartle-Haring. S., Brucker, P., & Hock, E. (2002). The impact of parental separation anxiety on identity development in late adolescence and early adulthood. *Journal of Adolescent Research, 17,* 439–450.

Bartolomucci, E., & Taylor, J. (1991). Preliminary reliability and validity of an instrument measuring separation–individuation outcomes. *Psychological Reports, 69,* 391–398.

Bellew-Smith, M., & Korn, J. H. (1986). Merger intimacy status in adult women. *Journal of Personality and Social Psychology, 50,* 1186–1191.

Bergman, A., & Harpaz-Rotem, I. (2004). Revisiting rapprochement in the light of contemporary developmental theories. *Journal of the American Psychoanalytic Association, 52,* 556–570.

Bettmann, J. E., Tucker, A., Behrens, E., & Vanderloo, M. (2017). Changes in late adolescents and young adults' attachment, separation, and mental health during Wilderness Therapy. *Journal of Child and Family Studies, 26,* 511–522.

Bjornsen, C. A. (2000). The blessing as a rite of passage in adolescence. *Adolescence, 35,* 357–363.

Blass, R. B., & Blatt, S. J. (1996). Attachment and separateness in the experience of symbiotic relatedness. *Psychoanalytic Quarterly, 65,* 711–746.

Blos, P. (1962). *On adolescence: A psychoanalytic interpretation.* New York, NY: Free Press.

Blos, P. (1967). The second individuation process of adolescence. *Psychoanalytic Study of the Child, 22,* 162–186.

Blos, P. (1968). Character formation in adolescence. *Psychoanalytic Study of the Child, 23,* 245–263.

Blos, P. (1970). *The young adolescent: Clinical studies.* New York, NY: Free Press.

Blos, P. (1971). The child analyst looks at the young adolescent. *Daedalus, 100,* 961–978.

Blos, P. (1976). When and how does adolescence end?' *Adolescent Psychiatry, 5,* 5–17.

Blos, P. (1979). *The adolescent passage: Developmental issues.* New York, NY: International Universities Press.

Blos, P. (1983). The *contribution of psychoanalysis to the psychotherapy of adolescents. Psychoanalytic Study of the Child, 38,* 577–600.

Blos, P. (1985). *Son and father: Before and beyond the Oedipus Complex.* New York, NY: Free Press.

Blos, P. (1989). The place of the adolescent process in the analysis of the adult. *Psychoanalytic Study of the Child, 44,* 3–18.

Blum, H. P. (2004). Separation–individuation theory and attachment theory. *Journal of the American Psychoanalytic Society*, *52*, 535–553.

Brandt, D. E. (1977). Separation and identity in adolescence. *Contemporary Psychoanalysis*, *13*, 507–518.

Chen, C. C., Richardson, G. B., Lai, M. H., Dai, C. L., & Hays, D. G. (2018). Development and cross-cultural validity of a brief measure of separation–individuation. *Journal of Child and Family Studies*, *27*, 2797–2810.

Choi, K. H. (2002). Psychological separation–individuation and adjustment to college among Korean American students: The roles of collectivism and individualism. *Journal of Counseling Psychology*, *49*, 468–475.

Christenson, R. M., & Wilson, W. P. (1985). Assessing pathology in the separation–individuation process by an inventory: a preliminary report. *Journal of Nervous and Mental Disease*, *173*, 561–565.

Colarusso, C. A. (1990). The third individuation: The effect of biological parenthood on separation–individuation processes in adulthood. *Psychoanalytic Study of the Child*, *45*, 170–194.

Colarusso, C. A. (1997). Separation–individuation processes in middle adulthood: The fourth individuation. In S. A. Akhatar & S. Kramer (Eds.), *The seasons of life: Separation–individuation perspectives* (pp. 285–318). Northvale, NJ: Aaronson.

Colarusso, C. A. (2000). Separation–individuation phenomena in adulthood: General concepts and the fifth individuation. *Journal of the American Psychoanalytic Association*, *48*, 1467–1489.

Coppolillo, H. P. (1984). Integration, organization, and regulation in late adolescence. In D. D. Brockman (Ed.), *Late adolescence: Psychoanalytic studies* (pp. 120–135). New York, NY: International Universities Press.

Delhaye, M., Kempemaers, C., Burton, J., Linkowski, P., Stroobants, R., & Goossens, L. (2012). Attachment, parenting, and separation–individuation in adolescence: A comparison of hospitalized adolescents, institutionalized adolescents, and controls. *The Journal of Genetic Psychology*, *173*, 119–141.

Dolan, B. M., Evans, C. and Norton, K. (1992). The separation–individuation inventory: Association with borderline phenomena. *Journal of Nervous and Mental Disease, 180*, 529–533.

Dzukaeva, V. (2014). Family characteristics of psychological separation from parents during late adolescence. *Procedia – Social and Behavioral Sciences*, *146*, 346–352.

Erreich, A. (2011). More than enough guilt to go around: Oedipal guilt, survivor guilt, separation guilt. *Journal of the American Psychoanalytic Association, 59*, 131–151.

Esman, A. H. (1980). Adolescent psychopathology and the rapprochement phenomenon. *Adolescent Psychiatry*, *8*, 320–331.

Esman, A. H. (1997). Obituary: Peter Blos (1903–1997). *International Journal of Psychoanalysis*, *78*, 813–814.

Feldberg, A. (1983). Adolescent separation, individuation, and identity (re)formation: Theoretical extensions and modifications. Unpublished doctoral dissertation, California School of Professional Psychology, Fresno, CA.

Friedlander, M. L., & Siegel, S. M. (1990). Separation–individuation difficulties and cognitive-behavioral indicators of eating disorders among college women. *Journal of Counseling Psychology, 37*, 74–78.

Greenberg, J. R., & Mitchell, S. A. (1983). *Object relations in psychoanalytic theory*. Cambridge, MA: Harvard University Press.

Grotevant, H. D., & Cooper, C. R. (1998). Individuality and connectedness in adolescent development: Review and prospects for research on identity, relationships, and context. In E. Skoe & A. von der Lippe (Eds.), *Personality development in adolescence: A cross-national and life-span perspective* (pp. 3–37). London: Routledge.

Hadiwijaya, H., Klimstra, T., Vermunt, J. K., Branje, S. J. T., and Meeus, W. H. J. (2017). On the development of harmony, turbulence, and independence in parent–adolescent relationships: A five-wave longitudinal study. *Journal of Youth and Adolescence, 46,* 1772–1788.

Hansburg, H. G. (1980a) *Adolescent separation anxiety: A method for the study of adolescent separation problems, Vol. 1.* New York, NY: Robert E. Krieger.

Hansburg, H. G. (1980b). *Adolescent separation anxiety: Separation disorders, Vol. 2.* New York, NY: Robert E. Krieger.

Hill, P. L., Burrow, A. L., & Summer, R. (2016). Sense of purpose and parent–child relationships in emerging adulthood. *Emerging Adulthood, 4,* 436–439.

Hock, E., Eberly, M., Bartle-Haring, S., Ellwanger, P., & Widaman, K. (2001). Separation anxiety in parents of adolescents: Theoretical significance and scale development. *Child Development, 72,* 284–298.

Hoffman, J. A. (1984). Psychological separation of late adolescents from their parents. *Journal of Counseling Psychology, 31,* 170–178.

Hofstede, G., Hofstede, G. J., & Minkov, M. (2010). *Cultures and organizations: Software of the mind* (3rd ed.). New York, NY: McGraw Hill Education.

Holmbeck, G. N., & Leake, C. (1999). Separation–individuation and psychological adjustment in late adolescence. *Journal of Youth and Adolescence, 28,* 563–581.

Holmbeck, G. N., & McClanahan, G. (1994). Construct and content validity of the separation–individuation test of adolescence: A reply to Levine. *Journal of Personality Assessment, 62,* 169–172.

Holmbeck, G. N., & Wandrei, M. L. (1993). Individual and relational predictors of adjustment in first-year college students. *Journal of Counseling Psychology, 40,* 73–78.

Humphreys, C. N., & Davidson, W. B. (1997). Individuation of self and stereotyping of others. *Psychological Reports, 81,* 1252–1254.

Jiang, L. C., Yang, I. M., & Wang, C. (2017). Self-disclosure to parents in emerging adulthood: Examining the roles of perceived parental responsiveness and separation–individuation. *Journal of Social and Personal Relationships, 34,* 425–445.

Johnson, P., Buboltz, W. C., & Seemann, E. (2003). Ego identity status: A step in the differentiation process. *Journal of Counseling and Development, 81,* 191–195.

Josselson, R. (1982). Personality structure and identity status in women viewed through early memories. *Journal of Youth and Adolescence, 11,* 293–299.

Josselson, R. (1987). *Finding herself: Pathways to identity development in women.* San Francisco, CA: Jossey-Bass.

Josselson, R. (1988). The embedded self: I and thou revisited. In D. K. Lapsley & F. C. Power (Eds.), *Self, ego, and identity: Integrative approaches* (pp. 91–106). New York, NY: Springer-Verlag.

Josselson, R. (2017). *Paths to fulfillment: Women's search for meaning and identity.* New York, NY: Oxford University Press.

Kalsner, L., & Pistole, M. C. (2003). College adjustment in a multiethnic sample: Attachment, separation–individuation, and ethnic identity. *Journal of College Student Development, 44,* 92–109.

Kavčič, T., & Zupančič, M. (2018). Types of separation–individuation in relation to mothers and fathers among young people entering adulthood. *Journal of Youth Studies, 22*(1), 66–86.

Kins, E., Beyers, W., & Soenens, B. (2012). When the separation–individuation process goes awry: Distinguishing between dysfunctional dependence and dysfunctional independence. *International Journal of Behavioral Development, 37*, 1–12.

Kins, E., Soenens, B., & Beyers, W. (2011). "Why do they have to grow up so fast?" Parental separation anxiety and emerging adults' pathology of separation–individuation. *Journal of Clinical Psychology, 67*, 647–664.

Kins, E., Soenens, B., & Beyers, W. (2012). Parental psychological control and dysfunctional separation–individuation: A tale of two different dynamics. *Journal of Adolescence, 35*, 1099–1109.

Koepke, S., Denissen, J. J. A. (2012). Dynamics of identity development and separation–individuation in parent–child relationships during adolescence and emerging adulthood: A conceptual integration. *Developmental Review, 32*, 67–88.

Komidar, L., Zupančič, M., Puklek Lepušček,M., & Bjornsen, C. (2016). Development of the short version of the Individuation Test for Emerging Adults (ITEA-S) and its measurement invariance across Slovene and US emerging adults. *Journal of Personality Assessment, 98*, 626–639.

Komidar, L., Zupančič, M., Sočan, G., & Puklek Lepušček, M. (2014). Development and construct validation of the Individuation Test for Emerging Adults. *Journal of Personality Assessment, 96*, 503–514.

Kroger, J. (1990). Ego structuralization in late adolescence as seen through early memories and ego identity status. *Journal of Adolescence, 13*, 65–77.

Kroger, J. (1995). The differentiation of "firm" and "developmental" foreclosure identity statuses: A longitudinal study. *Journal of Adolescent Research, 10*, 317–337.

Kroger, J. (1996). Identity, regression and development. *Journal of Adolescence, 19*, 203–222.

Kroger, J. (1998). Adolescence as a second separation–individuation process: A critical review of an object relations approach. In E. Skoe & A. von der Lippe (Eds.), *Personality development in adolescence: A cross-national and life span perspective* (pp. 172–192). London: Routledge.

Kroger, J., & Green, K. (1994). Factor analytic structure and stability of the separation–individuation test of adolescence. *Journal of Clinical Psychology, 50*, 772–779.

Kroger, J. & Haslett, S. J. (1988). Separation–individuation and ego identity status in late adolescence: A two-year longitudinal study. *Journal of Youth and Adolescence, 17*, 59–81.

Kroger, J., & Marcia, J. E. (2011). The identity statuses: Origins, meanings, and interpretations. In S. J. Schwartz, Luyckx, K., & Vignoles, V. (Eds.) *Handbook of identity theory and research* (pp. 31–53). New York, NY: Springer-Verlag.

Kruse, J., & Walper, S. (2008). Types of individuation in relation to parents: Predictors and outcomes. *International Journal of Behavioral Development, 32*, 390–400.

Laguerre, C. E., Vavassori, D., & Fernandez, L. (2015). Parental contributions and separation anxiety on adolescents' cannabis use. *Journal of Addictions Nursing, 26*, 3–7.

Lapsley, D. K., Aalsma, M. C., & Varshney, N. M. (2001). A factor analytic and psychometric examination of pathology of separation–individuation. *Journal of Clinical Psychology, 57*, 915–932.

Lapsley, D. K., & Edgerton, J. (2002). Separation–individuation, adult attachment style, and college adjustment. *Journal of Counseling and Development, 80*, 484–492.

Levine, J. B. (1994). On McClanahan and Holmbeck's construct validity study of the separation–individuation test of adolescence. *Journal of Personality Assessment, 62*, 166–168.

Levine, J. B., & Saintonge, S. (1993). Psychometric properties of the separation–individuation test of adolescence within a clinical population. *Journal of Clinical Psychology, 49*, 492–507.

Levine, J. B., Green, C. J., & Millon, T. (1986). Separation–individuation test of adolescence. *Journal of Personality Assessment, 50,* 123–137.

Levitz-Jones, E. M., & Orlofsky, J. L. (1985). Separation–individuation and intimacy capacity in college women. *Journal of Personality and Social Psychology, 49,* 156–169.

Mahler, M. S., Pine, F., & Bergman, A. (1975). *The psychological birth of the human infant.* New York, NY: Basic Books.

Marcia, J. E. & Bilsker, D. (1991). Adaptive regression and ego identity. *Journal of Adolescence, 14,* 75–84.

Marsden P., Meyer, C., Fuller, M., & Waller G. (2002). The relationship between eating psychopathology and separation–individuation in young nonclinical women. *Journal of Nervous and Mental Diseases, 190,* 710–713.

Maslach, C., Stapp, J., & Santee, R. T. (1985). Individuation: Conceptual analysis and assessment. *Journal of Personality and Social Psychology, 49,* 729–738.

Masterson, J. F. (1986). Creativity as a vehicle to establish a real self: Jean Paul Sartre, Edvard Munch, Thomas Wolfe. In J. F. Masterson (Ed.), *The real self: A developmental and object relations approach* (cassette recording 4). New York, NY: Masterson Group.

Mattanah, J. F., Brand, B. L., & Hancock, G. R. (2004). Parental attachment, separation–individuation, and college adjustment: A structural equation analysis of mediational effects. *Journal of Counseling Psychology, 51,* 213–225.

Mattanah, J. F., Lopez, F. G., & Govern, J. M. (2011). The contributions of parental attachment bonds to college student development and adjustment: A meta-analytic review. *Journal of Counseling Psychology, 58,* 565–596.

Mayseless, O., & Scharf, M. (2009). Too close for comfort: Inadequate boundaries with parents and individuation in late adolescent girls. *American Journal of Orthopsychiatry, 79,* 191–202.

McCarthy, J. B. (1995). Adolescent character formation and psychoanalytic theory. *American Journal of Psychoanalysis, 55,* 245–267.

McClanahan, G., & Holmbeck, G. N. (1992). Separation–individuation, family functioning, and psychological adjustment in college students: A construct validity study of the separation–individuation test of adolescence. *Journal of Personality Assessment, 59,* 468–485.

Meeus, W., Iedema, J., Maassen, G., & Engels, R. (2005). Separation–individuation revisited: On the interplay of parent–adolescent relations, identity and emotional adjustment in adolescence. *Journal of Adolescence, 28,* 89–106.

Milne, L. C., & Lancaster, S. (2001). Predictors of depression in female adolescents. *Adolescence, 36,* 207–223.

Minuchin, S. (1974). *Families and family therapy.* Cambridge, MA: Harvard University Press.

Offer, D., & Schonert-Reichl, K. A. (1992). Debunking the myths of adolescence: Findings from recent research. *Journal of the American Academy of Child and Adolescent Psychiatry, 31,* 1003–1014.

Orlofsky, J., & Frank, M. (1986). Personality structure as viewed through early memories and identity status in college men and women. *Journal of Personality and Social Psychology, 50,* 580–586.

Oznobishin, O., & Kurman, J. (2016). Family obligations and individuation among immigrant youth: Do generational status and age at immigration matter? *Journal of Adolescence, 51,* 103–113.

Papini, D. R., Micka, J. C., & Barnett, J. K. (1989). Perceptions of intrapsychic and extrapsychic functioning as bases of adolescent ego identity status. *Journal of Adolescent Research, 4,* 462–482.

Perosa, L. M., Perosa, S. L., & Tam, H. P. (1996). The contribution of family structure and differentiation to identity development in females. *Journal of Youth and Adolescence, 25,* 817–837.

Perosa, L. M., Perosa, S. L., & Tam, H. P. (2002). Intergenerational systems theory and identity development in young adult women. *Journal of Adolescent Research, 17,* 235–259.

Perrin, M. B., Ehrenberg, M. F., & Hunter, M. A. (2013). Boundary diffusion, individuation, and adjustment: Comparison of young adults raised in divorced versus intact families. *Family Relations: An Interdisciplinary Journal of Applied Family Studies, 62,* 768–782.

Pine, F. (1985). *Developmental theory and clinical process.* New Haven, CT: Yale University Press.

Pine, F. (1990). *Drive, ego, object, and self.* New York, NY: Basic Books.

Pine, F. (1992). Some refinements of the separation–individuation concept in light of research on infants. *Psychoanalytic Study of the Child, 45,* 179–194.

Pinquart, M., & Silbereisen, R. K. (2002). Changes in adolescents' and mothers' autonomy and connectedness in conflict discussions: An observation study. *Journal of Adolescence, 25,* 509–522.

Ponappa, S., Bartle-Haring, S., & Day, R. (2014). Connection to parents and healthy separation during adolescence: A longitudinal perspective. *Journal of Adolescence, 37,* 555–566.

Quintana, S. M. and Kerr, J. (1993). Relational needs in late adolescent separation–individuation. *Journal of Counseling and Development, 71,* 349–354.

Quintana, S. M., & Lapsley, D. K. (1990). Rapprochement in late adolescent separation–individuation: A structural equations approach. *Journal of Adolescence, 13,* 371–385.

Rhodes, B., & Kroger, J. (1992). Parental bonding and separation–individuation difficulties among late adolescent eating disordered women. *Child Psychiatry and Human Development, 22,* 249–263.

Rice, K. (1990). Attachment in adolescence: A narrative and meta-analytic review. *Journal of Youth and Adolescence, 19,* 511–538.

Rice, K. G. (1992). Separation–individuation and adjustment to college: A longitudinal study. *Journal of Counseling Psychology, 39,* 203–213.

Rice, K. G., Cole, D. A., & Lapsley, D. K. (1990). Separation–individuation, family cohesion, and adjustment to college: Measurement validation and test of a theoretical model. *Journal of Counseling Psychology, 37,* 195–202.

Saraiva, L. M., & Matos, P. M. (2012). Separation–individuation of Portuguese emerging adults in relation to parents and to the romantic partner. *Journal of Youth Studies, 15,* 499–517.

Sartre, J. P. (1964) *Words.* London: Hamish Hamilton.

Schafer, R. (1973). Concepts of self and identity and the experience of separation–individuation in adolescence. *Psychoanalytic Quarterly, 42,* 42–59.

Scharf, M. (2001). A "natural experiment" in child rearing ecologies and adolescents' attachment and separation representations. *Child Development, 72,* 236–251.

Smolak, L., & Levine, M. P. (1993). Separation–individuation difficulties and the distinction between bulimia nervosa and anorexia nervosa in college women. *International Journal of Eating Disorders, 14,* 33–41.

Stern, D. N. (1985). *The interpersonal world of the infant*. New York, NY: Basic Books.

Stey, P. C., Hill, P., & Lapsley, D. (2014). Factor structure and psychometric properties of a brief measure of dysfunctional individuation. *Assessment, 21*, 452–462.

Sugimura, K., Crocetti, E., Hatano, K., Kanlušonyté, G., Hihara, S., & Žukauskiené, R. (2018). A cross-cultural perspective on the relationships between emotional separation, parental trust, and identity in adolescents. *Journal of Youth and Adolescence, 47*, 749–759.

Usher, S. F. (2017). *Separation–individuation struggles in adult life: Leaving home*. New York, NY: Routledge.

Valls-Vidal, C., Alsina, A. G., Pérez-Testor, C., Guárdia-Olmos, & Iafrate, R. (2016). Young adults' individuation with mother and father as a function of dysfunctional family patterns, gender and parental divorce. *Journal of Divorce and Remarriage, 57*, 245–265.

Walzer, M. S., & Nottis, K. E. K. (2013). The effect of undergraduates' major, gender, race/ethnicity, and school year on teacher enmeshment. *College Student Journal, 47*, 677–688.

4 Identity as life story
Narrative understandings of adolescent identity development

One day a granddaughter asked her grandmother to tell her about her life. At the time, the granddaughter was moving from adolescence into adulthood. The grandmother, Sara, was nearing the end of her life. Sara gave her granddaughter a look as if it to say: "Do you really want to hear this?" The look back from her granddaughter was encouragement enough, and it was time for a story to be told and heard. Sara began her story about her life, not with her own childhood, but instead by explaining how her parents came to live in Cuba.[1] As Sara spoke, people appeared and exited her story – their ways of life, dispositions, motivations, and values were sketched out as she continued.

Sara said her father was easy-going, but strong and warm. He was also hard-working, lucky, and an adventurer. The adventurer part was not completely by choice, because Sara's father was a second-born son. During that time, it was the custom in Spain for only the first-born son to receive the family fortune. As a second-born son, Sara's father would have to find his own way in the world. He left home at 14 for Argentina and then returned to Spain when he was 18 years old. He was lucky enough to get the number 13 for his conscription number, which meant he was released from military service. So he left Spain again, but this time he went to Cuba.

The stories that Sara told that day were nuanced, and the emotional tone ranged from the comical and joyous to tragic and inconsolable, and they gave glimpses of memorable times such as her mother's trip from Spain to Cuba by ship – she was seasick and vowed never to be on the ocean again – as well as what everyday life was like for Sara growing up in the Cuban countryside before the revolution. Her story touched on influential characters like her father, mother, and brother – her mother was loving but had a temper, her brother was always in a hurry and loved gambling so much that his mother said that he would come home one day with no pants on (because he lost them to gambling).

For the part of Sara's story that is retold below, the insights that her granddaughter had were tacit and twofold. It should be expected that if a person lived long enough, unexpected things were likely to happen, and that meant that a person should value the moments and relationships that they have today, because they could be gone tomorrow. In terms of the unexpected, for instance, Sara's father's story had several moments where chance played a role – he was born a second son and was unexpectedly released from military service – free to go to Cuba when he did. Chance also collided with Sara's will when she told the story of trying to get back to Cuba to see her mother.

Sara said that when she heard that her mother had died, she tried to get back to the far east of Cuba – *to Guantanamo* – before her mother was buried, so she could see her face one last time. But, it seemed like everything was working against her. She went from Miami to Havana in a heavy rain by plane. She landed and wanted to take a second flight to Guantanamo. Sara was a new mother at the time and had her son Tony with her (the granddaughter's father). The pilot of the second flight told her that there was no way they were flying to Guantanamo that night because of the weather, so Sara took the train and in time reached home. Sara's mother had recently been buried when she arrived. The gravedigger and her father asked her if she wanted them to break the concrete covering her mother's grave so Sara could see her again, but she decided against it.

Except for starting her narrative in an unexpected place, Sara's story had many events that had a temporal coherence or order to them (McAdams & McLean, 2013), and her story had several themes that ran through it. To make meaning out of one's life, a person engages in cognitive and emotional processes like autobiographical reasoning, which involves connecting life events to psychological changes or stability in one's self, and can involve deriving wider life lessons and insights from life events[2] (Habermas & Köber, 2014). Life stories contain depictions of important moments and people. They speak to the roles of chance and a person's will (i.e., agency), goals, and values, as well as the larger push and pull of history, culture, and tradition in everyday people's lives and how losses are weathered, sometimes conquered, or left unresolved. Narrative identity researchers would say that Sara's story and the act of Sara telling her story to her granddaughter is a typical, even a necessary way for family members to bond and communicate, for the older generation to model values and insights that can be of help to the next generation, as well as a way for narrators to continue to make sense of themselves and their lives across a lifetime (McAdams & McLean, 2013). Indeed, it has been noted that the intergenerational narration of life stories creates an entrée into a family's identity, as well as demonstrating

> for children that telling and sharing the past is an important social activity. They [narrators] also convey that there are certain ways to tell these kinds of stories, focusing not just on what happened but why it was interesting, important, and emotional.
>
> (Fivush, Habermas, Waters, & Zaman, 2011, p. 324)

Different types of studies have been used to investigate narrative identity in adolescence and emerging adulthood, including those that document normative trends and how relationships are important to narrative identity development, as well as studies that clarify how narrative identity relates to other psychological constructs and outcomes. A number of innovative scholars have advanced the field of adolescent narrative identity development, among them, Monisha Pasupathi.

Pasupathi the person

Monisha Pasupathi, professor of developmental psychology at the University of Utah, is a leading scholar in the narrative identity field. She has conducted innovative research in several areas, such as a series of studies that map out the dynamic interaction between narrators and listeners. She also has been examining how these social processes relate to wider ideas about how narrative identity develops (Pasupathi, 2014). As she remarked, "what captivates me is the way people use narrating to build an identity" (Pasupathi, personal communication, July 11, 2018).

Pasupathi was born on the east coast of the United States but grew up in the American Midwest, in Ohio. Her parents were both Southerners. Her mother was from the deep south of the United States and her father was born in southern India. Pasupathi completed her undergraduate degree in psychology and English literature at Case Western Reserve University in Ohio and then went on to complete a doctoral degree in psychology at Stanford University. Following that time, she completed a post-doctoral research fellowship investigating wisdom at the Max Planck Institute in Berlin, Germany, before taking on a faculty position at the University of Utah.

In discussing professionally formative life events, she told a story about how a temporary holiday from her doctoral project led her to pursue an abiding interest in studying conversations, listeners, narrators, and the social construction of narrative identity.

> I was in grad school . . . I was in a personality program, studying emotional regulation across the adult development and aging . . . yet I kept hanging around with a psycholinguist named Herb Clark . . . He was interested in communication and the way that a speaker forms an utterance . . . Herb was working on this joint action model of language use. I loved this idea, and it had nothing to do with my dissertation work, but I just could not really let it go. And, I would go to Herb's lab meetings and one month he brought in a friend – her name was Janet Bavelas – who was also a psycholinguist. And he said, "Hey, I want to you come and meet Janet, and I want you to come and listen to her presentation – I know you guys are going to like each other because you both wander around all the time with your dogs." It is true, I had this Australian Shepherd who went everywhere with me in graduate school. So, I went to Janet's talk and she talked about a study in which people were asked to tell another person about a close call, a story about a time when they almost died. And what Janet did was change whether the person they were talking to paid attention or not. What she was able to show was that even though there was not a lot of back and forth – it was a monologue– the speaker is so dependent on the listener to be able to tell that story, that if you

disrupt the listener's attention, the speaker is not able to tell the story . . . I was completely blown away, could not stop talking about it. I was with a friend in the stairwell after that talk, a fellow graduate student and said it probably not only changes the story but also changes how they remember the story, and how they think about themselves over time. And that was the moment . . . the thing that captivated me was this talk from a very different discipline. They did not want to understand memory or the self or identity; they wanted to answer a particular question, how you produce a sentence . . . But being exposed to that work really changed everything in my life. I am forever grateful, and I don't know if I have to be grateful to Herb, Janet, or the dog?

(Pasupathi, personal communication, July 11, 2018)

After her early inspiration from theory and experiments conducted by psycholinguists, Pasupathi has worked systematically to shed considerable light on ways that listeners help to co-construct personal narratives, and to develop new ideas about other potential processes of change possibly involved in narrative identity development that include but also go beyond autobiographical reasoning[3] (Pasupathi, 2014).

In asking her about the very forward edge of narrative identity research, Pasupathi was excited about several ideas including the following:

Everyone who narrates their experiences does it in ways that are variable, whether people just tell redemptive stories all the time, but the variation in when you do and when you don't as a signature of personality and identity, that is a very challenging set of questions, within person variation in narrating. I think that it is a very important area for the field to address.

(Pasupathi, personal communication, July 11, 2018)

Pasupathi's ideas and research are referred to throughout this chapter, but for detailed research examples of her and other scholars' research in conversational narrative identity studies, see the later chapter section entitled: "Spill the tea! The social construction of narrative identity."

The nature of narrative identity

The stories that make up narrative identity are not a faithful rendering of every moment of our lives (Adler, Lodi-Smith, Philippe, & Houle, 2016; McAdams, 2015). We choose what is meaningful to us (McAdams, 2015). Regardless of the audience, and even if no one else is there to hear our story, our stories about ourselves are being worked on and such stories are argued to be fundamental to the human experience (McAdams, 2015). We work on our life stories in order to make some sense of it all (McAdams, 2015).

[The life story] is not synonymous with a case study; it is not simply any old thing that a person says when asked to talk about the self in a psychological experiment. The life story, instead, is an internalized and evolving structure of the mind – an integrative story about who I am, how I came to be, and where my life may be going.

(McAdams & Manczak, 2015, p. 425)

In the story of Siddhartha, which is referred to in Chapter 2, Siddhartha also considered what it means to seemingly change one's sense of identity as time passes across a lifetime, but also to remain the same in some essential ways. Siddhartha's new insights about the presence of the past and the future in one's identity experience in the here and now were gained by working as a ferryman along with his friend Vasudeva to help travelers cross a river later in his life (Hesse, 1951).

Optimal narrative identity

An optimal narrative identity is thought to help people find increasing meaning and purpose in life and a sense of unity within themselves across time and situations, but also to allow enough room for change so that new life experiences, lessons, and insights can be incorporated along the way (Fivush et al., 2011; McLean, 2008).

> Identity matters for people's functioning in the world – identities help people to see themselves moving from past to future, make commitments meaningful, and find common ground with others. Problems of continuity can be understood as incoherence in identity over time – irreconcilable differences between the me-that-was and the me-that-is.
>
> (Pasupathi, 2014, p. 21)

Narrative identity development acts as a conduit by which adolescents can move into a more adult-like space that values responsibility and purpose in one's life, as well as self-insight, understanding of life in general, and a sense of direction and purpose that guides one's future (de Silveira & Habermas, 2011). Later in this chapter, the theoretical proposition about what comprises optimal adolescent narrative identity development is examined in light of the available research evidence.

Narrative identity as part of life-span personality development

Narrative identity is not only of interest to psychologists but also to scholars working within cognitive neuroscience as well as the humanities, particularly in philosophy, literature, and linguistics (Pasupathi, personal communication, July 11, 2018). Since the 1980s, several psychologists have developed theories and advanced the use of methods to document different aspects of narrative identity. One prominent framework is the three-layer model of personality development which was put forward by Dan P. McAdams and colleagues (e.g., McAdams, 2015; McAdams & Manczak, 2015; McAdams & Olson, 2010; McAdams & Pals, 2006).

The three-layer framework aims to bring a greater synthesis between developmental and personality psychology (McAdams, 2015) and derives key concepts and research priorities from William James and Erik Erikson (e.g., the individual's search for continuity across time; Hammack, 2014). The framework also draws from Erikson's emphasis on lifespan developmental change (McLean & Pratt, 2006), as well as from classic and contemporary personality theorists such as Gordon Allport, Henry Murray, Paul Costa, and Robert McCrae (McAdams, 2015; McLean & Syed, 2014). The framework sets for itself an ambitious task in attempting to integrate a diverse set of more specific theories and research findings, some of which were intended to test and expand the framework and others that were not (McAdams & Olson, 2010). The three-layer framework explains how change takes place across different developmental domains and considers person-context interactions across different settings – all with the aim of proposing a comprehensive framework for the study of life-span personality development (McAdams, 2015).

Historically, it has been more typical that a body of knowledge would emerge for one of the framework layers (e.g., traits) without a concerted attempt to sort out distinctions and intersections between allied features and mechanisms involved in different facets of personality development (McAdams, 2015). Stated differently, the ingredients (i.e., psychological constructs and conceptions of how developmental change takes place) that make up the three-layer framework are a mix of the novel (e.g., narrative identity) and the familiar (e.g., traits or motives) within the discipline of psychology; the way that these ingredients are combined and integrated in the three-layer model is original and eclectic (McLean, 2017). In the history of psychology, eclectic frameworks have not always been successful, in that they have not always yielded the anticipated knowledge production and staying power. However, McAdams (1996) reflected on the value of the three-layer framework early in its development and the merits of trying to strike a successful balance between what McAdams (1996, p. 378) called "parochialism and the most promiscuous forms of eclecticism."

Specifically, in the three-layer framework, personality is conceptualized as being made up of traits, motivations/goals, and narrative identity (McAdams, 2015; McAdams & Manczak, 2015; McAdams & Olson, 2010; McAdams & Pals, 2006). These personality features or metaphorical layers in the framework have been called the self as a social actor (i.e., noticeable, socially important constellation of traits that typify a person), the self as an agent (i.e., a person acting in the world to fulfill goals based on motivations such as agency or connection), and the self as an autobiographical author (i.e., a person who is in the process of co-constructing a narrative identity that is made of one's life story and other important personal narratives; McAdams, 2015).

The three layers of personality – traits

The metaphor of three layers– one personality feature stacked on top of the other with traits at the bottom, motivation/goals (also called characteristic adaptations) in the middle, and narrative identity on top – paints a picture of the nature and development of these distinct yet intersecting personality features (McLean, 2017). Traits are at the foundation of the framework and they are thought to develop earlier in comparison to other layers and are posited to emerge out of temperament (McAdams & Manczak, 2015). Temperament has been conceptualized as an early developing building block of personality and consists of the usual ways that infants behave as well as how infants experience and express their emotions (negative to positive) as they interact with others and the environment (showing low to high impulsivity/control or regulation as well as low to high reactivity; Groh et al., 2017). Other ongoing psychological and social processes at work in the development of traits include how adept individuals are at social cognition, including forming attributions of others and impression management (McAdams, 2015).

Traits develop in childhood and become more solidified in adolescence and adulthood (McAdams & Olson, 2010). Traits are thought to be the substance of a person's individuality and provide a basis for one's social roles and reputation (McAdams & Olson, 2010). Theory and research about Costa and McCrae's (2017) big five trait theory have been used in descriptions of the three-layer framework (e.g., McAdams & Olson, 2010). In the big five theory, the essential traits are conscientiousness, agreeableness, neuroticism (CAN traits are important to the constancy or reliability of personality), as well as openness to experience and extraversion (OE traits are involved in the adaptability or plasticity of personality; i.e., CANOE), and each trait is a multi-dimensional construct made up of several facets (Costa & McCrae, 2017; McAdams, 2015).

Traits are dispositions that people can experience or exhibit in abundance or in moderation or only sporadically (relative to others), and together core traits, such as those in the big five, are predictive of a person's usual ways of thinking, feeling, and acting across a diversity of situations (Costa & McCrae, 2017). Traits are thought to help us to meet the demands of human social life (Costa & McCrae, 2017; McAdams & Manczak, 2015). Traits represent cues to let others know in rapid ways the kind of person they may be encountering (McAdams, 2015, p. 255; "the streamlined reputational signatures through which actors initially know each other and sort each other out"). While the idea of a trait, historically, has implied continuity, a meta-analysis of longitudinal studies has shown significant mean-level changes in some traits in adulthood (e.g., Roberts, Walton, & Viechtbauer, 2006). For example, it is not uncommon that as one moves from adolescence to middle adulthood conscientiousness and agreeableness are likely to increase for the typical person along with a decline in neuroticism (e.g., normative changes in CAN traits – this research finding has been called the maturity principle). Such changes are thought to be precipitated by the demands of and more experience with adult social roles (McAdams & Olson, 2010).

The three layers of personality – motives, goals, and characteristic adaptations

The next layer in the middle of the three-layer framework of personality development addresses how people act on their needs, motivations, and values/goals

(McAdams, 2015). Important developmental processes and transitions that have been hypothesized to make a motivated agent possible include children developing an understanding that other people can have their own unique wishes and thoughts, and that, in general, wishes and thoughts can be a reason why people behave, think, or feel as they do (i.e., theory of mind; Imuta, Henry, Slaughter, Selcuk, & Ruffman, 2016). Additionally, the age 5–7 shift, which heralds a noticeable transition which many children show through their behaviors, evidence of increasingly integrated and efficient cognitive, emotional, and social competencies that come with age (Sameroff & Haith, 1996).

> By age 8 or 9 years, many children have developed and articulated personal goals, and they see themselves as more or less self-determining, goal-directed agents whose aspirations take increasing space in consciousness and show increasing influence on social behavior. . . .Layered over the actor's developing dispositional profile is a slowly evolving motivational agenda, a program for striving that eventually will come to encompass personality's most salient goals, plans, values, and life projects.
>
> (McAdams & Manczak, 2015, p. 428)

People certainly have their own agendas in life, ranging from the esoteric to the more normative, that may, in turn, correspond to a person's phase in the life-span (e.g., achieving a balance between connection and independence from parents as an adolescent or wishing to preserve health and independence in late adulthood). Unlike the layer of the model that involves traits, this middle layer does not stop at describing what is normative or to be expected for most people but also pays substantial attention to the individual person's development (i.e., a person's goals which can be one of a kind; McAdams, 2015). Further, this middle layer has an emphasis on how values support the goals that people formulate for themselves (McAdams, 2015). For example, when people pursue a particular set of goals, their selection and efforts to actualize their goals in part reflect what values they hold (McAdams, 2015).

The three layers of personality – narrative identity

A concise but far reaching description of narrative identity is as follows:

> Narrative identity is the story that a person composes about how he or she came to be the person he or she is becoming – a selective reconstruction of the past integrated with the imagined future, providing a life in full with a sense of meaning, purpose, and temporal continuity . . .
>
> (McAdams, 2015, p. 259)

Another formulation which emphasized other nuances was given by Hammack (2010, p. 184) as follows: "Our personal narratives become cognitive and affective anchors for the life course – filters through which we make sense of the social world and our experience in it." Life stories and other personal narratives can be private at times and the object of introspection, but most stories end up going public at some point (McLean, 2005; McLean & Pasupathi, 2011; McLean, Pasupathi, & Pals, 2007). Once shared, our personal narratives end up on a metaphorical editor's desk (i.e., important people in our lives and our culture play this editorial role). The editor hears our tale and gives us a decision as to whether or not to reject, accept, or revise and resubmit our story (i.e., retell our story again but this time with some changes). Of course, we can then protest or accept the editor's decision. The cultural aspect of this editing job is called a master narrative (Hammack, 2008). Because master narratives are rooted in culture, this construct is addressed in Chapter 5.

In the three-layer framework, narrative identity is viewed as the top layer in the framework – the metaphor here is the self as the autobiographical author or storyteller (McAdams, 2015). While narrative identity is present and measurable in studies with adolescents, the full nuanced expression of one's narrative identity is not typically realized until sometime during adulthood (McAdams, 2015). Narrative identity is complex and has many features and processes involved in it. Narrative identity has been measured by analyzing life stories as well as personal narratives of different types such as self-defining memories (e.g., McLean, 2005). Autobiographical/episodic memory and narration skills are examples of some of the cognitive and sociocultural processes that can drive narrative identity development from childhood onwards (i.e., narration skills concern knowing how a story is told in one's culture and being able to execute that story with an audience; McLean, 2017). Narration and interpretative skills are fostered by reminiscence and storytelling about life events in the context of conversations with important others such as parents and friends (McLean & Jennings, 2012).

Processes that come to the forefront of narrative identity development, particularly in adolescence, include formal operational thinking (i.e., having a flexible command of deductive and inductive reasoning, abstract reasoning for example about time and causality) and autobiographical reasoning, which is more commonly used by adolescents than children (Fivush et al., 2011). Autobiographical reasoning spans cognitive and emotional domains of development; it is hypothesized to be a main driver of changes in narrative identity development and involves remembering one's life (i.e., the who, what, and where?), but also demands active organizing, reflecting, interpreting, and making meaning in the wider context of one's life experiences (Fivush et al., 2011; McLean, 2017).

To firmly grasp what narrative identity is in terms of how it is conceptualized and studied in the psychological research literature, it is helpful to consider how many researchers collect narratives from study participants. What are the questions and prompts used by narrative researchers and how are narratives typically analyzed? What is singled out as the main object of the analysis? These issues are described later in the chapter by considering different types of measures used in the field as well as by an in depth description of a selection of illustrative research studies.

The three layers of personality – distinctions and intersections

In terms of distinctions, the timing of the developmental emergence of the layers in the framework and mechanisms of change at work in the layers in some cases differ. Take as a case in point autobiographical reasoning, which is a driver of change in the development of narrative identity. Autobiographical reasoning is not directly at work in the emergence and functioning of traits; instead early temperament, social interactions, and evolutionary forces are posited to be essential to trait development (McAdams, 2015).

Another distinction has to do with time-orientation and which aspects of time (the past, present, and future) are emphasized in each layer. The present is thought to be important to all of the personality features in the framework (McAdams, 2015). Considering the present in relation to the future is hypothesized to be most relevant to the motivated agent who is in the process of formulating goals as well as the autobiographical author who also has to consider his or her story in light of what is likely to happen in the future (McAdams, 2015). A reflection on and integration of experiences in the past and present in relation to the what is expected in the future, (i.e., the full gamut of time orientations) is thought to be most pressing for the autobiographical author who is working on a narrative identity (McAdams, 2015).

Additional distinctions deal with research/knowledge emphasis, for example, whether the ambition is to explain personality development at the individual and/or group level. Traits concern nomothetic or group-oriented personality features (i.e., traits upon which we all vary). The layer concerning motivations and goals (i.e., self as agent) and narrative identity (i.e., the self as storyteller working on a narrative identity) attest to the uniqueness of individual development. In other words, this layer combines an idiographic, single person focused view, in terms of personality development explained at the individual level, one person and life at a time, with more shared processes of importance. For example, in the case of narrative identity, different forms of coherence (e.g., causal motivational coherence) can act as a shared universal driver of narrative identity development, but the meaning that is made of one's life story can be completely unique (i.e., "no one else has exactly the same collection of life experiences or ways of telling about those experiences"; Reese et al., 2017, p. 613). In terms of intersections, the layers are posited to come together to produce a "one of a kind person" (McAdams & Olson, 2010). Thus, in the three-layer framework, personality development is best understood by appreciating the distinctions but also empirically seeking to document potential intersections among these essential personality features (McAdams, 2015).

Criticism of the three-layer framework including narrative identity

How do the layers work?

It has been posited that layers in the three-layer framework of lifespan personality development may interact in a reciprocal manner in some instances (Lilgendahl, 2014).

Yet, empirical evidence for how the three layers are distinct and interact is just begin-ning (Adler et al., 2016; McLean, 2017). An example of what has been found thus far is some evidence for the distinctiveness of the trait and narrative identity layers (Adler et al., 2016). Consider several studies in which there is a simultaneous com-parison of the association between these two layers (i.e., traits and narrative identity) and well-being; results tend to show that each layer has a unique and non-redundant association with well-being (Adler et al., 2016). McLean (2017) concluded that peo-ple elevated on particular traits, such as neuroticism and openness to experience, are more likely to have a more negative emotional tone and more complexity in their personal narratives, respectively, based on findings across relevant studies. While the overall three-layer framework of personality development is original and conceptu-ally innovative and has inspired many new research studies designed to expressly test the framework, more research is needed in order to clarify the long-term knowledge generating potential of this approach.

Coherence and unity

Finding a sense of coherence in oneself over time is central to the theoretical conception of optimal narrative identity development (McAdams, 2015). Post modernism scholars such as Gergen (1991) have argued for the inevitability of discontinuous identities in light of new technologies and experiences that are typi-cal of late modern life. The notion of fragmentation of a person's identity into many potentially disparate and unrelated identities is in contrast to the focus on the search for continuity, coherence, or unity across time and parts of oneself in the narrative identity field. In a response to this idea of identity fragmenta-tion, Hammack (2014) noted the lack of empirical support for this postmodernist contention. Other scholars have been more accepting of the potential for the post-modernist position on discontinuous identities in that such an idea could be useful to examining identity in a particular type of situation, namely "to understand identity maintenance in problematic societal contexts" (Côté, 2014, p. 12). More empirical studies designed to directly address this question are likely to clarify this unresolved debate, but the indications of aspects of narrative identity devel-opment being associated with outcomes such as well-being and mental health (e.g., Adler et al., 2015) adds weight to the picture of optimal narrative identity development advocated by narrative identity scholars.

Embracing "and" thinking

In contemporary developmental science, value is placed on openness to the pos-sibility of "and" ways of thinking, rather than an automatic default into "either or thinking" (Overton, 2015). In the case of the narrative identity research field, there appears to be tension between the aim of documenting an individual life and generating conclusions from research studies that have broad applica-tion to people in general, (or individual versus population-focused research, also called ideographic versus nomothetic research). See Lundh (2015) for a historical review of these two different research aims. Although the individual's voice and the subjective meaning that one makes of life are highly valued in narrative identity research studies, the analysis of personal narratives in terms of how data are typically analyzed appears to have largely focused on generating nomothetic knowledge. The statement below by Adler and colleagues (2016, p. 146) described the general present state of the research field clearly: "research on narrative identity . . . strives to adopt a phenomenological outlook while seeking to produce generalizable knowledge about the self." What seems not to have been fully appreciated by the narrative identity field as yet, is how the study of an individual life (i.e., an ideographic focus on an individual life and lifting up the voice of participants who are the ultimate experts on their lives) could inform what has been learned by the field's nomothetic work, and vice versa.

The barriers to walking across the ideographic and nomothetic divide successfully appear to be more about resources rather than a value-based barrier. Personal narratives are a rich source of information – useful for a diversity of research purposes. As Josselson and Flum (2014, p. 8) noted "interviewees can offer detailed 'thick' descriptions about what they are struggling with, exploring, deciding, or avoiding." Yet, it takes substantial effort and resources to analyze personal narratives (Adler et al., 2016). If one takes on both ideographic and nomothetic research aims in a given study, then this task would likely demand more research resources. However, it may be a worthwhile undertaking, in that such a dual approach would challenge researchers to formulate research questions about how ideographic and nomothetic research findings concerning narrative identity may complement and depart from one another (Josselson & Flum, 2014). As more longitudinal studies of the same individuals across time are conducted in this field, innovative research findings that could provide a methodological exemplar to other areas of developmental science could come from a more explicit and frequent mixture of ideographic and nomothetic research aims within narrative identity research studies.

Methodology

Another challenge to the field has been the concern that the life story interview may artificially elicit autobiographical reasoning and the movement towards self-continuity, rather than capture a naturally occurring and necessary change process. In other words: ". . . the core identity attributes of stability and continuity may not be latent properties of personal narratives but instead are artifacts of the interview/event itself" (Seaman, Sharp, & Coppens, 2017, p. 2031). A potential approach to address this concern is to have more frequent inclusion of naturalistic (non-laboratory based) storytelling occasions as a complement to structured interviews in a laboratory-based setting (Adler et al., 2016), thereby obtaining a wider sampling of personal narratives under different situations. In terms of the analysis of personal narratives, constructs/variables such as coherence have varying names and are operationalized differently across researchers (Fivush et al., 2011).

In some cases there is a need for the field to coalesce on a "common language" (Adler et al., 2016, p. 169).

Measuring narrative identity

The measurement of narrative identity is diverse. One method is the life story interview[4] (McAdams, 2008). This interview covers several domains and times in a person's life. For example, asking a person to describe his or her life's high and low points as well as key transitions when life took a significant turn (McAdams, 2008) is one form such interviews can take. Timing is also important, and people can be asked about their lives in the past and present (e.g., early memories, emotional memories from different developmental periods, time when one faced a challenge, or learned something important) as well as in the future (McAdams, 2008). Finally, after describing and reflecting about oneself in light of key moments in one's past, present, and future, people can be asked about what take home messages or conclusions they draw about themselves (McAdams, 2008).

Prompts that encourage people to elaborate on the seasons of their lives and specific important moments include, for example, asking what happened, when it happened, who was there, and what does this experience reflect or show about you as a person (McAdams, 2008)? Other empirical studies that concern narrative identity examine personal narratives about discrete life experiences (i.e., time limited or rare experiences "examples might include religious conversion, the transition to parenthood, or the death of a significant other" Adler et al., 2016, p. 145) and/or narratives that are subjectively important or emotionally clear (positive or negative; e.g., McLean & Fournier, 2008; Pasupathi & Hoyt, 2009).

In terms of typical study procedures, participants can be asked questions in a one-on-one interview with a research assistant and give answers to structured or semi-structured questions verbally in order to assess features and processes related to a personal narrative or life story. The interview would be audio or video recorded, transcribed, and then the text coded. Some researchers opt to give the interview in a written format, in which case questions are read and a written response is given. Some researchers use both interview and written formats in the same study (e.g., Jennings, Pasupathi, & McLean, 2014). Other scholars have analyzed biographies of individuals and then applied life story techniques combined with other textual analysis approaches (e.g., Hammack, 2010). An innovative approach is to ask for personal narratives, but the questions are answered in the presence of someone else, such as a stranger, parent, friend, or romantic partner (Jennings et al., 2014; McLean & Pasupathi, 2011). The discussion that ensues of the answers to the interview questions between participants and the other person can then be audio/video recorded, transcribed, and analyzed. Here, the interest is to examine how listeners contribute to the co-construction of narrative identity (Pasupathi & Hoyt, 2009).

The transcript that is generated can then be analyzed by one or more coders for certain theory-based features indicative of narrative identity processes (e.g., meaning making – "the degree to which one learns something about oneself from reflecting on past events"; McLean & Breen, 2009, p. 702) or aspects of narratives hypothesized to be associated with other outcomes (e.g., emotional tone). The amount of text to be analyzed for each study participant can be considerable, and some scholars recommend that conceptual coding be done by humans instead of computers (which focus on more linguistic text analysis), as meaning making can be highly nuanced and difficult to assess by machine (Adler et al., 2016). It is common to find narrative identity researchers generating numerical ratings of the emotional tone (e.g., low to high) of a narrative (positive and/or negative), complexity and nuance, themes of agency, communion, redemption and contamination, evidence of coherence (including self-event connections) as well as growth goals (Adler et al., 2016). Coders' ratings can then be calibrated for reliability or consistency. Other textual analysis approaches can involve a qualitative coding of personal narratives. See Morgan and Korobov (2012) for an example of a study that used a thematic analysis approach (i.e., a completely qualitative approach), in which personal narratives about romance were discussed in the presence of friends.

Research findings on narrative identity in adolescence

Normative trends in adolescent narrative identity[5] development

Cross-sectional and longitudinal evidence supports the idea that children can easily describe particular events and times in their lives, but it is rare for children to tell an all-encompassing and nuanced life story when asked to do so (Fivush et al., 2011; Habermas & de Silveira, 2008; Peterson & McCabe, 1994). Metaphorically speaking, children can be adept reporters of the daily news of their lives, but are not as well equipped to be seasoned historians or biographers of their entire life story – just yet. Adolescence tends to be a turning point in which many young people's capabilities (e.g., cognitive, socio-emotional, linguistic, narration and interpretative skills) and life experiences as well as socio-cultural expectations coalesce, and it becomes more common for individuals to engage in autobiographical reasoning. Furthermore, their personal narratives evidence greater coherence (Fivush et al., 2011; Habermas & Bluck, 2000; Köber, Schmiedek, & Habermas, 2015).

A German longitudinal study (Köber & Habermas, 2017), with participants that ranged in age from children to adults, provided an in depth example of methods and selected findings within this research area. This study had two parts. The first part spanned eight years and had several occasions when a group of young participants were asked to provide their entire life story (i.e., from the earliest memory to the present) as well as to describe seven key events in their lives (Köber & Habermas, 2017). At the beginning of the study, there were four age groups – 8, 12, 16, and 20 years of age (*n* = 113; followed over eight years to ages 16, 20, 24, and 28 years, respectively); the second part of the study added two additional age groups – 40 and 65 years of age, (*n* = 58; followed over four years to the ages of 44 and 69 years, respectively.

Multiple coders read and rated transcripts of the narratives given by all study participants and generated numerical indices that represented stability (i.e., the percentage of narrative segments and events that came up more than once over time), as well as counts of the types of life events described (e.g., normative or non-normative). Ratings were given on a seven point scale indicating the degree to which participants had different indicators of coherence evident in their narratives. For example, was there an undefined to very clear and explicit chronological order to what happened (i.e., temporal coherence)? Was there a deep reflection over how one's story connected to changes in one's personality (i.e., causal-motivational coherence)? Was there a deep reflection by participants on how their narrative events related to broader lessons about life, oneself, or metaphors that served as a conceptual link across parts of the narrative (i.e., thematic coherence; Köber & Habermas, 2017)?

Study results were based on following individuals over time (e.g., within-subjects longitudinal growth curve analyses with three time points for the younger group), as well as analyses that included both the younger and older age groups (cross-sectional age comparisons with means difference tests). Highlights of some key results were that by age 16 years and onwards, completed life stories evidenced more stability in comparison to asking participants to provide seven key events in their lives (Köber & Habermas, 2017). Results also indicated that narrative identity was in flux from childhood until late adolescence and young adulthood, when a new degree of stability and insight into one's life story emerged. Even greater stability in narrative identity, however, was likely as one moved further into adulthood (Köber & Habermas, 2017). Older relative to younger participants' narratives had more stability, with fewer new events added and more normative life events contained in them (e.g., school graduations, etc., Köber & Habermas, 2017).

Other studies with cross-sectional age-related comparisons between younger and older adults are consistent with findings from the Köber and Habermas (2017) longitudinal study; older (middle aged and onwards) relative to younger adults (e.g., in their twenties and thirties) have evidenced more stability and thematic coherence in their narratives (e.g., McLean, 2008; McLean & Fournier, 2008). Regarding adolescents, other cross-sectional studies of North American adolescents' personal narratives have also indicated that older compared to young adolescents engaged in more meaning making (e.g., McLean, Breen, & Fournier, 2010; Soucie, Lawford, & Pratt, 2012).

Overall, the studies relevant to understanding age-related trends in narrative identity development from childhood through adulthood show that older relative to younger people are better at connecting their life experiences to their own personal and psychological development, deriving meaning from those experiences (i.e., are more likely to engage in autobiographical reasoning), as well as showing more stability in their life stories particularly if one is a midlife adult or older. There are a handful of relevant longitudinal studies on developmental trends in narrative identity development, particularly those that include adolescents, and most of the current research evidence involves cross-sectional age-related comparisons.

Person-context interactions and other psychological and social processes are thought to be essential to adolescent narrative identity development, and the next group of studies sheds light on the social construction of narrative identity.

Spill the tea![6] The social construction of narrative identity

Another main area of research attention in the narrative identity field concerns social interactions. Here, the focus is to capture personal narratives in real time and in the context of conservations typically with important others (Pasupathi & Hoyt, 2009). The narrative prompts in this type of study are not meant to chronicle an entire life time, but instead are designed to elicit more discrete life events and memories, such as asking participants for a self-defining memory. An example of a self-defining memory would be what I remember about a particularly vivid life event or an experience that was critical to how I became the person that I am today (e.g., McLean & Fournier, 2008) or asking participants to tell a friend in a laboratory setting about a previously untold happy or sad life event (e.g., Pasupathi & Hoyt, 2009).

There can be some overlap between life stories and other personal narratives (e.g., important events; Köber & Habermas, 2017). It is posited that personal narratives told in conversational settings, which represent a relational/social developmental context, can exert a gradual impact on how people construct their life stories (Pasupathi & Hoyt, 2009). Ways in which this process may occur are by listeners either encouraging or putting a damper on the interpretative and narrative skills of the narrator, as well as through narrators building up a history of expectation with different listeners about what happens in the storytelling moment. This process is an aspect of relational positioning, for example, when important and/or potentially emotionally charged events are disclosed, and the narrator's voice can be either heard and affirmed or dismissed (McLean & Jennings, 2012). Pasupathi and Hoyt (2009, p. 570) cogently stated the following on this issue:

> In the long run, repeated unresponsiveness likely serves to silence a particular aspect of identity within that specific relationship context, and perhaps to silence that aspect of identity more broadly . . . The extent of the impact will also depend on the individual's motivation and capacity to seek out alternative social relationships within which particular identities can be elaborated, reflected upon, and thus further developed . . .

The conversational narrative identity research literature includes cross-sectional, descriptive studies that aim to examine the ebb and flow of a conversation and studies in which the intentions and behaviors of narrators and/or listeners are systematically changed as part of an experiment; many of these studies are laboratory-based. The majority of studies in this area have been conducted with young adult North American university students and their romantic partners or friends, and some studies have also been conducted with adolescents and their friends and/or parents.

Descriptive conversational studies

There are numerous studies about parents' and their *children's*[7] reminiscences about events and people (e.g., Fivush, Reese, & Haden, 2006). General conclusions derived from these studies are that children's narration and interpretative skills are fostered by parents' support (e.g., attentive listening) for their child's storytelling and elaboration and by children being exposed to parents' elaborative and/or introspective storytelling style (Fivush et al., 2006, 2011; McAdams & McLean, 2013; McLean, 2017; McLean & Jennings, 2012). The descriptive conversational narrative identity research literature with adolescents is emerging, but study results thus far tend to be similar to the main findings of the parent-child reminisce research literature, with some caveats regarding adolescents' age and gender.

A cross-sectional descriptive study by McLean and colleagues provided an illustration of how mothers' support or scaffold narrative identity work in their adolescents, and how narrative identity may change as youth move towards the end of adolescence (McLean & Jennings, 2012; McLean & Mansfield, 2012). Scaffolding in this study referred to different types of parental engagement, such as affirming, challenging, or reinterpreting, in response to their adolescent's narrative (McLean & Jennings, 2012). In this study, adolescents were asked to provide personal narratives in the presence of a friend and/or their mother (McLean & Jennings, 2012). A sample of 22 adolescents spoke with both a friend and their mother, and study results indicated that more scaffolding by mothers was generally associated with more meaning making on the part of adolescents; furthermore, mothers scaffolded more often and differently in comparison to friends (McLean & Jennings, 2012).

With a larger and overlapping sample of 63 adolescents (aged 11–18 years, mean = 13 years), an additional study found that meaning making on the part of adolescents became more nuanced, likely due to a larger sample with a wider age range (McLean & Mansfield, 2012). In this latter study, adolescents discussed personal narratives in the presence of their mothers. Study results showed that early adolescents had mothers that scaffolded more than older adolescents, and that mothers' scaffolding was associated with greater meaning making by younger but not older adolescents (McLean & Mansfield, 2012). Thus, a general conclusion from McLean and colleagues' studies are that parental scaffolding maybe critical to setting the groundwork for narrative identity development in childhood though middle adolescence, but changes may occur that make the importance of parental scaffolding more qualified during late adolescence. It is also possible that a diverse array of listeners (e.g., friends and romantic partners) may play an increasingly important role in the social construction of narrative identity (McLean & Jennings, 2012; McLean & Mansfield, 2012). However, descriptive conversational narrative identity studies with adolescents are fewer in number than those with young adults, and more research, including longitudinal studies, is needed to further test this conclusion.

Experimental conversational studies

Experimental manipulations have also been part of narrative identity studies in social interaction research paradigms. In this case, listeners can be randomly assigned to different study conditions: The distracted listener, the engaged and responsive listener (what we might wish for in a good friend or a supportive parent), as well as the agreeable listener (who wholeheartedly supports the interpretations and meaning that narrators derive from their stories), or the contradictory listener who challenges and reinterprets the narrators' insights and lessons learned (e.g., Pasupathi & Hoyt, 2009; Pasupathi & Rich 2005). Returning to the story of Siddhartha, Vasudeva, the ferryman who was Siddhartha's companion towards the end of his life, exemplifies what an engaged listener can be like and the positive impact that this listener can have on one's narrative. Vasudeva's patience, presence of mind, and authentic involvement as a listener were obvious to Siddhartha, as he shared the ups and downs of his life to his friend and tried to make meaning of them (Hesse, 1951).

Descriptive and experimental conversational studies: general findings

Research findings from conservational studies on narrative identity, both descriptive and experimental, generally showed that more responsive listeners were generally associated with more interpretative work or meaning making on the part of the narrator (Jennings, Pasupathi, & McLean, 2014; McLean & Pasupathi, 2011; Pasupathi & Hoyt, 2009). Also, listeners who challenged the narrator's story along with giving support and providing a reinterpretation have also been linked with more meaning making on the part of the narrator (e.g., McLean & Pasupathi, 2011; Pasupathi & Hoyt, 2009).

Thus, available evidence points to a dynamic engagement on the part of narrators and listeners when personal narratives are told in a conversational setting; the products and experiences of this engagement are hypothesized to provide the material that can support narrative identity development more generally. Moreover, attentive skillful listeners can make a difference in terms of fostering a narrator's development, creating a forum for developmental change in how individuals see themselves and their life experiences. Engaged listening, which could involve being attentive, supportive, or supportive combined with challenging and offering new interpretations, tends to be associated with more elaboration and meaning making by narrators in studies with adolescents and young adults. It is important to note that for adolescents, there be a new availability of different listeners (e.g., romantic partners). More research is needed of how different listener responses may have different impacts on a life story presented in conversation.

Research evidence on what is an optimal narrative identity

Optimal narrative identity involves the interpretive and reflective work that a narrator utilizes to develop a coherent life story. What is thought to be gained in this process is a greater sense of self coherence across situations and time, as well as more meaning from one's life experiences. Empirically, it appears that interpretative, meaning making processes and features[8] should remain central to the theoretical conception of optimal narrative identity development; however, certain conditions must be considered for people in different age groups (Adler et al., 2016). Finally from an empirical standpoint, motivational (e.g., finding a sense of purpose through agency and/or communion) and some selected emotional aspects of narratives (e.g., increased redemption and decreased contamination themes) appear to merit greater emphasis in theoretical conceptions of optimal narrative identity development (Adler et al., 2015, 2016; Lilgendahl, 2014).

Going into the research evidence in more detail, Adler and colleagues (2016) conducted a systematic review and identified 30 studies that examined associations between indicators of narrative identity development and well-being. The studies included samples of adolescents and adults from the general as well as unique populations (e.g., adults who had experienced trauma or were undergoing psychotherapy, Adler et al., 2016). The majority of studies had a cross-sectional design and a few studies were longitudinal (Adler et al., 2016). The authors' qualitative examination of findings across studies indicated that a broad array of well-being indicators were significantly and positively associated with motivational themes in personal narratives. For example, a person narrated a past, present, or future-oriented striving after attaining a sense agency (working to shape one's life and life conditions) and/or connecting with other people, and thereby finding purpose in life; Adler et al., 2016). Well-being was also related to integrative themes in personal narratives that were characterized by learning about oneself or life in general from past events. Such learnings might include self-event connections, gaining a sense of resolution or insight, experience of psychological growth that can be of an assimilative (adding to the current view of oneself) or accommodative nature (a more dramatic reorganization), Adler et al., 2016). Furthermore, affective themes in personal narratives, particularly those moving from a negative to a positive interpretation of a series of connected life events (i.e., redemption) was associated with an indicator of well-being (Adler et al., 2016).

Other studies, the majority of which used adult samples, have also examined associations between narrative identity development and mental health outcomes and have shown initial evidence that increased themes of communion (Bauer & McAdams 2010), agency, and redemption (e.g., Adler et al., 2015) are prospectively associated with better mental health outcomes; themes of contamination (i.e., when good things go bad) are prospectively associated with poorer mental health over time (three to four years later). Adler et al. (2015, p. 493) noted that "whether the narrative of the agentic fighter is more myth than reality, for example, is not actually the central point when it comes to impacting [mental health]. Instead, the story itself may support and foster [mental health], regardless of the actual circumstances." While the aforementioned study results represent a promising start (e.g., Adler et al., 2015, 2016), there is a need for more longitudinal studies in varied cultural contexts that concern relations between narrative identity development and mental health, particularly studies that span adolescence and adulthood.

Current directions in narrative identity research

Developmental processes: what lies beyond autobiographical reasoning?

In addition to autobiographical reasoning, other possible processes of change may be important to bridging the interface between the personal narratives that are discussed in everyday conversations and a life story (Pasupathi, 2014). Pasupathi (2014) suggested that processes like tacit themes[9] and ways that people may communicate about their life experiences and narrative identity development by nonverbal means merit future investigation (e.g., gestures, eye contact, psychophysiology; Pasupathi, personal communication, July 11, 2018).

Research with a longitudinal perspective and global reach

As is the case with many research areas within psychology, the narrative identity field also is moving to include more longitudinal studies, particularly those that span early adolescence through adulthood, and a longitudinal emphasis would also benefit conversational narrative identity studies which, to date, have largely been cross-sectional or experimental (McLean & Mansfield, 2012). More longitudinal studies would allow for more systematic reviews and/or meta-analyses. Research studies in the narrative identity field have primarily been conducted in North America (some notable exceptions are studies conducted in Germany, New Zealand, Poland, Taiwan, and Sweden), and more studies with representative samples from across the globe would clearly advance the field (Fivush et al., 2011; Merrill & Fivush, 2016; Reese et al., 2017).

Narrative identity in relation to other identity indicators and theories

Some research studies have been conducted on how narrative identity works in relation to other identity perspectives, such as those that focus on the processes of identity exploration and commitment during adolescence and young adulthood (e.g., McLean & Pratt, 2006; McLean, Syed, Yoder, & Greenhoot, 2014). More research of this type would be valuable and would add an additional layer of innovation and integration to the field of identity studies in general (McLean & Pasupathi, 2012; Schwartz, Luyckx, & Crocetti, 2014; Seaman et al., 2017). In the next chapter section, this issue is discussed further in the context of the future development of identity-related interventions.

Implications for social response

Well designed and implemented interventions and policies that partner with young people to support their own identity development and future life prospects are essential (Ferrer-Wreder, Montgomery, Lorente, & Habibi, 2014; Montgomery, Hernandez, & Ferrer-Wreder, 2008). Currently, there exist only a handful of published research studies that describe interventions designed to expressly promote certain aspects of narrative identity development (e.g., Tseng, 2017) or explicitly examine how narrative identity development may change when other outcomes are altered as part of a prevention and/or treatment intervention (e.g., recovery from mental ill health – e.g., Adler, 2012; Adler & Hershfield, 2012). By and large, these studies have primarily been focused on adults, and they highlight the potential for narrative identity processes to be important to the promotion of positive outcomes and the reduction of problems. While there are some initial indications of promise, substantial descriptive and intervention research is needed in order to inform the ways that social institutions can systematically support youth in their narrative identity development.

Interventions designed to promote narrative identity in adolescents will require careful design given that different types of meaning making may have different relations to well-being in adolescence. For example, in studies with adults and children (who are supported by their parents in their interpretations), more meaning making in personal narratives and life stories (even when something negative may have happened) tended to be associated with greater well-being (McLean et al., 2010). However, in a study by McLean and colleagues (2010), some aspects of meaning making were related to better well-being, namely change connections (i.e., this is a type of a self-event connection in which participants explain how certain life events played a role in changes in themselves). Yet, a different indicator of meaning making called sophistication (i.e., "specific emotional, psychological, or relational insight from the event that applies to broader areas of the reporter's life") in early adolescent participants was associated with poorer well-being (McLean et al., 2010, p. 174).

The study authors suggested that self-event connections (e.g., change connections) may be cognitively and emotionally easier or developmentally appropriate for early adolescents, and are thereby are associated with better well-being, but that the more interpretative and introspective types of meaning making may be ill suited developmentally for early adolescents. Hence, the association with poorer well-being among early but not late adolescents may have arisen in this sample (McLean et al., 2010). This pattern of findings was also evident in a cross-sectional study with adolescents living in New Zealand (Reese et al., 2017).

If this finding is widely replicated in future research, and if there are lingering negative consequences for early adolescents who engage in more sophisticated meaning making into later adolescence and adulthood, then there would be important implications for the design of narrative identity-oriented interventions with adolescents. More introspective meaning making narratives could be beneficial to support late but not early adolescents. Or it may be the case, as other scholars have suggested, that this is a temporary, difficult period for these early adolescents "who are doing the hard work of identity exploration early on" and who later turn out to be fine or even better than fine, because they have a head start on other adolescents (Reese et al., 2017, p. 623). Thus, more longitudinal research studies with adolescent cohorts that include narrative identity processes and other outcomes such as well-being and varied indicators of health are vital to providing a sound basis for interventions to support the development of new narrative identity-related interventions for adolescents.

A parallel avenue to pursue along with longitudinal studies would be to include narrative identity development measurement in the outcome evaluation studies of existing identity interventions that have shown benefits in adolescent samples (e.g., Arango, Kurtines, Montgomery, & Ritchie, 2008; Eichas, Montgomery, Meca, & Kurtines, 2017; Kortsch, Kurtines, & Montgomery, 2008; Kurtines et al., 2008). A focus of a study such as this would be to examine what mediating or moderating role narrative identity related processes may play in intervention-related change for these existing evidence-based identity interventions. These types of interventions have already evidenced benefits in adolescent samples (Eichas et al., 2017). An aim could be to examine what role narrative identity related processes have in relation to other intervention targets for change and outcomes in identity interventions such as identity exploration.

Summary

Narrative identity involves a person's attempt to answer the following questions: Across time and the events of my life, among a diversity of other people and situations that I find myself in, what defines me? Who am I and what do I stand for across the epochs of my life? Indeed, the narrative identity perspective places particular value on developing one's own unique sense of unity or continuity over time and settings. One can put narrative identity in a wider three-layer framework of lifespan personality development that consists of traits, motivations/goals, and narrative identity (McAdams, 2015; McAdams & Manczak, 2015; McAdams & Olson, 2010; McAdams & Pals, 2006). Current research evidence shows that adolescence tends to be a developmental period in which it becomes increasingly more common for young people to show greater understanding of how their life experiences relate to who they are as a person as well as to tell personal narratives that are characterized by greater coherence and/or meaning making than are found among children (Fivush et al., 2011; Habermas & Bluck, 2000; Köber et al., 2015); these trends are likely to continue through adulthood (e.g., Köber & Habermas, 2017). Narrative identity research is young and a fast growing field within psychology (Adler et al., 2016), and there are likely to be many future advances in the field related to acceleration in the number of longitudinal and intervention studies with adolescents.

Notes

1 Köber and colleagues (2015, p. 261) stated in regards to temporal coherence that it serves to let the listener know

> when an event happened in the narrator's life . . . life narratives are expected to begin no later than with birth. Sometimes birth stories or earliest memories are told to foreshadow the global interpretation of life . . .

The personal narrative that starts off this chapter (i.e., Sara's story) was not collected as part of a scientific study. Sara's story was told to her granddaughter, who is the first author of this book (LFW), and is retold here for illustrative purposes. Sara began her own life story with her parents' story of how they came to live in Cuba. This break from what is typical in a life story can be called an anachrony (Köber et al., 2015), and could be a product of not following a systematic interview procedure and/or it could highlight the importance of family relationships and history which were fundamental to who Sara was and her culture (i.e., a master narrative – cf. Hammack, 2008 – of how a life story should be told in a Cuban or a Cuban American context). See Chapter 5 for more on master narratives.

2 McLean (2005, pp. 683–684) distinguished gaining insight and lesson learning in the quote below, in that lesson learning is about:

> a specific lesson from an event that could direct future behavior in similar situations . . . Gaining insight refers to gleaning meaning from an event that applies to greater areas of life than a specific behavior; with insight, there is often some kind of transformation in the understanding of oneself or others . . .

3 Autobiographical reasoning is multi-faceted and concerns how people see life events as formative to psychological changes or stability in themselves and/or connecting lived experiences to wider life lessons and/or insights (Habermas & Köber, 2014).

4 The questions and prompts for the life story interview can be found at the Foley Center website https://www.sesp.northwestern.edu/foley/instruments/interview/. The description of the life story interview questions and prompts in this book were paraphrased from this source.

5 An examination of existing empirical studies using a search engine often used in psychology called PsycINFO yielded 248 citations to empirical studies with the terms "narrative identity" or "autobiographical reasoning" referenced anywhere in the study. The identified empirical studies began to appear in the mid-1990s and about 32% were published in the last three years. Thus, the narrative identity field appears to be growing but it is a relevantly young (about two and a half decades old) area of inquiry within the discipline of psychology (Adler et al., 2016).

6 "Spill the tea!" or "what's the 411?" are slang phrases that can be used in an informal conversation to let other people know (these other people should also know the meaning of these phrases) that you would like to hear what they have to say about themselves and their experiences, and it can also be a request to hear about confidential or emotionally significant details about another person (i.e., gossip).

7 *Italics* were added in this sentence to emphasize that the reference here is specifically to children and not adolescents.

8 Coherence and meaning making are sometimes defined by different scholars in variable ways; in some cases these terms are clearly distinct and in other cases these terms appear to be conceptually merged which can lead to a lack of clarity in regards to making conclusions about the empirical associations of different narrative constructs (i.e., measured variables in studies) and correlates (i.e., well-being).

9 Tacit themes concern implicit recognition in storytelling that is essential to meaning making, but this recognition is more taken for granted than explicit (Pasupathi, 2014). For example, in the opening personal narrative told by Sara, her main theme was tacit and it was not part of her story telling style to step out of the narrative very frequently if at all to make meta-statements (i.e., statements about her statements) but from her story, the themes of what she was trying to convey were clear.

References

Adler, J. M. (2012). Living into the story: Agency and coherence in a longitudinal study of narrative identity development and mental health over the course of psychotherapy. *Journal of Personality and Social Psychology, 102,* 367–389.

Adler, J. M., & Hershfield, H. E. (2012). Mixed emotional experience is associated with and precedes improvements in psychological well-being. *PLoS ONE, 7*, 1–10.

Adler, J. M., Lodi-Smith, J., Philippe, F. L., & Houle, I. (2016). The incremental validity of narrative identity in predicting well-being: A review of the field and recommendations for the future. *Personality and Social Psychology Review, 20*, 142–175.

Adler, J. M., Turner, A. F., Brookshier, K. M., Monahan, C., Walder-Biesanz, I., Harmeling, L. H., . . . Oltmanns, T. F. (2015). Variation in narrative identity is associated with trajectories of mental health over several years. *Journal of Personality and Social Psychology, 108*, 476–496.

Arango, L. L., Kurtines, W. M., Montgomery, M. J., & Ritchie, R. (2008). A multi-stage longitudinal comparative design stage II evaluation of the changing lives program: The life course interview (RDA-LCI). *Journal of Adolescent Research, 23*, 310–341.

Bauer, J. J., & McAdams, D. P. (2010). Eudaimonic growth: Narrative growth goals predict increases in ego development and subjective well-being 3 years later. *Developmental Psychology, 46*, 761–772.

Costa, P. T., Jr., & McCrae, R. R. (2017). The NEO inventories as instruments of psychological theory. In T. A. Widiger (Ed.), *The Oxford handbook of the five factor model* (pp. 11–37). New York, NY: Oxford University Press.

Côté, J. E. (2014). Identity formation research from a critical perspective: Is social science developing? In K. C. McLean, & M. Syed (Eds.), *The Oxford handbook of identity development* [E-reader version] (pp. 1–22). New York, NY: Oxford University Press. doi: 10.1093/oxfordhb/9780199936564.013.015

De Silveira, C., & Habermas, T. (2011). Narrative means to manage responsibility in life narratives across adolescence. *The Journal of Genetic Psychology: Research and Theory on Human Development, 172*, 1–20.

Eichas, K., Montgomery, M. J., Meca, A., & Kurtines, W. M. (2017). Empowering marginalized youth: A self-transformative intervention for promoting positive youth development. *Child Development, 88*, 1115–1124.

Ferrer-Wreder, L., Montgomery, M. J., Lorente, C. C., & Habibi, M. (2014). Identify interventions for adolescents: Promoting optimal identity. In T. Gullotta & M. Bloom (Series Eds.), *The encyclopedia of primary prevention and health promotion* (pp. 1278–1287). New York, NY: Springer.

Fivush, R., Habermas, T., Waters, T. E. A., & Zaman, W. (2011). The making of autobiographical memory: Intersections of culture, narratives and identity. *International Journal of Psychology, 46*, 321–345.

Fivush, R., Reese, E., & Haden, C. A. (2006). Elaborating on elaborations: Role of maternal reminiscing style in cognitive and socioemotional development. *Child Development, 77*, 1568–1588.

Gergen, K. J. (1991). *The saturated self: Dilemmas of identity in contemporary life*. New York, NY: Basic Books.

Groh, A. M., Narayan, A. J., Bakermans-Kranenburg, M. J., Roisman, G. I., Vaughn, B. E., Fearon, R. M. P., & IJzendoorn, M. H. (2017). Attachment and temperament in the early life course: A meta-analytic review. *Child Development, 88*, 770–795.

Habermas, T., & Bluck, S. (2000). Getting a life: The emergence of the life story in adolescence. *Psychological Bulletin, 126*, 748–769.

Habermas, T., & de Silveira, C. (2008). The development of global coherence in life narratives across adolescence: Temporal, causal, and thematic aspects. *Developmental Psychology, 44*, 707–721.

Habermas, T., & Köber, C. (2014). Autobiographical reasoning is constitutive for narrative identity: The role of the life story for personal continuity. In K. C. McLean, & M. Syed (Eds.), *The Oxford handbook of identity development* [E-reader version] (pp. 1–31). New York, NY: Oxford University Press.doi: 10.1093/oxfordhb/9780199936564.013.010

Hammack, P. L. (2008). Narrative and the cultural psychology of identity. *Personality and Social Psychology Review, 12,* 222–247.

Hammack, P. L. (2010). The political psychology of personal narrative: The case of Barack Obama. *Analyses of Social Issues and Public Policy, 10,* 182–206.

Hammack, P. L. (2014). Theoretical foundations of identity. In K. C. McLean, & M. Syed (Eds.), *The Oxford handbook of identity development* [E-reader version] (pp. 1–37). New York, NY: Oxford University Press. doi: 10.1093/oxfordhb/9780199936564.013.027

Hesse, H. (1951). *Siddhartha.* New York, NY: New Directions Publishing Corp.

Imuta, K., Henry, J. D., Slaughter, V., Selcuk, B., & Ruffman, T. (2016). Theory of mind and prosocial behavior in childhood: A meta-analytic review. *Developmental Psychology, 52,* 1192–1205.

Jennings, L. E., Pasupathi, M., & McLean, K. (2014). "Intricate lettings out and lettings in": Listener scaffolding of narrative identity in newly dating romantic partners. *Self and Identity, 13,* 214–230.

Josselson, R., & Flum, H. (2014). Identity status: On refinding the people. In K. C. McLean, & M. Syed (Eds.), *The Oxford handbook of identity development* [E-reader version] (pp. 1–26). New York, NY: Oxford University Press. doi: 10.1093/oxfor dhb/9780199936564.013.019

Köber, C., & Habermas, T. (2017). How stable is the personal past? Stability of most important autobiographical memories and life narratives across eight years in a lifespan sample. *Journal of Personality and Social Psychology, 113,* 608–626.

Köber, C., Schmiedek, F., & Habermas, T. (2015). Characterizing lifespan development of three aspects of coherence in life narratives: A cohort-sequential study. *Developmental Psychology, 51,* 260–275.

Kortsch, G., Kurtines, W. M., & Montgomery, M. J. (2008). A multistage longitudinal comparative (MLC) design stage II: Evaluation of the changing lives program (CLP): The possible selves questionnaire-qualitative extensions (PSQ-QE). *Journal of Adolescent Research, 23,* 342–358.

Kurtines, W. M., Ferrer-Wreder, L., Berman, S. L., Lorente, C. C., Briones, E., Montgomery, M. J., . . . Arrufat, O. (2008). Promoting positive youth development: The Miami youth development project (YDP). *Journal of Adolescent Research, 23,* 256–267.

Lilgendahl, J. P. (2014). The dynamic role of identity processes in personality development: Theories, patterns, and new directions. In K. C. McLean, & M. Syed (Eds.), *The Oxford handbook of identity development* [E-reader version] (pp. 1–31). New York, NY: Oxford University Press. doi: 10.1093/oxfordhb/9780199936564.013.026

Lundh, L-G. (2015). The person as a focus for research. The contributions of Windelband, Stern, Allport, Lamiell, and Magnusson. *Journal for Person-Oriented Research, 1,* 15–33.

McAdams, D. P. (1996). What this framework can and cannot do. *Psychological Inquiry, 7,* 378–386.

McAdams, D. P. (2008). *The life story interview.* Evanston, IL: The Foley Center for the Study of Lives, Northwestern University. Retrieved from www.sesp.northwestern.edu/ foley/instruments/interview

McAdams, D. P. (2015). Three lines of personality development: A conceptual itinerary. *European Psychologist, 20,* 252–264.

McAdams, D. P., & Manczak, E. (2015). Personality and the life story. In M. Mikulincer, P. R. Shaver, M. L. Cooper & R. J. Larsen (Eds.), *APA handbook of personality and social psychology* (pp. 425–446). Washington, DC: American Psychological Association.

McAdams, D. P., & McLean, K. C. (2013). Narrative identity. *Current Directions in Psychological Science, 22,* 233–238.

McAdams, D. P., & Olson, B. D. (2010). Personality development: Continuity and change over the life course. *Annual Review of Psychology, 61,* 517–542.

McAdams, D. P., & Pals, J. L. (2006). A new big five: Fundamental principles for an integrative science of personality. *American Psychologist, 61,* 204–217.

McLean, K. C. (2005). Late adolescent identity development: Narrative meaning making and memory telling. *Developmental Psychology, 41,* 683–691.

McLean, K. C. (2008). Stories of the young and the old: Personal continuity and narrative identity. *Developmental Psychology, 44,* 254–264.

McLean, K. C. (2017). And the story evolves: The development of personal narratives and narrative identity. In J. Specht (Ed.), *Personality development across the lifespan* (pp. 325–338). San Diego, CA: Elsevier Academic Press.

McLean, K. C., & Breen, A. V. (2009). Processes and content of narrative identity development in adolescence: Gender and well-being. *Developmental Psychology, 45,* 702–710.

McLean, K. C., Breen, A. V., & Fournier, M. A. (2010). Constructing the self in early, middle, and late adolescent boys: Narrative identity, individuation, and well-being. *Journal of Research on Adolescence, 20,* 166–187.

McLean, K. C., & Fournier, M. A. (2008). The content and processes of autobiographical reasoning in narrative identity. *Journal of Research in Personality, 42,* 527–545.

McLean, K. C., & Jennings, L. E. (2012). Teens telling tales: How maternal and peer audiences support narrative identity development. *Journal of Adolescence, 35,* 1455–1469.

McLean, K. C., & Mansfield, C. D. (2012). The co-construction of adolescent narrative identity: Narrative processing as a function of adolescent age, gender, and maternal scaffolding. *Developmental Psychology, 48,* 436–447.

McLean, K. C., & Pasupathi, M. (2011). Old, new, borrowed, blue? The emergence and retention of personal meaning in autobiographical storytelling. *Journal of Personality, 79,* 135–164.

McLean, K. C., & Pasupathi, M. (2012). Processes of identity development: Where I am and how I got there. *Identity: An International Journal of Theory and Research, 12,* 8–28.

McLean, K. C., Pasupathi, M., & Pals, J. L. (2007). Selves creating stories creating selves: A process model of self-development. *Personality and Social Psychology Review, 11,* 262–278.

McLean, K. C., & Pratt, M. W. (2006). Life's little (and big) lessons: Identity statuses and meaning-making in the turning point narratives of emerging adults. *Developmental Psychology, 42,* 714–722.

McLean, K. C., & Syed, M. (2014). The field of identity development needs an identity: An introduction to The Oxford handbook of identity development. In K. C. McLean, & M. Syed (Eds.), *The Oxford handbook of identity development* [E-reader version] (pp. 1–19). New York, NY: Oxford University Press. doi: 10.1093/oxfordhb/9780199936564.013.023

McLean, K. C., Syed, M., Yoder, A., & Greenhoot, A. F. (2016). The role of domain content in understanding identity development processes. *Journal of Research on Adolescence, 26,* 60–75.

Merrill, N., & Fivush, R. (2016). Intergenerational narratives and identity across development. *Developmental Review, 40,* 72–92.

Montgomery, M. J., Hernandez, L., & Ferrer-Wreder, L. (2008). Identity development and intervention studies: The right time for a marriage? *Identity: An International Journal of Theory and Research, 8,* 173–182.

Morgan, E. M., & Korobov, N. (2012). Interpersonal identity formation in conversations with close friends about dating relationships. *Journal of Adolescence, 35,* 1471–1483.

Overton, W. F. (2015). Processes, relations, and relational-developmental-systems. In W. F. Overton, P. C. M. Molenaar, & R. M. Lerner (Eds.), *Handbook of child psychology and developmental science: Theory and method* (pp. 9–62). Hoboken, NJ: John Wiley & Sons.

Pasupathi, M. (2014). Autobiographical reasoning and my discontent: Alternative paths from narrative to identity. In K. C. McLean, & M. Syed (Eds.), *The Oxford handbook of identity development* [E-reader version] (pp. 1–30). New York, NY: Oxford University Press. doi: 10.1093/oxfordhb/9780199936564.013.002

Pasupathi, M., & Hoyt, T. (2009). The development of narrative identity in late adolescence and emergent adulthood: The continued importance of listeners. *Developmental Psychology, 45,* 558–574.

Pasupathi, M., & Rich, B. (2005). Inattentive listening undermines self-verification in personal storytelling. *Journal of Personality, 73,* 1051–1086.

Peterson, C. & McCabe, A. (1994). A social interactionist account of developing decontextualized narrative skill. *Developmental Psychology, 30,* 937–948.

Reese, E., Myftari, E., McAnally, H. M., Chen, Y., Neha, T., Wang, Q., . . . Robertson, S. (2017). Telling the tale and living well: Adolescent narrative identity, personality traits, and well-being across cultures. *Child Development, 88,* 612–628.

Roberts, B. W., Walton, K. E., & Viechtbauer, W. (2006). Patterns of mean-level change in personality traits across the life course: A meta-analysis of longitudinal studies. *Psychological Bulletin, 132,* 1–25.

Sameroff, A. J. & Haith M. M. (Eds.) (1996). *The five to seven year shift: The age of reason and responsibility.* Chicago, IL: University of Chicago Press.

Schwartz, S. J., Luyckx, K., & Crocetti, E. (2014). What have we learned since Schwartz (2001)? A reappraisal of the field of identity development. In K. C. McLean, & M. Syed (Eds.), *The Oxford handbook of identity development* [E-reader version] (pp. 1–45). New York, NY: Oxford University Press. doi: 10.1093/oxfordhb/9780199936564.013.028

Seaman, J., Sharp, E. H., & Coppens, A. D. (2017). A dialectical approach to theoretical integration in developmental–contextual identity research. *Developmental Psychology, 53,* 2023–2035.

Soucie, K. M., Lawford, H., & Pratt, M. W. (2012). Personal stories of empathy in adolescence and emerging adulthood. *Merrill-Palmer Quarterly, 58,* 141–158.

Tseng, W. (2017). An intervention using Lego Serious Play on fostering narrative identity among economically disadvantaged college students in Taiwan. *Journal of College Student Development, 58,* 264–282.

5 Identity as rooted in society and culture

> I thought about my ethnic identity a lot through high school. In my early teens, I always felt embarrassed by my parents, who emigrated here when I was seven. I didn't think much about it before then, but by my early teens they kept wanting me to follow their [cultural] and family traditions, and it made me feel really uncomfortable around my friends. So I went through a time of just wanting to forget everything about my Somali background and become "all American." But gradually I came to realize that I am Somali and I shouldn't try to deny it. Seeing other African Americans on TV doing important things started to make me feel kind of proud . . . and now I feel good about myself and being a Somali American.
>
> (Charlie, an 18-year-old college freshman)

This passage comes from an interview undertaken by Kroger in 2006 to obtain background material for her subsequent writing on ethnic identity development during adolescence. Charlie's statement gives us a glimpse of what it is like to belong to more than one world. There are many possible components of social identity, also sometimes called collective identity, which could be based on one's generation, gender, sexuality, ethnicity, nationality and even a person's support of a sports team or other special interest. Social identity deals with the question of "what group do I belong to?" (Worrell, 2014, p. 3) and can be seen from different angles: Individuals interacting with groups, groups interacting with each other, and people and groups embedded in a sociocultural and historical change (Spears, 2011).

To provide an illustration, consider a fictional young man with a Roma heritage[1] living in Berlin. This young man may see himself mostly as a cosmopolitan city dweller that spends a good part of his day laughing at the same internet memes that every other teenager in Germany is laughing at this week. But, how does he make sense of himself as a global citizen, as part of his generation, and in relation to the wider German society? How does he relate to other ethnocultural groups in Berlin? Each of these social groups can be a place where a sense of confusion or belonging and meaning can be found. Azmitia (2014) likened the many different possible components of social identity to boxes that we carry around. While juggling different identity boxes, this fictional young man may also be cultivating what is distinctive and meaningful about himself as an individual. In other words, he is also likely working on just being himself and figuring out who that is – that is, co-constructing his personal identity which reflects our individuality and how "one's individual goals and beliefs guide one's decisions and behaviors" (Schwartz et al., 2014, p. 63).

This chapter address the question of how adolescent identity development progresses as young people learn how to be themselves while still navigating and finding a psychological home in different social and cultural worlds. This chapter will focus on the development of ethnic identity as one example of how sociocultural forces are important to identity development during adolescence. In short, ethnic identity involves the intersection of personal and social identity (Cross et al., 2017), and may be more or less salient to a given adolescent depending on the adolescent and her or his sociocultural context. Ethnic identity also involves a person's psychological and social association with an ethnocultural group. Ethnocultural groups are often defined by a shared geographical and/or genealogical origin as well as elements of a common culture based on the particulars and history of the ethnocultural group in question (Liebkind, Mähönen, Varjonen, & Jasinskaja-Lahti, 2016; Worrell, 2014).

Sociocultural approaches to identity

An historic debate that lies underneath relevant theory, measurement, and information about identity concerns the degree to which individuals can exercise agency (e.g., free will, make choices about who they are) in the midst of their identity development (Burkitt, 2011). Ethnic and cultural identity makes an encounter with this debate inevitable. Are people indeed exploring identity options or making choices about who they are or are social groups and wider forces (e.g., social mobility and opportunity structures, power relations among groups in a particular society) dictating who we even have the possibility to consider becoming? This person versus context debate (see Table 5.1) has implications for how identity itself has been conceptualized by different theorists and within varied disciplines (Burkitt, 2011; Galliher, McLean, & Syed, 2017; Seaman, Sharp, & Coppens, 2017).

There is now a clearer recognition of the importance of examining how individuals can shape their identity along with the ways that society and culture work to co-construct a person's identity (e.g., Galliher, Rivas-Drake, & Dubow, 2017; Hammack, 2014; Seaman et al., 2017). The word co-construct implies that that there is a bi-directional association and that the individual and context are both essential when one wants to understand human development, in any domain of development (Kurtines, Azmitia, & Alvarez, 1992; Magnusson, 1996; Overton, 2013). The context can include social institutions, cultural activities, practices, and beliefs, historical times and conditions, and social interactions between people (Bronfenbrenner & Morris, 2006).

In present-day developmental science, the importance of person–context interactions is largely uncontroversial.[3] Yet, the devil is in the details, empirically speaking, and person–context interactions are complex (Kaplan & Garner, 2017)

Table 5.1 Dualisms in the study of identity development[2]

The individual shapes identity	The context (including culture) shapes identity
Identity is interior or inside the person	Identity as assigned to a person
My thoughts and emotions about myself	A predefined identity is offered that may (or may) not fit me
Personal identity	Social identity
The unique life I live and person that I am in my own eyes	National, ethnic, gender/occupation, group intersections
Identity process	Identity content
Exploration and meaning making	
Change in individuals	Change in groups
The unique life course of the individual person	Inter-group relations, power dynamics (meaning of groups changing in a society across generations)

and empirically challenging to address in a research study and a theoretical model of identity development. Ultimately, person–context interactions have been embraced because such interactions offer a more realistic framework to understand human development. Some identity theories and theories about theories (i.e., meta-theories) applied to identity studies are now exploring the specifics of how bi-directional person–context interactions may work in the case of identity development (Kaplan & Garner, 2017; Seaman et al., 2017).

The sociocultural tradition within the field of human development offers practical ways out of the person versus context debate (Rogoff, 2016; Rogoff, Dahl, & Callanan, 2018). This tradition derives several key ideas from Lev Vygotsky's scholarly work on the development of mental processes (Holland & Lachicotte, 2007; Penuel & Wertsch, 1995; see also van der Veer, 2012, for more on Vygotsky more generally). Several of Vygotsky's ideas that continue to have currency as part of the developmentally oriented sociocultural perspective include his views of human development as embedded in a particular sociocultural context and historical moment, development happening when people interact with each other, as well as when they engage in cultural practices (emphasizing how people's use and adaptation of symbols and tools can move development forward; Rogoff et al., 2018). Where the contemporary sociocultural tradition in human development goes beyond Vygotsky is in the proposition that the developing person and context are actually inseparable (Rogoff et al., 2018). Thus, many present-day sociocultural researchers that have a developmental orientation would likely reject:

> the assumption of a boundary between people and the events in which they engage, a boundary that divides the individual and the context/culture into separate entities . . . Crucially for the study of lived experience, people do not

simply participate. They participate IN some event. And while they are doing so they are IN that process, along with their companions, building on ways of life of prior generations of their cultural communities, in the particular contexts in which they engage.

(Rogoff et al., 2018, p. 7)

In addition to Vygotsky, the sociocultural tradition in human development also has clear connections to cultural psychology. This sub-field within psychology has championed the discovery and documentation of contextual diversity for its own sake (Shweder, 2011; Valsiner, 2012). Cultural psychology does not discount that idea that universal developmental processes can exist as ways to explain human development (e.g., exploration and commitment as a universal identity process in the Erikson and Marcia traditions), but it is also an ideal within cultural psychology that one should also not assume uniformity/universality (i.e., a developmental process), unless it is actually empirically documented in a diversity of cultures found across the globe (Hammack, 2008; Rogoff et al., 2018). Cultural psychology also recognizes the perverseness and complexity of the cultural and social context in relation to human development and advocates a bi-directional relation between the person and culture, and challenges identity researchers to not assume that culture's importance to identity development can be reduced down into a single variable that is a static characteristic of the person, and the ways that culture is at work in identity development should be captured by more than one research method (Hammack, 2008).

Some scholars have applied lessons learned from the sociocultural tradition in human development to identity, and the result is that there is greater theoretical synergy achieved between a person's identity-related choices and meaning making (which implies some degree of agency) and consideration of the roles that other people, signs/symbols, and additional aspects of context play in shaping identity development (e.g., Holland & Lachicotte, 2007; Penuel & Wertsch, 1995; Seaman et al., 2017). This fusion of identity and sociocultural ideals is valuable to advancing identity research because it has a clear stance on the importance of the cultural and historical moment and how individual actions in the world come together to make identity formation possible. Sociocultural approaches in the field of human development can be seen as a complement and not necessarily at odds with other theoretical perspectives and frameworks that speak to adolescent identity development such as Erik Erikson's psychosocial theory (Penuel & Wertsch, 1995). However, this type of sociocultural approach will have a stronger focus on studies of identity development as identity issues are encountered in a given adolescent's everyday life in a particular culture. Furthermore, this approach would challenge identity researchers to have a deep understanding of a person's lived experience as a basis for the development of valid identity measures (Rogoff et al., 2018). A sociocultural approach to identity would also imply more emphasis on examining how people use what they have at hand to foster their identity (Rogoff et al., 2018). For instance, how do adolescents talk about who they are with others in person or on social media? What are the important identity-related cultural rituals for a particular adolescent? What are the everyday institutional policies or practices young people may encounter at home or school that can foster or inhibit their identity development? In sum, there is a great deal to be gained by taking an integrative approach that transcends the historic person versus context debate by fusing ideas from developmental science, sociocultural theories, and cultural psychology and then applying them to the study of identity development (Seaman et al., 2017; Verkuyten, 2016).

Adolescent ethnic identity development

Within this broader framework of ideas, we now switch to the integrative model for ethnic and racial identity (ERI) development (Umaña-Taylor et al., 2014) as a focal point that is in keeping with the sociocultural tradition but has its own unique theoretical inspiration and history. The integrative model for ERI development encompasses a selection of allied but historically separate theories, concepts, and operationalizations (Umaña-Taylor et al., 2014). It includes ideas and propositions from prior theories that are developmental (Phinney, 1989, 1990; Phinney & Baldelomar, 2011; Phinney & Ong, 2007). It also draws from other theories that speak to the African American experience in the United States, in which there is the possibility of change in ERI in response to life experiences that could or could not happen (i.e., non-developmental changes). These theories that were originally focused on the African American experience are well attuned to describing what ERI consists of (i.e., what it feels like) and how social identity functions in the midst of a wider society that has power differentials between social groups (e.g., racial identity theory, and the multidimensional model of racial identity; see Cross, 1991; Helms, 1990; Sellers, Smith, Shelton, Rowley, & Chavous, 1998).

The integrative model is also based on a more general social psychology theory called social identity theory[4] (Tafjel & Turner, 1986; Spears, 2011), which also emphasizes how intergroup relations and power dynamics between social groups can be formative to a person's identity. The integrative model for ERI development (Umaña-Taylor et al., 2014) incorporates concepts from theories that have already been addressed earlier in this book (e.g., Erikson's life-span psychosocial theory and Marcia's identity status model as described in Chapter 2 and narrative identity in Chapter 4). Thus, concepts from Eriksonian and narrative identity approaches are brought back into this chapter, but now as seen through the lens of ethnicity identity development and sociocultural forces that may contribute to adolescent identity development.

Rivas-Drake the person

Deborah Rivas-Drake, Professor of Psychology and Education at the University of Michigan, is a leading scholar in the ERI field. Rivas-Drake is one of the co-developers of the integrative model for ERI development and is the co-author of a popular book entitled *Below the surface: Talking with teens about race, ethnicity, and identity* (Rivas-Drake & Umaña-Taylor, 2019). Her book offers a primer on adolescent ERI for adults who care for youth.

Rivas-Drake was born in New York City. In a conversation with her, she remembered a move that she made with her family from her childhood home in Queens, New York to Hollywood, Florida during adolescence. She identified this transition as one of the sparks behind her longstanding interest in identity and context. Queens was and remains one of the most culturally diverse counties in the United States, and Hollywood, Florida, at the time of Rivas-Drake's move (pre-hurricane Andrew), was a mostly White and non-Latino community. Rivas-Drake's own cultural background is Latina and she remembered the move to Florida as a teenager because it was "really a culture shock . . . a moment where I thought about the context and how different it was from where I was before, and how much it affected . . . how I thought of myself and who I am, where I belonged and who I belonged to" (Rivas-Drake, personal communication, November 21, 2019).

Rivas-Drake returned to New York City, and as a first generation college student, she completed her undergraduate degree in psychology at Pace University. She then went on to earn a doctoral degree in education and psychology at the University of Michigan and had a National Science Foundation supported postdoctoral research fellowship at New York University's Center for Research on Culture, Development and Education. Rivas-Drake had her first faculty appointment at Brown University and some years later, she returned to her doctoral alma mater for a faculty position at the University of Michigan.

Rivas-Drake's research studies, many of which are highlighted in this chapter, illustrate how present-day researchers are working in diverse ways to shed new light on how adolescent ethnic and/or racial identity development unfolds in person–context interactions. Her focus has been on how ethnic and/or racial identity is "constructed in relationships and in relation to other people, primarily family, school contexts . . . adults in schools, and peers" (Rivas-Drake, personal communication, November 21, 2019). Rivas-Drake's research has explored the ways that ethnic and/or racial identity can be an asset, in other words how and when can it be a psychological and/or social resource, in different settings and in varied moments in everyday life. Based on her research, she learned that:

> [R]eally . . . anything is only ever an asset, if your context is letting it be an asset . . . if you're able to draw on it or if people are . . . allowing you to bring that part of yourself to the context or to the experience in a way that is productive, and positive, and healthy.
> (Rivas-Drake, personal communication, November 21, 2019)

In asking Rivas-Drake about what ideas are at the very front edge of identity research and about what research projects she was presently working on, she said the following:

> [T]here has been a move. I think a lot of momentum is around asking about the role of context . . . I am trying to get deeper into what is happening in

schools, and actually what are adults doing that send messages, any kind of message, about how much your identity can be an asset there . . .

(Rivas-Drake, personal communication, November 21, 2019)

She also went on to discuss several innovations such as the use of network analysis of friendships as well as mixed method research in studies of adolescent ethnic and/or racial identity development. She also described several new studies that she is working on. They were wide ranging studies, but shared a common concern about how to unpack the complexity of contexts that matter for adolescent identity development, such as the adolescents' life at home or school. In her remarks, Rivas-Drake made clear the challenges incumbent upon researchers who attempt to address identity in terms of person–context interactions:

> [It's] really hard, because you definitely have to go beyond self-reports. . .you definitely have to have a multi-disciplinary view. Because something like a school context – it's multilevel, multilayered, there's pedagogy, there's climate, there's curriculum, there are just so many ways to understand the school context, that if you really want to understand how it informs identity . . . you have to get into all of that . . .
>
> (Rivas-Drake, personal communication, November 21, 2019)

Looking into the future, Rivas-Drake was focused on continuing programs of research that advance adolescent ERI development and their implications for academic and sociopolitical development, was enthusiastic about mentoring students and early career scholars and was ambitious in her efforts to have impact beyond academia to better connect with youth themselves as well as adults who care for young people (e.g., parents, teachers, etc.). Rivas-Drake had several key points that she was working on communicating to both academic and general audiences, for example:

> What we are saying about kids' identity is that it can only be facilitated . . . if . . . people are willing to start asking themselves, What do *I* need to know about my own practices and the way that *I* engage with people who are different from me, in order to not put up a barrier to it [ethnic and/or racial identity][5] being something that kids can express and that I can recognize as an asset?
>
> (Rivas-Drake, personal communication, November 21, 2019)

Rivas-Drake's ideas and research are referred to throughout this chapter, but for detailed research examples of her theory and research efforts with colleagues, see the later chapter sections entitled "The integrative model for ethnic and racial identity development" and "Research findings on ethnic identity development in adolescence."

The nature of culture and cultural identity

Ideas about culture, ethnicity, nationality, race, and identity are often confounded with one another in ways that obscure rather than illuminate. It is vital to reflect on what these concepts have in common and how they are distinct. The next three chapter sections are dedicated to clarifying key terms and concepts encountered in the psychological study of ethnic identity.

Regarding culture, there are many formulations about what culture consists of and how it is at work in our lives (Azmitia, 2014). Many conceptualizations of culture involve the proposition that it is made up of stories and history as well as values and beliefs that are expressed in daily life through rituals, lifestyle preferences, diet, dress, art, architecture, socialization and institutional practices (Azmitia, 2014). Culture is also often taken for granted in our language and social interactions (Hammack, 2008). Further, culture can have an intergenerational presence, with some aspects of culture being held dear for generations, while other parts are discarded or reinterpreted as time passes (Azmitia, 2014). Shweder (2011) noted that culture is evident when a group of people have mutual "understandings of what is true, good, and valuable" and a shared vision in terms of "their conceptions of self, society, and nature" (p. 14). Importantly, the culture that individuals share is not experienced in a uniform way and people in some cases only adopt aspects of a culture that are consistent with their own sensibilities and experiences (Hammack, 2008). Hoare (1991, p. 45) put it well, when she stated:

> Culture has long been conceptualized as that which is integral to the way persons construct and perceive their reality . . . The person is embedded in a society that anchors and sponsors identity . . . Different societies and cultures forge, within their citizens, a unique way of shaping and sensing reality . . . identity both absorbs and reflects culture.

Jensen, Arnett, and McKenzie (2011) described cultural identity as deciding on and taking one's place in a cultural community. Cultural identity involves personal and social identity and is broad because it could apply equally well to a wide range of cultural communities (Jensen et al., 2011) such as a particular generation and the zeitgeist that characterizes its spirit (e.g., the gig economy of millennials) or be descriptive of what unites a group of indigenous people together.

The nature of ethnic identity

A way to get one's bearings when encountering the concept of ethnic identity is to get acquainted with different types of acculturating peoples and societies (Phinney, 1990). Acculturation is an inevitable part of ethnic identity. Acculturation happens when groups of people (including individuals) navigate different social and cultural worlds (Berry & Sam, 2016). It occurs at individual, group, and societal levels (Berry & Sam, 2016). Acculturation involves a bi-directional interchange (or relation), and there is recognition that change is taking place as a result of face-to-face (and even virtual/remote) contact between peoples and cultures (Berry & Sam, 2016).

Acculturation psychology (e.g., Sam & Berry, 2016) offers several lucid concepts that are helpful to better understand ethnic identity. For example, acculturation psychology has a history of examining issues such as ethnic identity from a global rather than a single national standpoint (e.g., Liebkind et al., 2016). Acculturation strategies (e.g., assimilation, integration, separation, and marginalization – these terms are explained later in the chapter) are also salient when considering ethnic identity. It should be noted that acculturation speaks to a broad range of experiences and social connections that include but also go beyond ethnic identity.

Indeed, acculturation has an impact on a wide range of people in different life circumstances, including those in the mainstream host or receiving society as well as individuals who are making a new home for many different reasons. For instance, sojourners such as exchange students or temporary workers are new comers with a more recent arrival in a host or receiving society and will only have a short stay in their new home. Others who experience acculturation include people who voluntarily (i.e., immigrants) or are forced (i.e., refugees/those seeking asylum) to make their home in a new society (Berry & Sam, 2016). Acculturation also can happen for groups that have a long standing history in a particular society but have been able to retain elements of their own group's cultural distinctiveness (Berry & Sam, 2016). These sedentary or long standing groups include indigenous peoples and ethnocultural groups (Berry & Sam, 2016).

At the individual psychological level, people are changing in terms of how they behave, think, and feel (Berry & Sam, 2016). Acculturation strategies involve attitudes and behaviors about how people are responding to the changes around them and include the acculturation strategies of assimilation (i.e., from a ethnocultural group perspective this situation would be one in which the person's original culture is lost and the new culture is adopted), integration (i.e., a person is able to strike a balance between two or more cultures and selected aspects of these cultures are kept in a unique, personal blend), separation (i.e., where the original culture is kept and the new culture is avoided), and marginalization (i.e., not finding one's psychological home in either the original or new culture; Berry & Sam, 2016; Jensen et al., 2011). Acculturation expectations are what the new host/receiving society promotes as a way that newcomers and sedentary groups can exist in that society (e.g., multiculturalism, segregation; Berry & Sam, 2016). Acculturation strategies and expectations have been considered along with cultural and/or ethnic identity in empirical studies and theoretical work (cf. Jensen et al., 2011; Liebkind et al., 2016; Phinney, 1990; Schwartz, Montgomery & Briones, 2006).

As noted earlier, this chapter focuses primarily on adolescent identity development in relation to ethnocultural groups. Ethnocultural groups usually have as a central feature a shared geographical and/or genealogical origin (Liebkind et al., 2016) as well as other aspects of a common culture that can be specific and defining to a particular ethnocultural group (Worrell, 2014). The origin of an ethnocultural group can be based in fact or can be speculative and the stuff of legend (Liebkind et al., 2016). The diaspora(s) that is at the heart of an ethnocultural group's origin can go back millennia, or, by contrast, can be just a single generation or two back in time (Liebkind et al., 2016).

Ethnic identity is therefore rooted in the individual's psychological and social connection to an ethnocultural group. Yet, these social groups are themselves dynamic and have a life of their own outside of the individual's perception of them. Stated differently, ethnocultural groups are not static and set forever in time, but instead are created by people (i.e., socially and historically constructed and reworked over time; Liebkind et al., 2016). To illustrate the global pervasiveness of ethnocultural groups, consider the following explanation of what ethnocultural groups are:

> peoples who have a long history of settlement are the descendants of earlier waves of immigrants who have settled into recognizable groups, often with a sense of their own cultural heritage . . . These ethnocultural groups can be found the world over, for example in French- and Spanish-origin communities in the New World, in the groups descended from indentured workers (such as Chinese and Indian communities in the Caribbean), from those who were enslaved (such as African Americans) and in Dutch and British immigrant groups in Southern Africa, Australia and New Zealand.
>
> (Berry & Sam, 2016, p. 19)

Thus, a large part of ethnic identity development for adolescents is about figuring out who one is in relation to an ethnocultural group and coming to terms with how that group affiliation has bearing on one's relations to other social groups in society (Umaña-Taylor, 2015).[6] It should be noted that there is no one completely accepted definition of ethnic identity in the psychological research literature (Umaña-Taylor, 2011). However, the formulation used in this chapter is one that is commonly used by theorists and researchers in the field (e.g., Phinney, 1990; Schwartz et al., 2006; Umaña-Taylor et al., 2014). Further elaboration about the nature of ethnic identity and its development are provided in the description of the integrative model for ERI development among adolescents which appears later in this chapter.

Ethnic identity in relation to national identity

Like ethnic identity, national identity can also be a social identity that holds special importance for a person (Schwartz et al., 2006). National identity would involve typically the question of who am I in relation to a national government or governments (Liebkind et al., 2016). For instance, what does it mean to be me to be British and/or European, or a German but also Turkish or Nigerian? With a national identity, what it means to be part of a nation, in other words the national consciousness, spirit, and aspects of a shared culture such as values, is dynamic and is also updated as people and events on the ground change. A national identity can bring together groups of people who may not share a similar geographic and/or genealogical origin, and the spirit of some national identities may prioritize multiculturalism (e.g., Ward & Mak, 2016) or other master narratives. A master narrative can concern the story of a people, which can be reflected in or resisted against in individual life stories (McLean & Syed, 2016). These easily recognizable stories have immediate currency in a given social group and can be found in biographies of important people in that culture, in the meaning of rituals, or in the arch and ending of a movie or other media (Hammack & Toolis, 2016). Master narratives make a group distinctive and make clear what are the dearly held values and ideals of a group (Hammack & Toolis, 2016; McLean & Syed, 2016). These ideas will be discussed further in later sections of this chapter.

National identity can unite but it can also divide us from one another, even in the same nation. For example, people may have a sense of belonging, connection, and have mastered key parts of a national culture, but still are treated as foreigners or new comers. A qualitative study of Germans adolescents and young adults with an African heritage conducted by Hubbard and Utsey (2015) illustrated some of the different ways that people encounter the intersection of different components of social identity in their daily lives. For example, in the Hubbard and Utsey (2015) study, one study participant stated:

> I like to hear people ask me where I'm from, and when I tell them, one parent is from Finland, one is from Nigeria, but I grew up in Germany, then I feel special. I'm comfortable with that and I'm proud of it.
>
> (Hubbard & Utsey, 2015, pp. 99–100)

As is evident from the statement above, elements of social identity can intersect in unique and meaningful ways.

The intersection between ethnic and national identity is sometimes seen through the prism of a majority (dominant/more powerful) versus minority (non-dominant/less powerful) group relations (Berry & Sam, 2016) which has also been called "oppositional group processes" (Wainryb & Recchia, 2014, p. 3). While the majority versus minority way of conceptualizing national and ethnic identity and intergroup relations may be reflective of the situation in some nations and it is also a central theme in social identity theory (Tajfel & Turner, 1986). It is important to recognize that numerical size and/or position and power of a social group do not always go hand in hand (Adams & Abubakar, 2016). For example, in some national contexts having one numerically large majority group is uncommon (e.g., in the nations of Zambia or Namibia and in present-day South Africa; Adams et al., 2018; Adams & Abubakar, 2016). In other situations, the numerical minority group can hold the most social, cultural, and economic power (e.g., "the White group during apartheid South Africa"; Adams & Abubakar, 2016, p. 361). Further, acculturation can also sometimes take place among groups that do not have a substantial power differential (Berry & Sam, 2016).

Intersections between minority/majority group status and ethnic and national identity may not necessarily pattern themselves in the same ways across nations. For researchers, the concept of a minority and majority group can be useful when used to describe study participants' group affiliations, but researchers should also not assume an uncritical use of such terms. Use of the majority and minority distinction by researchers should be informed by a thorough appreciation of the history and current interactions between culture-related social groups in the national context relevant to the study in question (e.g., Adams et al., 2018).

Ethnic identity in relation to racial identity

A reason to reflect on the construct (or conceptualization) of racial identity is because of the historical role that it has played in theoretical and measurement approaches to adolescent ethnic identity development (Schwartz et al., 2014). Worrell (2014) noted that race as a biological construct has been abandoned in scientific circles, because it does not accurately explain variations in visible physical attributes of humans (i.e., this is called phenotype variation). For instance, variations in visible physical characteristics such as skin color, facial and hair features are wider within than across supposed racial groups (Worrell, 2014).[7] Even if one just focuses on what people appear to look like to others (i.e., phenotypic characteristics) in a group of people in general, there is a litany of problems in the reliability and validity of the measurements of these characteristics (López, Walker, & Yildiz Spinel, 2015).

Erikson (1975) described a concept called pseudo-speciation. In this case, Erikson noted "the tendency of humans to ignore the fact that they are a single species" (Kay, 2018, p. 265). Erikson's remarks about pseudo-speciation (or prejudice and discrimination) are also relevant when considering what continued psychological studies on how people perceive the concept of race may mean or yield:

> While man is obviously one species, he appears and continues on earth split up into groups (from tribes to nations, from castes to classes, from religions to ideologies) . . . we recognize here the human propensity to bolster one's own sense of inner mastery by bunching together and prejudging whole classes of people . . . In case you are now already lustily berating your favorite adversary . . . I must warn you that insight demands first of all the recognition of the fact that a human propensity such as has just been described is shared in some more or less form by all of us.
>
> (Erikson, 1975, pp. 175–176)

Given that the concept of race is steeped in ethical problems, it is not scientifically useful as a way to explain why people look differently from each other, and can be a catalyst for prejudice, discrimination, and in the words of Erikson (1975), pseudo-speciation. What place could the study of racial identity have in contemporary research on adolescent identity development (Verkuyten, 2016)?

Some scholars (e.g., Way & Rogers, 2014; Worrell, 2014) have contended that racial identity can be important to the study of identity development because racism exists all over the world, for all age groups (cf. Del Carmen Dominguez Espinosa & Dantas, 2016; Umaña-Taylor, 2016). Further, individuals' subjective views of themselves in terms of racial identity can be reflective of existing power differentials between social groups, and could be important to understanding the social reality that people encounter in their daily lives (Way & Rogers, 2014). Racial identity would involve a consideration of who one is in connection with a racially defined social group in a given society (Rivas-Drake et al., 2014a, 2014b). Racial identity would not just involve affiliation or ascription by others of a person to a racial group, but would also concern that person's understanding and possibly their engagement in a shared culture that comes along with what it is like to be part of that racial group (Worrell, 2014).

Thus, racial identity has been called "subjective, self-ascribed" (Schwartz et al., 2014, p. 59) and is considered to be psychologically, socially, and historically constructed (Worrell, 2014). Racial identity would also be rooted in how individuals are perceived and treated in racial terms by others (i.e., racialized experiences; Umaña-Taylor et al., 2014). Scholars have also made arguments for the consideration of racial and ethnic identity as a combined construct based on empirical grounds, in that there are some studies that include the measurement of ERI in the same study and/or in a meta-analysis (e.g., Smith & Silva, 2011); stark delineations between these constructs do not appear to be warranted due to high significant positive correlations, and in some situations both constructs are related to adjustment in similar ways (Rivas-Drake et al., 2014a). However, such findings have primarily been demonstrated in study samples from the United States and may or may not generalize further.

The main focus of this chapter is on adolescent ethnic identity development. However, it is recognized that racial identity may enter into ethnic identity development, depending on the young person's life experiences and social reality. Arguably, young people themselves are the most credible informants as to whether racial and/or ethnic identity (Schwartz et al., 2014) are important, or if other components of social identity, such as religious identity, are more salient (Verkuyten, 2016). Studies illustrative of these points are highlighted later in this chapter (e.g., Daha, 2011).

The integrative model for ethnic and racial identity development

Umaña-Taylor et al. (2014, p. 23) defined ethnic and racial identity (ERI) "as a multidimensional, psychological construct that reflects the beliefs and attitudes that individuals have about their ethnic–racial group memberships, as well as the processes by which these beliefs and attitudes develop over time." ERI development is thought to unfold as part of a normative life-span developmental process. It is posited that ERI development is particularly salient for those who have more than one ethnic and/racial background (i.e., bi-ethnic) *or* for individuals who are part of an ethnocultural and/or racial group that has less sociocultural power in society (Umaña-Taylor et al., 2014). In this model, there is a consideration of identity content (e.g., beliefs that have a cognitive developmental and social basis) and change processes (e.g., what my ethnocultural group means to me changes and/or is maintained as I explore, make meaning, and commit/resolve; Umaña-Taylor et al., 2014). The developmental domains of ERI involve the whole person, including affect, behavior, and cognition; ERI development is thought to take shape in an interaction between the developing individuals and their contexts (e.g., at home, in peer groups, in school, and via media; Umaña-Taylor et al., 2014).

As Umaña-Taylor and colleagues (2014) noted, this model is based on prior theories about social and ethnic/racial identity including cognitive and psychosocial developmental theories (e.g., Piaget, Erikson with extensions by Marcia and Phinney), as well as the inclusion of concepts from social identity theory (Tajfel & Turner, 1986) and from Cross (1971). In an extension of the integrative model, Cross and colleagues (2017) added more emphasis on content, namely focusing on different kinds of situations in which people enact their ethnicity or other social identity affiliations in everyday life and in relationships. An illustration of an enactment is code switching which involves changing one's language, accent, and/or behaving in ways that signify to others a person's competence in a particular cultural context (Cross et al., 2017).

The integrative model includes a description of how ERI should normatively change from childhood through young adulthood. In childhood, children might understand concepts such as ethnicity in more concrete terms, which differs from the more nuanced, abstract appreciation of ethnicity they are likely to have in adolescence (Rivas-Drake et al., 2014b), as well as what I and other people begin to call me in terms of my ethnicity (i.e., the self and others' group identifications/labelling; Umaña-Taylor et al., 2014). ERI in childhood may also concern the ethnocultural knowledge based on a child's own experience and through socialization (Umaña-Taylor et al., 2014). The content and processes involved in childhood center on "ethnic categorization, knowledge, and behaviors" (Umaña-Taylor et al., 2014, p. 28).

In adolescence, young people's cognitive and socio-emotional capabilities, such as perspective taking and social comparison, deepen and become more integrated, and adolescents also have a wider range of life experiences and knowledge of their societies (Umaña-Taylor et al., 2014). These growing capacities and experiences combine with normative sociocultural transitions to make it more likely that adolescents will attempt to explore and commit to a personally meaningful vision of what it means for them to be part of an ethnocultural or racial group (i.e., exploration – engaging in reflection, seeking experiences or other people to discuss and possibly try out new possibilities together; commitment/resolution – deciding on a way of living in and relating to the group; Rivas-Drake et al., 2014b).

Identity exploration and commitment are thought to work alongside other developmental change processes such as collective self-verification, which concerns the notion of whether or not the adolescent fits group ideals of what it means to belong or be considered part of the group. Collective self-verification lies at the interface between individuals' subjective perception of group belonging and the reception they get from the social feedback of other group members (Umaña-Taylor et al., 2014). Illustrative of this idea, a participant in an interview study with adolescents and emerging/young adults, who had an indigenous Mapuche heritage and was living in the Chilean cities of Temuco and Santiago, stated: "I **don't** know the pronunciation of words, therefore I'm LIKE **embarrassed** to say that I am (Mapuche). Because, **no**, I **don't** know, I feel **bad** because there are people that do know and I **don't**" (Oteíza & Merino, 2012, p. 307).[8]

Identity content is also of importance. For example, salience (i.e., an event happens to me that makes me think about myself in relation to my group), certainty (i.e., even though my group may have less social power and I have experienced discrimination based on my group affiliation, to what degree do I remain committed to this group?), private regard or affirmation (i.e., do I feel proud and/or good about my group? Rivas-Drake et al., 2014a) are all important facets to the content of one's identity. It is also posited that adolescents will develop a deeper understanding of how their group is viewed by others (i.e., public regard), have greater insight into intergroup relations and power dynamics between groups, and have a more accurate sense of the implications of those dynamics for themselves than will younger children (Umaña-Taylor et al., 2014).

From childhood to adolescence, ERI development shifts from understanding how sociocultural categories and labels work and might apply to oneself; ERI also involves an adolescent experiencing what it means to be part of one's ethnocultural group, of putting their capabilities and knowledge to use so they can put their own distinctive signature on ERI. In the integrative model, similar to the acculturation strategy of marginalization, one potential response to the encounter with ERI is to negate it from one's overall identity (i.e., identity self-denial). It is thought that adults encounter the same processes and content that were at work in adolescence, but have the additional challenge to infuse their ERI – where it fits, has meaning, and adds richness – into other facets of their identity (Umaña-Taylor et al., 2014). Relative to adolescents, adults should also be better prepared to engage in meaning making (e.g., searching for coherence across time and situations as part of narrative identity development) in regards to their ethnicity (Umaña-Taylor et al., 2014).

An optimal sense of ethnic identity

Ethnic identity will not be relevant to all adolescents. However, for those adolescents that are connected to an ethnocultural group, a well-developed ethnic identity should be an asset that allows people to successfully navigate, adapt to, and even thrive within the sociocultural worlds that mean the most to them (Umaña-Taylor et al., 2014). An interview study with 55 second generation Iranian American adolescents conducted by Daha (2011, p. 555) provided several illustrations, in adolescents' own words, about how social identity works for them as a resource. For example, one participant remarked:

> Being an Iranian among all the kids at school shows that I am an individual. [My culture] is related to my authenticity here in America.
>
> (Boy, 16½ years old)

Another participant stated:

> Culture is very important to me. I feel like it gives a little bit of perspective to me. I view things with 2 angles. I feel like I have sort of a self-identity that is deeper. More layers to it. I think culture has given me that aspect.
>
> (Boy, 18 years old)

In an ideal situation, adolescents who are part of an ethnocultural group (or a racial or national minority) go through a multi-faceted process of learning more about their group and its place in their society, come to a self-defined sense of what that group affiliation means to them, and end with a positive evaluation of their group (Rivas-Drake et al., 2014a). Adolescents as they transition into adulthood should make meaning of what their group signifies in their lives, and they should ideally experience more coherence and unity between personal and social identity as well as across the different components of social identity.

Criticism of the integrative model of ethnic and racial identity development

The integrative model sets the stage for a movement past the fragmentation that has historically characterized research on ethnic and/or racial identity (Rivas-Drake et al., 2014a). Fragmentation is related to the confusion in terminology, differential conceptualization of key constructs and their measurement, and has resulted in an inability to generate insights that encompass the research literature as a whole (Rivas-Drake et al., 2014a). Although the model has several strengths, some limitations are that narrative identity development is acknowledged in the model but not addressed in detail.

Another open question about this model concerns the tradition in most theories about ERI, including the integrative model, that take as a starting point the proposition that culture-related social identity would be of most importance to the development of those in a minority social position (e.g., Phinney, 1990; Umaña-Taylor, 2011; Umaña-Taylor et al., 2014). However, this is an empirical question that has not yet been thoroughly examined. For example, consider the Identity Project (Umaña-Taylor, Douglass, Updegraff, & Marsiglia, 2018a; Umaña-Taylor, Kornienko, Douglass Bayless, & Updegraff, 2018b). Its universal intervention approach has shown positive benefits in the Identity Project intervention trial for adolescents in groups with minority and majority social positions in the United States (Umaña-Taylor et al., 2018a, 2018b). See the chapter section entitled "Implications for social response" for more details about the Identity Project. The widespread benefits of this intervention challenge the proposition that ethnic and/or racial identity is only important to those adolescents in a minority social position. Different kinds of cultural identity could also be of particular importance to the identity development of those in the sociocultural mainstream or majority in a society. Research on culture-related social identity does exist in majority groups, but much more research on this topic is needed. Such a research direction would be consistent with acculturation theory (e.g., Berry & Sam, 2016), which sees acculturation as relevant and happening to those in the minority and majority groups alike.

Another limitation of the integrative model surrounds the issue of its current generalizability. The model is designed to speak most directly to ethnocultural groups and other minority groups living in the United States and is therefore attuned to and reflective of this context. The model was highlighted in this chapter because it also has the potential to have value beyond the United States – not likely in its exact current form, but as adapted to better reflect the wide variation in acculturating peoples and societies (Verkuyten, 2016).

Other catalysts that could guide subsequent iterations of the integrative model could be systematic programs of research aimed at gaining new insights about ethnic identity from participatory action research (PAR) that is culturally grounded and youth-guided with an insider view of a given culture as a foundation for further theory development. A participatory action research study conducted by Bhabha and colleagues (2017) provided an illustration of this kind of research. The study was conducted with 20 Roma and non-Roma adolescents who worked in pairs along with input from adult researchers to create, implement, and complete a descriptive study about how adolescents and their families as well as policy makers in Serbia view youth opportunities and barriers surrounding school and work (Bhabha et al., 2017). The study was impressive in a number of regards; some 300 adolescents, 57 parents, and 40 policy members/ other adult youth stake holders were interviewed as study participants. Results from study participants highlighted the nature of struggles faced by Roma youths, in particular, to participate and succeed in school and work. For youth researchers, the project gave an opportunity for some to engage in identity work in a supportive setting:

> I have always had trouble with my identity. The project provided me with a starting point for thinking about this. Even when I am with somebody I have known since primary school, I still feel the need to declare my nationality. People tell me that they know, but I still feel the need to say explicitly that I am Roma . . . I have never talked about these insecurities and challenges before, and preparing for the interviews was a good starting point for these kinds of conversations . . .
>
> (Bhabha et al., 2017, p. 208)

Later in this chapter, other studies with adolescents living outside of the United States are highlighted in order to showcase innovative studies on ethnic and other forms of collective identity development in different national contexts.

Measuring ethnic identity

There are many options if one wants to use a survey to measure ethnic and/or racial identity, with a quantitative approach. The Multigroup Ethnic Identity Measure (MEIM) and the Ethnic Identity Survey (EIS) are highlighted in this section because these surveys have been used in many ERI studies and measure parts of the integrative model, namely the identity processes of exploration and commitment/resolution as well as positive group affect (viewed as identity content).

The MEIM has a ubiquitous presence in the ethnic identity research literature (e.g., Smith & Silva, 2011). This instrument was created and refined by Jean Phinney and colleagues (Phinney, 1989, 1990; Phinney & Ong, 2007) and is based on Phinney's theory of ethnic identity development, which has its roots in Erikson's ideas about identity exploration and commitment as well as the identity status model as developed by Marcia (1966), but is now applied to ethnic identity development. Phinney's theory (1990) and the MEIM are also derived from social identity theory's emphasis on having a positive evaluation of one's social group (Phinney, 1990).

Phinney (1990) proposed that ethnic identity development would become particularly important during adolescence for ethnic minority youth. The developmental process is thought to start with an unexamined ethnic identity, which could mean that ethnic identity is not on the adolescent's radar screen (diffusion) or that the adolescent has uncritically adopted external views about what ethnicity should mean in life (foreclosure) to movement towards a period of exploration of ethnicity (moratorium) to an authentic, self-defined and internalized sense of one's own ethnicity and how it fits into one's wider identity and society at large (achievement; Phinney, 1990).

Different editions of the MEIM exist and range from six to 20 items (Schwartz et al., 2014). There has been variability in the different editions of the MEIM used across studies and variation among researchers in how they work with the MEIM items to create different scale scores (i.e., to specify what the MEIM is exactly measuring, working to get close correspondence between item content, how people typically interpret and respond to items, and theory; Schwartz et al., 2014). The availability and widespread use of the MEIM has brought the study of ethnic identity development into many adolescent research initiatives that did not have a primary focus on identity development (Umaña-Taylor, Yazedjian, & Bámaca-Gómez, 2004). Use of the MEIM has, for example, mainstreamed inquiries of ERI development into more general adolescent studies on a wide range of topics. The popularity of the MEIM among researchers could be linked to some of its virtues such as a history of good scale reliability (Umaña-Taylor et al., 2004). The MEIM is also relatively brief, so it is feasible to add this instrument to a larger assessment battery, but it still offers a multi-dimensional scale that is indicative of the rich concept of ethnic identity rather than just an ethnic label or identification. The MEIM is also not restricted for use with one particular ethnocultural or racial group and therefore could be used in many parts of the world, as was done in the International Comparative Study of Ethno-Cultural Youth (Berry, Phinney, Sam, & Vedder, 2006). As more studies with the MEIM were conducted over the years, the variation in how researchers worked with the MEIM has continued (Schwartz et al., 2014). As studies accumulated, more was learned about the MEIM's factor structure. In some cases, a consistent picture of the factor structure did not emerge or the dimensions/ scales that were identified did not always correspond with Phinney's (1989, 1990) original formulations of the multidimensional structure of ethnic identity development (Schwartz et al., 2014).

The Ethnic Identity Scale (EIS) represents another main quantitative indicator of ERI. The EIS has several parallels to the MEIM, such as sharing a similar theoretical basis and not being group specific (Douglass & Umaña-Taylor, 2015; Umaña-Taylor et al., 2004). Like the MEIM, the EIS also has different versions ranging from nine to 17 items. The EIS provides scale scores of ethnic identity exploration, resolution (i.e., identity commitment), and affirmation (i.e., positive-affect for one's group) with generally good reliability. Evidence for the factor structure of the EIS is building, but appears promising thus far.

Prevailing recommendations are that it is most informative to report indices of ethnic identity development (that reflect identity process and content) as separate scale scores (Schwartz et al., 2014). Composite and profile scores can certainly be used if such scores fit the research questions and aims, but a composite score on its own (e.g., strong ethnic identity score that combines exploration, commitment, and affirmation into a total score) will likely not tell a complete story, particularly if the study is longitudinal and the research question is about normative changes in components of ERI development over time or the research aim focuses on understanding the connection between ERI and adaptation (Schwartz et al., 2014).

Beyond the sole use of surveys to measure ERI development, there are many innovative mixed-method approaches, such as the quantitative analysis of friendship networks in combination with survey-based assessments (e.g., Rivas-Drake, Umaña-Taylor, Schaefer, & Medina, 2017; Santos, Kornienko, & Rivas-Drake, 2017), as well as a multi-level integration method that combines experience sampling methods (e.g., setting a time frame, for example seven days, and asking participants to respond to a few questions at a set time during each day in that time frame, with the questions answered in light of what has happened so far that day – "How much did you feel like a member of your racial/ethnic group today?"). Registry (e.g., how ethnically diverse is the adolescent's school) and self-reported data about ERI, such as the MEIM (e.g., Douglass & Yip, 2015, p. 214) are additional mixed-methods approaches used to study ERI. Other methods used in ERI studies have included interviews on life story, turning point, or other life event narratives (e.g., Hammack, 2006; Komolova, Pasupathi, & Wainryb, 2018) as well as narratives in combination with ERI self-reported surveys (e.g., Syed & Azmitia, 2010). Semi-structured interviews that are not rooted in a narrative identity framework have also been used in ERI studies (Bhabha et al., 2017; Way & Rogers, 2014).

Research findings on ethnic identity development in adolescence

The psychological ERI research literature is vibrant and expanding.[9] The first subsection here provides a brief overview of an assortment of research studies with adolescents living in different parts of the world. These studies use different theoretical and research methods. The aim of this subsection is to demonstrate the global relevance of ERI development. The other two subsections that follow address what is known thus far about normative trends in ERI development and what evidence exists about what is optimal ERI development (i.e., the ERI–adaptation connection).

Empirical illustrations of ethnic and national identity's global relevance

Several cross-sectional studies concerning ethnic and/or national identity have been conducted with adolescents in many countries (e.g., Aydinli-Karakulak & Dimitrova, 2016; Dimitrova et al., 2017a, 2017b, 2018; Dimitrova, Aydinli, Chasiotis, Bender, & Van de Vijver, 2015; Dimitrova, Ferrer-Wreder, & Trost, 2015). A key study is the International Comparative Study of Ethno-Cultural Youth conducted by Berry and colleagues (2006). This was a large cross-sectional study of 7,977 adolescents. The adolescents included those with a relatively recent immigration history and those without such a history (i.e., mainstream youth) living in 13 countries (e.g., Australia, France, Finland, Norway, Sweden, United States, Portugal: Berry et al., 2006). The study combined ideas from acculturation psychology, such as measurement of acculturation attitudes and behaviors, along with developmental views of ethnic identity (i.e., Phinney, 1990, and use of the MEIM) as well as measurement of national identity and other intercultural constructs (Berry et al., 2006).

Using cluster analysis, researchers identified four acculturation profiles, the most common of which was an integration profile which included 36.4% of the immigrant youth in the study and was characterized by engagement in heritage or origin and national cultures, including elevated ethnic and national identity development (Berry et al., 2006). This profile was significantly associated with better psychological and sociocultural adaptation/adjustment (Berry et al., 2006). Girls were more likely than boys to be in the integration profile (Berry et al., 2006). Other acculturation profiles identified were an ethnic (22.5%), diffuse (22.4%), and national profile (18.7%). The diffuse profile was significantly connected with reduced adaptation/adjustment and boys were more likely, than girls to be in this profile (Berry et al., 2006).

A more recent multi-national, cross-sectional study by Dimitrova and colleagues (2017b) also illustrated the benefits of examining ethnic identity across different cultural and national settings. The Dimitrova et al. (2017b) study differed from the International Comparative Study of Ethno-Cultural Youth (Berry et al., 2006) in that it was designed to speak to the well-being of adolescents in a settled ethnocultural group within Europe, who have a distinct history, rather than many different groups of immigrant youth acculturating in a wide range of receiving or host societies. The Dimitrova et al. (2017b) study involved measuring adolescents' engagement in their ethnic, national, family, and religious identity (e.g., centrality, positive group affect, involvement in group activities). The sample consisted of 1,221 middle adolescents (52% Roma, 48% mainstream) living in Bulgaria, the Czech Republic, Kosovo, and Romania (Dimitrova et al., 2017b).

This study has advantages over previous works, such as measurement of several components of collective identity, inclusion of ethnic minority and majority youth, and measurement of ethnic and national identity in ethnic minority youth. For participants in general, results revealed that being more engaged in family and religious identity was associated with feeling better (i.e., elevated well-being) and that engagement in national identity was not significantly connected to adolescents' well-being (Dimitrova et al., 2017b). An important finding was that greater engagement in Roma identity was related to feeling worse (i.e., lower well-being) among Roma adolescents living in Bulgaria and Kosovo (Dimitrova et al., 2017b), and ethnic identity engagement by Roma adolescents was not associated with well-being in the Czech Republic and Romania. Researchers suggested that improvements in the life conditions of Roma peoples in Bulgaria and Kosovo may be particularly neglected relative to the other nations in this study (Dimitrova et al., 2017b). This is an important study because study results for Roma youth depart from the wider research literature that supports a positive association between ERI development and many indicators of adolescent adaptation and thriving.

The final set of illustrative studies in this section moves to a description of innovative qualitative studies that concern ethnic and/or national identity among adolescents; some of these studies are conducted with youth exposed to political conflict. As an illustration of these types of studies, one can look to a longitudinal study conducted by Hammack (2006) with 30 Israeli and Palestine adolescents who came to the United States to take part in a two or three week intensive peer encounter experience. Data collection included field work, participant observation, as well participants completing life story interviews and a life line drawing before and after the peer encounter experience in the United States and up to two years later. Thematic content analysis revealed several themes relevant across participants in both the short and long term, such as changes in narratives from seeing the out group in a more connected and less polarized light, to experiencing confusion, and in some cases repolarization. The outgroup would be Palestinians for the Israelis youth and the outgroup would be Israelis for Palestinian youth. A statement from one of the participants illustrates how personal and national identity was changing:

> By the end of the camp, I was ready to make peace . . . But when I went back home, I just realized that this is wrong . . . You can't be making friends with them. They're killing you! . . . The whole thing is wrong . . . I think that peace now is like giving up . . . After what I've been through, I changed this year. Last year I believed in peace . . . But now I grew up a little and have

pride. I got to know new people back home – Palestinians – and they talked to me and I really respect them . . . They woke me up to what I had done – that it was wrong.

(Hammack, 2006, p. 358)

Hammack (2006) noted that it was common for adolescents in this study to come back to an in-group orientation, even if they had experienced a period when they perceived more connection with their out-group.

This study highlights how young people's efforts to construct a coherent life story and to make meaning out of their life experiences can run up against national master narratives. A master narrative does not have to be about a national identity or sensibility, but it can be. Master narratives are the well-worn stories that immediately ring a bell in a given culture (Hammack & Toolis, 2016; McLean & Syed, 2016). Hammack (2010, p. 184) described master narratives as giving people a way in which to do the following:

> understand collective experience . . . master stories are accessible through cultural products and practices, including media, educational materials, and life-course rituals. They include central messages about the nature and meaning of social categories, including gender, race, and ethnicity.

In the case of Israeli and Palestinian master narratives elements of these shared stories were echoed in some participants' life story narratives in the aforementioned Hammack (2006) study, and for example included discussion about the value of standing up against existential threats, resistance against oppression as well as redemption and contamination themes; Hammack & Toolis, 2016). For some in the United States, a common master narrative may be stories of redemption such as persevering against all odds, and a terrible situation turning out for the best (Hammack, 2010). Yet, in other subcultures in the United States and other national cultures, such as in Sara's story (see Chapter 4), masters narratives may concern weathering losses (e.g., Komolova, Pasupathi, & Wainryb, 2018).

Normative trends in ethnic and racial identity development: Quantitative longitudinal studies

This section concerns what can learned from longitudinal studies of ERI.[10] The studies described here include quantitative measurement of ERI-related processes and/or content and come primarily from the United States. Even though variability is evident, the general consensus is that different aspects of ERI are likely to grow across adolescence (e.g., French, Seidman, Allen, & Aber, 2006; Huang & Stormshak, 2011; Hughes, Del Toro, & Way, 2017; Kim, Bámaca-Colbert, Jian, & Gonzales-Backen, 2017; Pahl & Way, 2006).

A study conducted by Huang and Stormshak (2011) provided an illustration of a longitudinal study of ERI development in adolescence. This study was conducted in the Pacific Northwest region of the United States and included

379 adolescents who self-identified as having an ethnic, racial, or indigenous background (i.e., Latino, African American, Asian, American Indian, mixed ethnicity; Huang & Stormshak, 2011). Positive group affect, ERI-related exploration and commitment, and ethnic group behaviors were measured annually by way of the MEIM, and ERI indices were combined into a single score (Huang & Stormshak, 2011).

Researchers identified six trajectories as youth moved from 6th to 9th grade (approximately 12 to 15 years old; trajectories were not moderated by gender; Huang & Stormshak, 2011). Growth in ERI was evidenced by 47.3% of the sample who could be described by trajectories that showed growth in ERI at a moderate or sharp pace (47.3%). Stability was also evident in the 30.1% of adolescents who had a high stable ERI trajectory (i.e., these youth had explored and sorted out ERI issues early on in their adolescence and stayed that way). Researchers attributed this high stability trajectory to the location of the study, which tended towards ethnic homogeneity and may have led some adolescents to an earlier than typical navigation of ERI questions as a minority living in a majority setting. Other less frequently occurring trajectories included a low stable (4.5%) pattern or decline in ERI (18.1%) at a moderate or sharp pace. Some trajectories were more or less common with youth in different minority groups. This study offers a multifaceted picture of ERI development in cultural minority adolescents who live in a relatively ethnically homogeneous region of the United States (Huang & Stormshak, 2011). Results from other longitudinal studies in more ethnically heterogeneous regions of the United States (e.g., Hughes et al., 2017) also support a general normative trend towards growth in aspects of ERI during adolescence.

Another interesting set of findings from longitudinal ERI studies concerns factors that could be important to later changes in ERI. For example, factors associated with subsequent growth in ERI included whether or not adolescents' parents were born abroad, whether or not families socialized children about their ethnic group, adolescents' friends were supportive of their group, friends became more similar on ERI development over time (Else-Quest & Morse, 2015; Kim et al., 2017; Santos et al., 2017; Umaña-Taylor, Zeiders, & Updegraff, 2013). How different people, experiences, and other aspects of context may support or inhibit ERI development is only just beginning to be outlined in the research literature (e.g., Yip, Seaton, & Sellers, 2010). Syed, Juang, and Svensson (2018) proposed a model of how settings where ERI is relevant can be conceptualized, and such a model could help to improve the measurement and theoretical incorporation of context into future ERI studies.

Research evidence on optimal ethnic and racial identity development

Several studies speak to a diverse array of benefits associated with ERI development in adolescents and adults. For instance, a 10-month longitudinal study with two cohorts of 140 Turkish/German children and adolescents indicated, in the older cohort (13 to 15 years old), that when ethnic identity exploration was low and commitment was elevated (reminiscent of foreclosure) that youth would have fewer cross-ethnic friends (Spiegler, Verkuyten, Thijs, & Leyendecker, 2016). Researchers suggested that supporting national minority youths' identity explorations around their group affiliations could facilitate a greater reaching out and connection between youth with different ethnicities (Spiegler et al., 2016). A longitudinal study of 125 Israeli adolescents that have a recent immigration history from the former Soviet Union, also showed that from 8th to 10th grade, group centrality (i.e., how important the national minority group is in your life) and positive group affect were associated prospectively with less peer-rated aggression (Benish-Weisman, 2016). Longitudinal studies conducted in the United States also support a positive prospective association between indicators of ERI development and a diverse range of outcomes such as adolescents having a closer connection to their families and adolescents perceiving more benefits around pursuing education (e.g., Kiang & Fuligni, 2009; Mroczkowski & Sánchez, 2015).

Turning now to meta-analyses and narrative reviews, Smith and Silva (2011) conducted an important meta-analysis that examined the ERI – adaptation connection, with adaptation measured in terms of well-being, self-esteem, and mental health. Participants were primarily typical (non-clinical) samples of people identifying with a minority group living in either the United States or Canada (e.g., African American, Asian American, Latino, Native American: Smith & Silva, 2011). The meta-analysis included 184 studies, including 41,626 adults and youth with an average age of 22.9 years old (Smith & Silva, 2011). The studies often used the MEIM as a composite/total score that could include exploration, commitment, and/or affirmation (i.e., positive group affect). Results showed that higher levels of ERI were associated with higher well-being, self-esteem and less depression and behavior problems. The ERI – adaptation connection was applicable to both males and females; however associations were stronger for those younger than 40 years old (Smith & Silva, 2011). This later result supports the idea that ERI should have particular developmental salience for adolescents and emerging or young adults.

A meta-analysis of 46 studies conducted by Rivas-Drake and colleagues (2014a) examined the importance of positive ethnic–racial affect (i.e., having a good/proud feeling about one's own ethnic–racial group, operationalized as affirmation, private regard, pride in varying surveys with different theoretical origins) to adaptation (i.e., as indexed by for example academic achievement, mental health and symptoms, social competence, and well-being). As in the Smith and Silva (2011) meta-analysis, most studies in the meta-analysis by Rivas-Drake et al. (2014a) were cross-sectional and a handful of studies were longitudinal. Studies of the Rivas-Drake et al. (2014a) meta-analysis included children or adolescents from a main ethnic and/or racial groups in the United States (i.e., African American, Latino, Asian American youth, studies with indigenous youth were not included in this meta-analysis). The primary results showed significant associations between positive ethnic–racial affect and different indicators of adaptation (e.g., less depression, greater social competence), as well as reduced health risk (e.g., less substance use). As in the Smith and Silva (2011) meta-analysis, the positive associations between ERI and adaptation held for boys and girls as well as across ethnic/racial groups.

Rivas-Drake and colleagues (2014b) also conducted a narrative review of the United States ethnic/racial minority and indigenous adolescent ERI research literature, but in this case, they were able to include a wider array of ERI indicators, in comparison to the aforementioned meta-analysis on positive affect (Rivas-Drake et al., 2014a); the ERI indicators included identity exploration, commitment (resolution), centrality, positive affect, and public regard. An illustrative finding from this review was that adolescents' ERI development was positively associated with psychosocial functioning and mental health; these associations were found across most of the ethnic/racial groups included in the review (Rivas-Drake et al., 2014b).

In summary, along with a growing number of longitudinal studies on ERI development, the two meta-analyses and a narrative review provide converging evidence that ERI development can serve as a developmental asset for young people. However, the weight of this evidence is primarily for adolescents in minority groups in North America. Evidence for a positive ERI development – adaptation connection also exists outside of North America (e.g., Berry et al., 2006; Spiegler et al., 2016). However, there may be exceptions to this general conclusion based on the particular ethnocultural or national minority group considered and in some contexts (e.g., Dimitrova et al., 2017b).

The present-day salience of ethnic identity

To get a sense of the present-day importance of ethnic and national identity, consider that according to a United Nations report, 3.4% of the world's population are international immigrants (United Nations, 2017). This represents a 50% increase in the number of international immigrants since 2000 (United Nations, 2017). International immigrants include people who are fleeing their homes as refugees or as asylum seekers as well as individuals on the move to pursue educational or work opportunities (United Nations, 2017). In developed regions of the world, 12 out of every 100 people are international immigrants (United Nations, 2017). Berry and Sam (2016, p. 2) concluded that "there is hardly any country that is currently not affected by migration in one way or another, either as a sender or as a receiver." As Berry and Sam remind us, acculturation has always been part of the human experience. It is also the case that many nations in various parts of the world began as a culturally diverse (Berry & Sam, 2016). However, recent historic increases in the movement of people, including international immigration, means that acculturation, ethnic and national identity and their relations to adolescent well-being and adaptation are likely to command sustained attention into the future.

Current directions in ethnic identity research and theory

Empirical efforts are under way that will improve our understanding of the ways that context, such as interpersonal and school/neighborhood level factors are important to adolescent ethnic identity development (e.g., Oyserman &

Yoon, 2009; Rivas-Drake et al., 2017; Santos et al., 2017). More longitudinal ethnic identity development studies, with direct measurement of context, outside of the United States are important to these efforts. Studies about the ERI development – adaptation connection in different ethnocultural, indigenous, and national minority groups could also focus on what surviving, doing well, and/or what thriving means for youth in their ecology and how social identity relates to this adaptation. This approach would be in keeping with the idea of adaptive culture (García Coll et al., 1996; Perez-Brena, Rivas-Drake, Toomey, & Umaña-Taylor, 2018), which challenges researchers to seek out a close understanding of the young person's social reality and also allows for the possibility that youth can take diverse pathways to arrive at adaptation and thriving.

Importantly, there are also some exemplar studies and findings that hint at the insights to be gained by designing research that can document the timing of how changes in exploration and commitment sequence themselves in relation to each other and how these identity process changes may be linked with changes in identity content (e.g., positive group affect or the salience of ethnicity). Studies by Hughes and colleagues (2017) and Wang, Douglass, and Yip (2017) offer a glimpse of what this temporal unpacking may look like in multi-ethnic United States-based samples.

Implications for social response

Several courses of action can be taken from the ERI research literature. On the basis of descriptive research findings, it has been recommended that national governments and other stakeholders in the welfare of youth find ways to encourage immigrant youth to retain and explore their culture of origin and to provide abundant opportunities for these youth to be meaningfully involved in the national society/culture (Berry et al., 2006). But, what, in particular, appears to be promising as a way to support youth in their ERI development? Interventions specifically designed to support ERI development offer several practical techniques and insights.

The focus on ERI development and its promotion has played the leading role in some interventions (e.g., the Identity Project: Umaña-Taylor et al., 2018a, 2018b; Sisters of Nia: Belgrave et al., 2004; Young Empowered Sisters: Thomas, Davidson, & McAdoo, 2008). One can also find interventions in which ERI has had a supporting role as a component in a larger intervention initiative (e.g., the Seventh Generation Program: Moran & Bussey, 2007). Frequently occurring actions/activities across relevant interventions include the creation of time and the opportunity to discuss identity, culture, and ethnicity in personal terms in a supportive context with peers and an engaged adult (Umaña-Taylor et al., 2018b). Other common intervention activities included a chance to learn about the ethnic and/or racial group (or groups) culture and history, take part in cultural activities as well as different types of exercises and discussions aimed at helping adolescents' personalize and make meaning of how their group relates to them and make sense of intergroup relations. Such interventions typically last for a few months and have a small group format and a trained adult intervention leader. Pre- to post-test intervention benefits of such interventions, relative to a comparison or control group, have included positive changes in aspects of awareness raising, self-concept, activism, values, and facets of ERI development (e.g., Belgrave et al., 2004; Thomas et al., 2008).

To date, one of the more rigorous and larger scale intervention trials of an ERI specific intervention was conducted by Umaña-Taylor and colleagues (2018a, 2018b). These researchers developed and tested the Identity Project in a randomized controlled trial with pre, post, and a one year follow up. The Identity Project is a universal school-based intervention conducted with 218 middle adolescents self-identifying as African American, Black, Latino, Asian American, American Indian or Native American and White. The intervention was given as part of an elective course in schools and the control condition was an active control that concerned learning more about post high school educational and job possibilities.

The intervention consisted of activities that promoted greater knowledge about what ERI is and how it develops, awareness raising about different cultural traditions and symbols, group histories and intergroup relations, a reflection on one's own family history as well as photo voice activities with a story board and group discussion (Umaña-Taylor et al., 2018a). Intervention-related benefits included pre to posttest change ERI related exploration which was associated with a later increase in ERI related resolution and then changes up to one year later in overall identity coherence, improved grades, and more academic engagement and self-esteem and reduced depressive symptoms (Umaña-Taylor et al., 2018b). The Identity Project was implemented as a universal intervention, and therefore it appears highly promising and beneficial to a wide range of youth in the study, including those in the cultural minority and majority. This type of intervention merits further development through effectiveness trials and cross-national replication studies.

Summary

Sociocultural approaches to adolescent identity development generally emphasize the role that social and/or cultural group memberships play in the identity formation process of adolescence. Ethnic identity development lies at the intersection of personal and social identity, and it has been offered as an illustration of how social and cultural forces can be at work in the person context interactions that are at the heart of identity development for many adolescents. Much more research is needed on adolescent ethnic identity development in various parts of the world. Yet, what can be concluded thus far is that across the developmental period of adolescence, individuals are likely to explore who they are in relation to the cultures and social groups that mean the most to them. For many youth, engagement in questions around social identity is associated with better adaptation and well-being. There are also several types of activities and settings that offer promising ways to support young people as they address this challenge/opportunity.

Notes

1 Roma are a diverse ethnocultural group that has many subgroups that go by different names such as Roma, Stinti, Kale as well as other names (Flecha & Soler, 2013). Roma people live all over the world, but have their largest numerical concentrations in Europe and Eastern Europe in particular (e.g., Romania and Bulgaria; Dimitrova, Sam, & Ferrer-Wreder, in press). Roma peoples have their genealogical origins in Northern India, but have in many cases a centuries long history and a distinct socio-cultural presence in many of the countries in which they live (i.e., a sedentary ethnocultural group for generations in several nations). Roma peoples, including youth, have many substantial strengths and evidence thriving, yet Roma people have also been historically subjected to severe discrimination and persecution by majority and other minority groups in the countries in which they live (Dimitrova & Ferrer-Wreder, 2017; Dimitrova, Sam, & Ferrer-Wreder, in press). See Kyuchukov (in press) to learn more about research with Roma heritage youth living in Berlin.
2 Information in Table 5.1 is based on the work of several scholars such as Burkitt (2011), Seaman et al. (2017), and Spears (2011).
3 Developmental science came to prominence in the 1990s (e.g., Magnusson & Cairns, 1996) and has continued to help to resolve some of the dualisms (i.e., either/or ways of thinking and conceptualizing) characteristic of the history of psychology as a field. A bi-directional association recognizes that the context in which we live is non-ignorable, powerful, and intimately at work in our lives, *but* it is also the case that individuals have the capacity to push back against the context and to a greater or lesser degree, depending on the timing and particular circumstances involved, and to move their own life course in another direction. There are many frameworks in which bi-directional person–context interactions are advocated, including the bioecological model of human development (Bronfenbrenner & Morris, 2006), the critical co-constructivist perspective (Kurtines et al., 1992), holistic–interactionistic systems views (Magnusson, 1996), and relational–developmental systems (Overton, 2013).
4 Social identity theory (Tajfel & Turner, 1986) posits that people can form a social group on even the most trivial or minimal of grounds as part of an experiment, but also in our daily experience, more consequential social groups that we affiliate with will have an impact on our own identity as we strive to keep a positive view of ourselves and our group even in the midst of de-valuation by other social groups (Spears, 2011).
5 In this quote, the text in *[brackets and italics]* was added by Laura Ferrer-Wreder.
6 Illustrating the concept of ethnic identity further, one could ask what does belonging to a particular ethnic group mean to me in terms of the totality of who I am as a person at a particular moment in my life (as an adolescent or as an adult, as a parent or as a child; Umaña-Taylor et al., 2014)? How do I fit in and/or depart from all that comes with being part of this group? If I am part of this group, what does that mean for how I will relate to other groups that I come into contact with?
7 For an interesting study on genealogical DNA testing and changes or stability in individuals' subjective meaning of their racial identity over time, see the study by Lawton and Foeman (2017).
8 The formatting in this quote was preserved and appears as it does in the original article. The quote appears in the article in Spanish and a translated English edition made by the study authors.
9 For instance, a non-systematic search of the PsycInfo database can provide a wide angle view of the field. With a search that required that the words "ethnic identity" or "racial identity" be in the title of the document would show that in the 1950s and 1960s only a handful of scholarly documents were published in each decade (i.e., books, journal articles, dissertations, etc.). This was followed by substantial, successive increases in the number of documents published per decade from the 1970s up through the 1990s, and from the 2000s to the present there have been approximately 2,853 scholarly documents published thus far.

10 At the time of writing this chapter, a cursory search of the PsycInfo database identified 72 records, when the search required that the words "ethnic identity" or "racial identity" or "ethnic–racial identity" be in the document title and that the study in question had to be longitudinal with children and/or adolescents in the study sample and the document should be peer reviewed.

References

Adams, B., & Abubakar, A. (2016). Acculturation in Sub-Saharan Africa. In D. Sam & J. Berry (Eds.), *The Cambridge handbook of acculturation psychology* (pp. 355–374). Cambridge: Cambridge University Press.

Adams, B. G., Naudé, L., Nel, J. A., Van de Vijver, F. J. R., Laher, S., Louw, J., & Tadi, F. (2018). When there are only minorities: Identity and in-group/out-group orientations of emerging adults in four South African ethnocultural groups. *Emerging Adulthood, 6,* 7–16.

Aydinli-Karakulak, A., & Dimitrova, R. (2016). Brief report: When does identity lead to negative affective experiences? A comparison of Turkish–Bulgarian and Turkish–German adolescents. *Journal of Adolescence, 47,* 125–130.

Azmitia, M. (2014). Reflections on the cultural lenses of identity development. In K. C. McLean, & M. Syed (Eds.), *The Oxford handbook of identity development* [E-reader version] (pp. 1–20). New York, NY: Oxford University Press. doi: 10.1093/oxfordhb/9780199936564.013.033

Belgrave, F. Z., Reed, M. C., Plybon, L. E., Butler, D. S., Allison, K. W., & Davis, T. (2004). An evaluation of sisters of Nia: A cultural program for African American girls. *Journal of Black Psychology, 30,* 329–343.

Benish-Weisman, M. (2016). Brief report: Ethnic identity and aggression in adolescence: A longitudinal perspective. *Journal of Adolescence, 47,* 131–134.

Berry, J. W., Phinney, J. S., Sam, D. L., & Vedder, P. (2006). Immigrant youth: Acculturation, identity, and adaptation. *Applied Psychology: An International Review, 55,* 303–332.

Berry, J., & Sam, D. (2016). Introduction. In D. Sam & J. Berry (Eds.), *The Cambridge handbook of acculturation psychology* (pp. 1–8). Cambridge: Cambridge University Press.

Bhabha, J., Fuller, A., Matache, M., Vranješević, J., Chernoff, M. C., Spasić, B., & Ivanis, J. (2017). Reclaiming adolescence: A Roma youth perspective. *Harvard Educational Review, 87,* 186–224.

Bronfenbrenner, U., & Morris, P. A. (2006). The bioecological model of human development. In R. M. Lerner, & W. Damon (Eds.), *Handbook of child psychology: Theoretical models of human development* (pp. 793–828). Hoboken, NJ: John Wiley & Sons.

Burkitt, I. (2011). Identity construction in sociohistorical context. In S. J. Schwartz, K. Luyckx & V. L. Vignoles (Eds.), *Handbook of identity theory and research* (pp. 267–283) New York, NY: Springer Science + Business Media.

Cross, W. E., Jr. (1971). The Negro-to-Black conversion experience. *Black World, 20,* 13–27.

Cross, W. E. Jr. (1991). *Shades of Black.* Philadelphia, PA: Temple University Press.

Cross, W. E., Jr., Seaton, E., Yip, T., Lee, R. M., Rivas, D., Gee, G. C., Roth, W., & Ngo, B. (2017). Identity work: Enactment of racial-ethnic identity in everyday life. *Identity: An International Journal of Theory and Research, 17,* 1–12.

Daha, M. (2011). Contextual factors contributing to ethnic identity development of second-generation Iranian American adolescents. *Journal of Adolescent Research, 26,* 543–569.

Del Carmen Dominguez Espinosa, A., & Dantas, S. (2016). Acculturation in Central and South America. In D. Sam & J. Berry (Eds.), *The Cambridge handbook of acculturation psychology* (pp. 227–247). Cambridge: Cambridge University Press.

Dimitrova, R., Aydinli, A., Chasiotis, A., Bender, M., & Van de Vijver, F. J. R. (2015). Heritage identity and maintenance enhance well-being of Turkish-Bulgarian and Turkish-German adolescents. *Social Psychology, 46*, 93–103.

Dimitrova, R., Buzea, C., Taušová, J., Uka, F., Zakaj, S., & Crocetti, E. (2018). Relationships between identity domains and life satisfaction in minority and majority youth in Albania, Bulgaria, Czech Republic, Kosovo, and Romania. *European Journal of Developmental Psychology, 15*, 61–82.

Dimitrova, R., & Ferrer-Wreder, L. (2017). Positive youth development of Roma ethnic minority across Europe. In N. J. Cabrera, & B. Leyendecker (Eds.), *Handbook on positive development of minority children and youth* (pp. 307–320). New York, NY: Springer Science + Business Media.

Dimitrova, R., Ferrer-Wreder, L., & Trost, K. (2015). Intergenerational transmission of ethnic identity and life satisfaction of Roma minority adolescents and their parents. *Journal of Adolescence, 45*, 296–306.

Dimitrova, R., Musso, P., Naudé, L., Zahaj, S., Solcova, I. P., Stefenel, D., Uka, F., Jordanov, V., Jordanov, E., & Tavel, P. (2017a). National collective identity in transitional societies: Salience and relations to life satisfaction for youth in South Africa, Albania, Bulgaria, the Czech Republic, Kosovo and Romania. *Journal of Psychology in Africa, 27*, 150–158.

Dimitrova, R., Sam, D., & Ferrer-Wreder, L. (Eds.). (in press). *Roma minority in a global context: Resources for positive youth development.* Oxford: Oxford University Press.

Dimitrova, R., Van de Vijver, F. J. R., Taušová, J., Chasiotis, A., Bender, M., Buzea, C., Uka, F., & Tair, E. (2017b). Ethnic, familial, and religious identity of Roma adolescents in Bulgaria, Czech Republic, Kosovo, and Romania in relation to their level of well-being. *Child Development, 88*, 693–709.

Douglass, S., & Umaña-Taylor, A. J. (2015). A brief form of the ethnic identity scale: Development and empirical validation. *Identity: An International Journal of Theory and Research, 15*, 48–65.

Douglass, S., & Yip, T. (2015). Adolescent ethnic identity in context: Integrating daily diaries, biannual surveys, and school-level data. In C. E. Santos, & A. J. Umaña-Taylor (Eds.), *Studying ethnic identity: Methodological and conceptual approaches across disciplines* (pp. 203–233). Washington, DC: American Psychological Association.

Else-Quest, N., & Morse, E. (2015). Ethnic variations in parental ethnic socialization and adolescent ethnic identity: A longitudinal study. *Cultural Diversity and Ethnic Minority Psychology, 21*, 54–64.

Erikson, E. H. (1975). *Life history and the historical moment.* New York, NY: W. W. Norton & Company.

Flecha, R. & Soler, M. (2013). Turning difficulties into possibilities: Engaging Roma families and students in school though dialogic learning. *Cambridge Journal of Education, 43*, 451–465.

French, S. E., Seidman, E., Allen, L., & Aber, J. L. (2006). The development of ethnic identity during adolescence. *Developmental Psychology, 42*, 1–10.

Galliher, R. V., McLean, K. C., & Syed, M. (2017). An integrated developmental model for studying identity content in context. *Developmental Psychology, 53*, 2011–2022.

Galliher, R. V., Rivas-Drake, D., & Dubow, E. F. (2017). Identity development process and content: Toward an integrated and contextualized science of identity. *Developmental Psychology, 53*, 2009–2010.

García Coll, C. G., Crnic, K., Lamberty, G., Wasik, B. H., Jenkins, R., García, H. V., & McAdoo, H. P. (1996). An integrative model for the study of developmental competencies in minority children. *Child Development, 67*, 1891–1914.

Hammack, P. L. (2006). Identity, conflict, and coexistence: Life stories of Israeli and Palestinian adolescents. *Journal of Adolescent Research, 21*, 323–369.

Hammack, P. L. (2008). Narrative and the cultural psychology of identity. *Personality and Social Psychology Review, 12*, 222–247.

Hammack, P. L. (2010). The political psychology of personal narrative: The case of Barack Obama. *Analyses of Social Issues and Public Policy, 10*, 182–206.

Hammack, P. L. (2014). Theoretical foundations of identity. In K. C. McLean, & M. Syed (Eds.), *The Oxford handbook of identity development* [E-reader version] (pp. 1–37). New York, NY: Oxford University Press. doi: 10.1093/oxfordhb/9780199936564.013.027

Hammack, P. L., & Toolis, E. E. (2016). Putting the social into personal identity: The master narrative as root metaphor for psychological and developmental science. Commentary on McLean and Syed. *Human Development, 58*, 350–364.

Helms, J. E. (1990). *Black and White racial identity: Theory, research, and practice.* Westport, CT: Greenwood Press.

Hoare, C. H. (1991). Psychosocial identity development and cultural others. *Journal of Counseling & Development, 70*, 45–53.

Holland, D., & Lachicotte, Jr., W. (2007). Vygotsky, Mead, and the New Sociocultural Studies of Identity. In H. Daniels, M. Cole, & J. Wertsch (Eds.), *The Cambridge Companion to Vygotsky* (pp. 101–135). Cambridge: Cambridge University Press.

Huang, C. Y., & Stormshak, E. A. (2011). A longitudinal examination of early adolescence ethnic identity trajectories. *Cultural Diversity and Ethnic Minority Psychology, 17*, 261–270.

Hubbard, R. R., & Utsey, S. O. (2015). A qualitative study of biracial identity among Afro-Germans living in Germany. *Identity: An International Journal of Theory and Research, 15*, 89–112.

Hughes, D. L., Del Toro, J., & Way, N. (2017). Interrelations among dimensions of ethnic-racial identity during adolescence. *Developmental Psychology, 53*, 2139–2153.

Jensen, L. A., Arnett, J. J., & McKenzie, J. (2011). Globalization and cultural identity. In S. J. Schwartz, K. Luyckx & V. L. Vignoles (Eds.), *Handbook of identity theory and research* (pp. 285–301). New York, NY: Springer Science + Business Media.

Kaplan, A., & Garner, J. K. (2017). A complex dynamic systems perspective on identity and its development: The dynamic systems model of role identity. *Developmental Psychology, 53*, 2036–2051.

Kay, A. (2018). Erikson online: Identity and pseudospeciation in the internet age. *Identity: An International Journal of Theory and Research, 18*, 264–273.

Kiang, L., & Fuligni, A. J. (2009). Ethnic identity and family processes among adolescents from Latin American, Asian, and European backgrounds. *Journal of Youth and Adolescence, 38*, 228–241.

Kim, P. S. Y., Bámaca-Colbert, M. Y., Jian, N., & Gonzales-Backen, M. (2017). Friends' cultural orientation as a mediator between familial ethnic socialization and ethnic identity among Mexican-origin adolescent girls. *Cultural Diversity and Ethnic Minority Psychology, 23*, 291–299.

Komolova, M., Pasupathi, M., & Wainryb, C. (2018). "Things like that happen when you come to a new country": Bosnian refugee experiences with discrimination. *Qualitative Psychology*. Advance online publication.

Ktena, N. (2018). Why does everybody love moth memes? It's the one-sided love story that we can all relate to. Retrieved from www.bbc.co.uk/bbcthree/article/45ce5960-31a2-4223-a426-c3414df5ec79

Kurtines, W. M., Azmitia, M., & Alvarez, M. (1992). Science, values, and rationality: Philosophy of science from a critical co-constructivist perspective. In W. M. Kurtines, M. Azmitia & J. L. Gewirtz (Eds.), *The role of values in psychology and human development* (pp. 3–29). Oxford: John Wiley & Sons.

Kyuchukov, H. (in press). Changes of language and identity among Bulgarian Muslim Roma migrant youth in Berlin, Germany. In R. Dimitrova, D. Sam, & L. Ferrer-Wreder (Eds.), *Roma minority in a global context: Resources for positive youth development*. Oxford: Oxford University Press.

Lawton, B., & Foeman, A. (2017). Shifting winds: Using ancestry DNA to explore multiracial individuals' patterns of articulating racial identity. *Identity: An International Journal of Theory and Research, 17*, 69–83.

Liebkind, K., Mähönen, T., Varjonen, S., & Jasinskaja-Lahti, I. (2016). Acculturation and identity. In D. Sam & J. Berry (Eds.), *The Cambridge handbook of acculturation psychology* (pp. 30–49). Cambridge: Cambridge University Press.

López, I., Walker, L. H. M., & Spinel, M. Y. (2015). Understanding the association between phenotype and ethnic identity. In C. E. Santos, & A. J. Umaña-Taylor (Eds.), *Studying ethnic identity: Methodological and conceptual approaches across disciplines* (pp. 119–148). Washington, DC: American Psychological Association.

Magnusson, D. (1996). Interactionism and the person approach in developmental psychology. *European Child & Adolescent Psychiatry, 5*, 18–22.

Magnusson, D., & Cairns, R. B. (1996). Developmental science: Toward a unified framework. In R. B. Cairns, G. H. Elder Jr. & E. J. Costello (Eds.), *Developmental science* (pp. 7–30) New York, NY: Cambridge University Press.

Marcia, J. E. (1966). Development and validation of ego-identity status. *Journal of Personality and Social Psychology, 3*, 551–558.

McLean, K. C., & Syed, M. (2016). Personal, master, and alternative narratives: An integrative framework for understanding identity development in context. *Human Development, 58*, 318–349.

Moran, J. R., & Bussey, M. (2007). Results of an alcohol prevention program with urban American Indian youth. *Child and Adolescent Social Work Journal, 24*, 1–7.

Mroczkowski, A. L., & Sánchez, B. (2015). The role of racial discrimination in the economic value of education among urban, low-income Latina/o youth: Ethnic identity and gender as moderators. *American Journal of Community Psychology, 56*, 1–11.

Oteíza, T., & Merino, M. E. (2012). Am I a genuine Mapuche? Tensions and contradictions in the construction of ethnic identity in Mapuche adolescents from Temuco and Santiago. *Discourse & Society, 23*, 297–317.

Overton, W. F. (2013). A new paradigm for developmental science: Relationism and relational-developmental systems. *Applied Developmental Science, 17*, 94–107.

Oyserman, D., & Yoon, K. (2009). Neighborhood effects on racial–ethnic identity: The undermining role of segregation. *Race and Social Problems, 1*, 67–76.

Pahl, K., & Way, N. (2006). Longitudinal trajectories of ethnic identity among urban Black and Latino adolescents. *Child Development, 77*, 1403–1415.

Penuel, W. R., & Wertsch, J. V. (1995). Vygotsky and identity formation: A sociocultural approach. *Educational Psychologist, 30*, 83–92.

Perez-Brena, N., Rivas-Drake, D., Toomey, R. B., & Umaña-Taylor, A. J. (2018). Contributions of the integrative model for the study of developmental competencies in minority children: What have we learned about adaptive culture? *American Psychologist, 73*, 713–726.

Phinney, J. S. (1989). Stages of ethnic identity development in minority group adolescents. *Journal of Early Adolescence, 9*, 34–49.

Phinney, J. S. (1990). Ethnic identity in adolescents and adults: Review of research. *Psychological Bulletin, 108*, 499–514.

Phinney, J. S., & Baldelomar, O. A. (2011). Identity development in multiple cultural contexts. In L. A. Jensen (Ed.), *Bridging cultural and developmental approaches to psychology: New syntheses in theory, research, and policy* (pp. 161–186). New York, NY: Oxford University Press.

Phinney, J. S., & Ong, A. D. (2007). Conceptualization and measurement of ethnic identity: Current status and future directions. *Journal of Counseling Psychology, 54*, 271–281.

Rivas-Drake, D., Seaton, E. K., Markstrom, C., Quintana, S., Syed, M., Lee, R. M., Schwartz, S. J., Umaña-Taylor, A. J., French, S., & Yip, T. (2014a). Ethnic and racial identity in adolescence: Implications for psychosocial, academic, and health outcomes. *Child Development, 85*, 40–57.

Rivas-Drake, D., Syed, M., Umaña-Taylor, A., Markstrom, C., French, S., Schwartz, S. J., & Lee, R. (2014b). Feeling good, happy, and proud: A meta-analysis of positive ethnic–racial affect and adjustment. *Child Development, 85*, 77–102.

Rivas-Drake, D. & Umaña-Taylor, A. J. (2019). *Below the surface: Talking with teens about race, ethnicity, and identity*. Princeton, NJ: Princeton University Press.

Rivas-Drake, D., Umaña-Taylor, A. J., Schaefer, D. R., & Medina, M. (2017). Ethnic-racial identity and friendships in early adolescence. *Child Development, 88*, 710–724.

Rogoff, B. (2016). Culture and participation: A paradigm shift. *Current Opinion in Psychology, 8*, 182–189.

Rogoff, B., Dahl, A., & Callanan, M. (2018). The importance of understanding children's lived experience. *Developmental Review, 50*, 5–15.

Sam, D., & Berry, J. (2016). Conclusions: Where are we and where are we headed? In D. Sam & J. Berry (Eds.), *The Cambridge handbook of acculturation psychology* (pp. 525–531). Cambridge: Cambridge University Press.

Santos, C. E., Kornienko, O., & Rivas-Drake, D. (2017). Peer influence on ethnic-racial identity development: A multi-site investigation. *Child Development, 88*, 725–742.

Schwartz, S. J., Montgomery, M. J., & Briones, E. (2006). Toward an interdisciplinary study of acculturation, identity, and culture. *Human Development, 49*, 42–43.

Schwartz, S. J., Syed, M., Yip, T., Knight, G. P., Umaña-Taylor, A. J., Rivas-Drake, D., & Lee, R. M. (2014). Methodological issues in ethnic and racial identity research with ethnic minority populations: Theoretical precision, measurement issues, and research designs. *Child Development, 85*, 58–76.

Seaman, J., Sharp, E. H., & Coppens, A. D. (2017). A dialectical approach to theoretical integration in developmental–contextual identity research. *Developmental Psychology, 53*, 2023–2035.

Sellers, R. M., Smith, M. A., Shelton, J. N., Rowley, S. A. J., & Chavous, T. M. (1998). Multidimensional model of racial identity: A reconceptualization of African American racial identity. *Personality and Social Psychology Review, 2*, 18–39.

Shweder, R. A. (2011). Commentary: Ontogenetic cultural psychology. In L. A. Jensen (Ed.), *Bridging cultural and developmental approaches to psychology: New syntheses in theory, research, and policy* (pp. 303–310). New York, NY: Oxford University Press.

Smith, T. B., & Silva, L. (2011). Ethnic identity and personal well-being of people of color: A meta-analysis. *Journal of Counseling Psychology, 58*, 42–60.

Spears, R. (2011). Group identities: The social identity perspective. In S. J. Schwartz, K. Luyckx & V. L. Vignoles (Eds.), *Handbook of identity theory and research* (pp. 201–224). New York, NY: Springer Science + Business Media.

Spiegler, O., Verkuyten, M., Thijs, J., & Leyendecker, B. (2016). Low ethnic identity exploration undermines positive interethnic relations: A study among Turkish immigrant-origin youth. *Cultural Diversity and Ethnic Minority Psychology, 22*, 495–503.

Syed, M., & Azmitia, M. (2010). Narrative and ethnic identity exploration: A longitudinal account of emerging adults' ethnicity-related experiences. *Developmental Psychology, 46*, 208–219.

Syed, M., Juang, L. P., & Svensson, Y. (2018). Toward a new understanding of ethnic-racial settings for ethnic-racial identity development. *Journal of Research on Adolescence, 28*(2), 262–276.

Tajfel, H., & Turner, J. (1986).The social identity theory of intergroup behavior. In W. Austin & S. Worchel (Eds.), *Psychology of intergroup relations* (pp. 7–24). Chicago, IL: Nelson-Hall.

Thomas, O., Davidson, W., & McAdoo, H. (2008). An evaluation study of the Young Empowered Sisters (YES!) Program: Promoting cultural assets among African American adolescent girls through a culturally relevant school-based intervention. *Journal of Black Psychology, 34*, 281–308.

Umaña-Taylor, A. J. (2011). Ethnic identity. In S. J. Schwartz, K. Luyckx & V. L. Vignoles (Eds.), *Handbook of identity theory and research* (pp. 791–801). New York, NY: Springer Science + Business Media.

Umaña-Taylor, A. J. (2015). Ethnic identity research: How far have we come? In C. E. Santos, & A. J. Umaña-Taylor (Eds.), *Studying ethnic identity: Methodological and conceptual approaches across disciplines* (pp. 11–26). Washington, DC: American Psychological Association.

Umaña-Taylor, A. J. (2016). A post-racial society in which ethnic-racial discrimination still exists and has significant consequences for youths' adjustment. *Current Directions in Psychological Science, 25*, 111–118.

Umaña-Taylor, A. J., Douglass, S., Updegraff, K. A., & Marsiglia, F. F. (2018a). A small-scale randomized efficacy trial of the identity project: Promoting adolescents' ethnic–racial identity exploration and resolution. *Child Development, 89*, 862–870.

Umaña-Taylor, A. J., Kornienko, O., Douglass Bayless, S., & Updegraff, K. A. (2018b). A universal intervention program increases ethnic-racial identity exploration and resolution to predict adolescent psychosocial functioning one year later. *Journal of Youth and Adolescence, 47*, 1–15.

Umaña-Taylor, A. J., Quintana, S. M., Lee, R. M., Cross, W. E., Rivas-Drake, D., Schwartz, S. J., Syed, M., Yip, T., & Seaton, E. (2014). Ethnic and racial identity during adolescence and into young adulthood: An integrated conceptualization. *Child Development, 85*, 21–39.

Umaña-Taylor, A. J., Yazedjian, A., & Bámaca-Gómez, M. (2004). Developing the ethnic identity scale using Eriksonian and social identity perspectives. *Identity: An International Journal of Theory and Research, 4*, 9–38.

Umaña-Taylor, A. J., Zeiders, K. H., & Updegraff, K. A. (2013). Family ethnic socialization and ethnic identity: A family-driven, youth-driven, or reciprocal process? *Journal of Family Psychology, 27*, 137–146.

United Nations (2017). Population facts. No. *2017/* 5, December. Retrieved from: www. un.org/en/development/desa/population/publications/pdf/popfacts/PopFacts_2017-5.pdf

Valsiner, J. (2012). Psychology courting culture: Future directions and their implications. In J. Valsiner (Ed.), *The Oxford handbook of culture and psychology* (pp. 1092–1104). New York, NY: Oxford University Press.

Van der Veer, R. (2012). Cultural-historical psychology: Contributions of Lev Vygotsky. In J. Valsiner (Ed.), *The Oxford handbook of culture and psychology* (pp. 58–68). New York, NY: Oxford University Press.

Verkuyten, M. (2016). Further conceptualizing ethnic and racial identity research: The social identity approach and its dynamic model. *Child Development, 87*, 1796–1812.

Wainryb, C., & Recchia, H. (2014). Youths' constructions of meanings about experiences with political conflict: Implications for processes of identity development. In K. C. McLean, & Syed, M. (Ed.), *The Oxford handbook of identity development* [E-reader version] (pp. 1–33). New York, NY: Oxford University Press. doi: 10.1093/oxfordhb/9780199936564.013.008

Wang, Y., Douglass, S., & Yip, T. (2017). Longitudinal relations between ethnic/racial identity process and content: Exploration, commitment, and salience among diverse adolescents. *Developmental Psychology, 53*, 2154–2169.

Ward, C., & Mak, A. (2016). Acculturation theory and research in New Zealand and Australia. In D. Sam & J. Berry (Eds.), *The Cambridge handbook of acculturation psychology* (pp. 314–336). Cambridge: Cambridge University Press.

Way, N., & Rogers, O. (2014). "They say black men won't make it, but I know I'm gonna make it": Ethnic and racial identity development in the context of cultural stereotypes. In K. C. McLean & M. Syed (Eds.), *The Oxford handbook of identity development* [E-reader version] (pp. 269–285). New York, NY: Oxford University Press. doi: 10.1093/oxfordhb/9780199936564.013.032

Wiggins, B. E., & Bowers, G. B. (2015). Memes as genre: A structurational analysis of the memescape. *New Media & Society, 17*, 1886–1906.

Worrell, F. C. (2014). Culture as race/ethnicity. In K. C. McLean, & M. Syed (Eds.), *The Oxford handbook of identity development* [E-reader version] (pp. 249–268). New York, NY: Oxford University Press. doi: 10.1093/oxfordhb/9780199936564.013.029

Yip, T., Seaton, E. K., & Sellers, R. M. (2010). Interracial and intraracial contact, school-level diversity, and change in racial identity status among African American adolescents. *Child Development, 81*, 1431–1444.

6 Intersectionality, and the confluence of gender and sexual identity

> Last week I went in to take the written test for my driver's license. The form said I had to check whether I was male or female. I always hate that kind of question – like there are only those two gender options! For me, it's kind of a fluid sort of thing – whether I feel male or female, or maybe nothing at all . . . it's all kind of uncertain for me right now . . .
>
> (Sam, 17-year-old high school student)

Intersectionality and identity integration, two topics discussed in this chapter, challenge researchers to avoid disaggregating, isolating, or statistically controlling away the nuance described in the quote above. This is a challenging mantle to take up in actual research practice, and such issues are explored in this chapter. It should be noted that this chapter and the next (Chapter 7) are unique in focus and organization. They are dedicated to the examination of novel extensions and the mapping of where the edges of our knowledge are in selected identity-related research areas. This chapter is an exploration of the particular novel extension of intersectionality and identity integration as it relates to adolescent gender and sexual identity development.

Briefly, intersectionality is a framework to guide research (Cole, 2009). It encourages researchers to attend to the social and power structures as well as a person's total identity package across a variety of personally salient life domains and areas (Cole, 2009). Identity integration is based on Eriksonian psychosocial theory and focuses on individuals' sense of continuity in their identity across contexts and time (Syed & McLean, 2016). The concepts of intersectionality and identity integration are first addressed in detail here in this chapter. These concepts are not only applicable to gender and sexual identity development but are highly relevant to identity development in general and have implications for several topics addressed at varied points of this book, including Chapter 5.

In this chapter, the first section is an overview of intersectionality and identity integration. Then, there is an explanation of other ideas important to understanding the psychological research literature on adolescent gender and sexual identity development. To give further life to these concepts, they are seen in light of a selected theory about gender or sexual identity. Theories and the psychological research literatures on gender and sexual identity development have developed in parallel to one another (Diamond, Pardo, & Butterworth, 2011). This second chapter section reflects this division, in that key concepts relevant to gender identity are addressed first and are then followed by concepts relevant to sexual identity. In these sections, there is also a critical reflection on the past and current meaning of these concepts as they are used in the psychological research literature on adolescence. This segment is followed by a chapter section in which two key research examples are discussed in detail in order to provide a concrete illustration of themes and/or research practices consistent with intersectionality and/or identity integration, as well as to demonstrate possibilities for the future research in this area. A summary statement concludes the chapter.

Bridging ideas: intersectionality and identity integration

Intersectionality

Intersectionality has transdisciplinary importance, and it is relevant to psychology, as well as legal, feminist, critical race, and women's studies (Collins, 2000; Parent, DeBlaere, & Moradi, 2013). It has also been important to the ongoing struggles for civil rights movements for many groups (Cole, 2009; Crenshaw, 1991):

> Intersectionality has traveled far from its historical moorings in the reflections of Black feminists such as Sojourner Truth (1851) and the Combahee River Collective (1977). It has journeyed through the academy in the work of Black feminist scholars such as Kimberlé Crenshaw (1989, 1991) and Patricia Hill Collins (1991) and in recent years has landed within diverse disciplines, including psychology.
>
> (Bowleg & Bauer, 2016, p. 337)

Intersectionality is not a psychological theory designed to explain how identity development progresses across adolescent and adult life, but it can be viewed as a framework that aims to promote social justice – and one central avenue to achieving this aim is to conduct scientific research on how power and social position are at work in people's lives (Bowleg & Bauer, 2016; Syed, 2010). For example, aspects of Erikson's (1968) life-span psychosocial theory and the concept of identity integration (Syed & McLean, 2016), would be able to pick up where intersectionality leaves off, because intersectionality is a framework to guide research rather than an explanation for why we should expect people to strive to make sense of who they are across contexts and time.

From the perspective of intersectionality, one facet or component of identity does not take precedence over another. It is the total package of how people put together their identity in combination with what society deems as important (in regards to identity), and this is the subject of inquiry (Diamond & Butterworth, 2008). By making use of the tenants of intersectionality, many studies have provided new insights into the experience and implications of what it is like for a person to belong to more than one world and/or cultural community (e.g., Bowleg, 2013; Parent et al., 2013). Parent and colleagues (2013, p. 640), in reference to conclusions reached by Stewart and McDermott (2004), concisely summed up several of the core ideas of intersectionality as focusing on "nonhomogeneity of groups, location of persons within power structures and acknowledgement of the relations between those structures, and the unique effects of identifying within more than one group." Regarding nonhomogeneity of groups, this means that people who see themselves as part of a social group will have similarities but will also come to that group with important differences in their life experiences and access to opportunities. Individuals who identify with the social category of women, for example, could include older and younger women who grew up with different life chances and values, as well as women who are indigenous or who identify with two ethnocultural groups, women with differing ability status, and/or affluent women or women who live in poverty and so on.

From a research perspective, Cole (2009, p. 176) challenged researchers to ask themselves "Who is included within this category?" For example, if researchers intend to learn more about adolescents as part of study, where does the study sample of adolescents come from (what time period is the study conducted in, what country, what region, is the sample recruited from a school or a recreation group)? Who ends up in that study sample, and are they representative of the wider population of interest? What are these adolescents' life conditions and access to opportunities?

Expanding the idea of diversity even further and considering diversity within and across the intersection of different social categories, salient identity facets for a particular person could center on that individual's physical ability, ethnicity, culture, religion, social class, educational background, generation and age, as well as immigration experience, gender, sexuality. Is the combination of gender, sexuality, and religion most self-defining for a given person's identity? Or is the confluence of social class, immigration experience, and where the person is in the life-span –most important for understanding another person's identity? The search for answers to such questions is worthwhile, because variations in health and educational or other life outcomes have been shown to differ by a person's total identity package (e.g., Fine, 2015).

Scholars working with an intersectional approach would also argue that finding answers to the aforementioned questions have considerable value because the unique content of individuals' total identity package can be essential to gaining insight into people's subjective experiences of themselves. Put differently, what is it like from an individual's perspective to have to navigate multiple identity classifications? A statement made by a participant in Bowleg's (2013, p. 762) study illustrates this point well:

> The combination of the two [identities; being Black and gay] has caused me
> to look a little deeper within myself and to find definition from within and

also to just to love on a different level or beyond what people may think in terms of the stereotypes and judgments people make upon my life.

The intersectional approach demands that researchers embrace the complexity and distinctiveness of a person's identity as a whole and incorporate such a consideration into the scientific process. For example, Cole (2009) challenged researchers to be aware of intersectional considerations from the beginning of a study, when hypotheses and research questions are formulated (e.g., hypotheses consider the possibility of within group variation) and when a sample is recruited (e.g., are less studied subgroups included in the study sample). An intersectional approach would also be important to the later steps of a study when findings are considered in light of what happened in the study and how the study results fit into the wider research literature (Cole, 2009). This approach would mean that study findings are not over generalized beyond the study sample, interpretations are not just about individuals being fundamentally different from one another, but also consider that differences in psychological outcomes may also be due to differences in life circumstances/opportunities (Cole, 2009).

Intersectionality is also very clear about the importance of power and appreciating where people find themselves in a social hierarchy due to their identity (Cole, 2009). As stated by Bowleg and Bauer (2016, p. 337), "no attention to power, no intersectionality." If a particular combination of social identity components comes along with social privileges and/or discrimination, then it is vital to understand that unique confluence of benefits and barriers and to recognize that these identity pluses and minuses will not simply be additive or segregated in a person's life experience, but that they are conflated with one another (Cole, 2009). In terms of research practice, this means that the realities of inequality are recognized as part of the life experience of study participants (Cole, 2009). Structural inequality between people based on their identity is given due consideration when researchers attempt to explain the "why" behind their study results (Cole, 2009).

Identity integration

Identity integration as described by Syed and McLean (2016) is rooted in Erikson's (1968) descriptions of the role of continuity in identity development across context and time. In Syed and McLean's (2016) revisiting and elaboration of this idea, there are four types identity integration: Contextual, temporal, ego, and person-society. Contextual integration concerns the ways in which people bring harmony or make peace out of who they are across different areas or domains of their lives (Syed & McLean, 2016). Temporal integration is often captured as part of narrative identity studies, in which people reflect on and describe how they make sense of who they are across their past, present, and expected future (Syed & McLean, 2016). Ego integration is viewed as the combination of both contextual and temporal integration (Syed & McLean, 2016). In other words, how do people come to a workable co-existence between personally and socially important facets of their identity over the course of their lives (Syed & McLean, 2016)? Person-society integration refers to the degree of fit that one's identity has with what is expected within an individual's society and culture (e.g., master narratives; McLean, Shucard, & Syed, 2017), as well as the expectations of important others (i.e., friends, family, romantic partners; Syed & McLean, 2016).

A statement made by a participant in Diamond's (2005) longitudinal study illustrates what it is like when who you are runs against what may be expected, and instances when person-society integration requires a great deal of attention and forethought to make it work. The quote below comes from a participant named Lori. From adolescence through emerging adulthood, Lori evidenced substantial active exploration and commitment in regards to gender and sexual identity. Lori stated:

> I do want to mess with people to help them think about why they need to shove people in these categories and for those who don't fit we're going to torture them. And so I'm used to someone going, "what's up with that?", and kind of going through that educational process and explaining things.
>
> (Diamond & Butterworth, 2008, p. 374)

Arguably, identity integration seeks to explain how people can pull different parts of their identities together across context and time into authentic and meaningful infusions that are their own, as well as acknowledge the role that other people and wider socio-cultural factors may play in inhibiting or fostering such integration.

Key concepts and reflections about gender identity

Physiological sex, gender, gender identity, and Bussey's theory

As historical times and social structures change, ideas about physiological sex and gender are also undergoing reconsideration (Magnusson & Marecek, 2018). Diamond and colleagues (2011, pp. 25–26) provided several clear formulations of concepts important to the study of gender, when they stated that:

> Sex is most often used to describe one's status as male or female . . . determined biologically via sex chromosomes and assessed at birth by the appearance of external genitalia (which generally suffices, except for rare disorders of sexual differentiation in which there may be disjunctures between chromosomal sex and genital morphology). In contrast, gender refers to the trait characteristics and behaviors culturally associated with one's sex . . . Gender also refers to a person's subjective judgements and inferences about sex including stereotypes, roles, presentation, and expressions of masculinity and femininity . . . Gender identity represents a person's sense of self as a boy/man or a girl/woman. As such, it carries an expected set of role behaviors, attitudes, dress style, and appearance.

Further, gender identity development emphasizes "the processes by which individuals relate to whichever conceptions of gender are prevailing in their social contexts – including how individuals come to see themselves in gender-differentiated ways and adopt gender-differentiated behaviors in the first place" (Bussey, 2011, p. 605).

Physiological sex and gender are viewed by some contemporary psychologists as socio-historical and cultural constructions created by people and open to change (e.g., Hegarty, Ansara, & Barker, 2018; Magnusson & Marecek, 2018). This constructed view of sex and gender has been advocated in light of observed physiological variation in humans – in criteria sometimes used to determine physiological sex (e.g., sex chromosomes, external genitalia). A constructed view has also been based on how sex and gender have historically been differentially formulated by cultures in various parts of the world, which may have long had more than two categories for physiological sex and have more contingent or context/role specific designations to determine a person's sex (Hegarty et al., 2018; Magnusson & Marecek, 2018).

Gender plays a substantial role in everyday life and is a defining consideration in the distribution of social power within many societies (Magnusson & Marecek, 2018; Rieger & Savin-Williams, 2012). Research studies concur that children come to understand gender as a social category and will eventually attempt to see themselves in relation to how gender is conceptualized in their culture, and come to adopt a gender identity that is in line with or diverges from societal expectations (Diamond et al., 2011). Identity issues and questions regarding gender can remain relevant throughout a person's life and can also be significantly reevaluated as the place and value of gender shifts and changes in a given society (Bussey, 2011).

There are many disciplines, frameworks, and more specific theories relevant to the study of gender and/or sexual identity development such as feminist psychology (Magnusson & Marecek, 2018), dynamical systems models (Diamond, 2018; Diamond et al., 2011), gender schema theory (Bem, 1981), differential developmental trajectories (Savin-Williams, 2011), social identity theory (Tajfel & Turner, 1986), life course theory (Elder, 1998), social cognitive theory (Bandura, 2008), the identity status model (Marcia, 1966), and narrative identity approaches (Hammack & Cohler, 2011). Many of these perspectives would agree that gender identity and sexual identity are in many cases interrelated but not the same phenomena. These perspectives would also embrace a view of gender and sexual identity as multi-dimensional, multi-determined, and open to change over time, but precisely what dimensions are emphasized and the particulars of how and when change takes place and how much change is possible can be points of difference.

One can take Bussey's (2011) theory as illustrative of a model in which the dynamic nature of gender identity takes center stage. This model is an extension of Bandura's (2008) social cognitive model. Bussey (2011) posited that certain factors interact to co-create gender identity and are instrumental to change in gender identity over time. These factors include aspects of people at the individual level, as well as behavioral and environmental levels. *Individual factors* include how people understand their physical sex and gender, self-regulation, agency, and other socio-cognitive processes such as self-efficacy. *Behavioral factors* include what people do – how gender is signified by individuals' behaviors, by doing or enacting gender in everyday life, people selecting environments. *Environmental factors* include social, cultural, historical, and structural – how other people react to a person's gender identity as well as how others might model gender, how groups can come together to actualize change as it regards the welfare of gender-related groups, and the social benefits and disadvantages related to gender in a society. These three multi-dimensional factors, the person, behavior, and environment – are thought to combine and mutually influence one another (Bussey, 2011). In this model, developmental change in gender identity is considered to be ongoing and continuous (Bussey, 2011).[1]

Diversity in gender and gender identity: beyond either/or conceptualizations

A mutually exclusive (i.e., one or the other – only female or male), two category approach to conceptualizing physiological sex and gender has been challenged for a number of reasons (Hegarty et al., 2018; Magnusson & Marecek, 2018). The two gender only way of seeing the physical sex and gender of a person does not encompass the bodies and life experience of all people (Diamond et al., 2011; Hegarty et al., 2018). For example, people with a gender-variant identity encompass the many ways in which people make sense of who they are in terms of their bodies and gender, including for instance individuals who are and live on a relatively permanent basis as a gender different from their birth sex assignment (e.g., from female to male or male to female), which may or may not involve physical changes to a person's body (Diamond et al., 2011). Other people with a gender-variant identity may identify in terms of a non-binary identity and may reject gender as self-defining (i.e., gender-nonconforming) or may identify somewhere in between or above gender with a unique combination of elements of masculinity and femininity put together by the person in a relatively permanent or in a more variable and fluid way (i.e., transgender as well as other self-descriptions that people use including genderqueer, gender fluid, and/or gender expansive; Diamond, 2018; Diamond & Butterworth, 2008; Hegarty et al., 2018; White, Moeller, Ivcevic & Brackett, 2018). Across the life-span, people whose birth sex assignment and gender identity match (i.e., cisgender) as well as people with a gender-variant identity both are likely to engage in exploration and questioning about what gender means in their lives (Diamond et al., 2011). As with identity development in general, adolescence and emerging adulthood are prime times to engage in such questioning and identity work in these areas can extend well into adulthood.

Key concepts about sexual identity and reflections on the intersection of sexual and gender identity

Sexuality, sexual identity, and Dillon and colleagues' theory

Relative to the past, sexuality and sexual identity are viewed in a more multi-dimensional and diverse light (Diamond, 2018). Sexual identity is a wide construct that encompasses a number of other facets and developmental processes (Savin-Williams, 2011). An important part of sexual identity is sexuality itself which involves "sexual needs, sexual values, modes of sexual expression, preferred characteristics of sexual partners, preferred sexual activities and behaviors" (Dillon, Worthington, & Moradi, 2011, p. 27). Other dimensions of sexual identity include sexual orientation and sexual orientation identity (Dillon et al., 2011). According to Savin-Williams (2011, p. 672), "sexual orientation is a deeply rooted predisposition toward erotic or sexual fantasies, thoughts, affiliations, affection or bonding with members of one's sex, the other sex, both sexes, or, perhaps, neither sex (asexuality)."

Sexual orientation identity involves a self-recognition of one's sexual orientation as part of one's identity (Dillon et al., 2011). In psychological studies, sexual orientation has been defined and measured in a number of ways (Morgan, 2013). In such studies, people have been asked to self-identify as heterosexual (i.e., opposite sex-oriented preferences, sexual fantasy, attraction, and/or behavior) or homosexual (i.e., same sex-oriented preferences, sexual fantasy, attraction, and/or behavior), and in some cases as bisexual (i.e., opposite and same sex-oriented preferences, sexual fantasy, attraction, and/or behavior; Morgan, 2013). Intermediate sexual orientation categories/labels have also begun to be used more frequently in psychological studies such as mostly heterosexual and mostly homosexual in addition to the aforementioned categories of heterosexual, homosexual, and bisexual (Diamond, 2018; Morgan, 2013; Savin-Williams, 2011).

Over the last several decades, there have been many theories that concern sexual identity development (Morgan, 2013). Theories about adolescent, emerging adult, and young adult identity development already described in this book such as the identity status and narrative identity perspectives also have been applied to gender and sexual identity development, with the processes of identity exploration and commitment as well as autobiographical reasoning, meaning making, and the navigation of different master narratives highlighted as important to what it means to engage in gender and sexual identity development (e.g., Dillon et al., 2011; Hammack & Cohler, 2011).

The model of sexual identity development described next, as an illustrative theory, by Dillon and colleagues (2011) relies in part on ideas from Erik Erikson and James Marcia's identity status model. Dillon and colleagues' (2011) theory consists of concepts such as personal and social identity, exploration and commitment, and identity status. The patterns of change in Dillon's model are relatively cyclical, as they are in Marcia's model of identity development through adulthood, but starting points in the two models differ (a foreclosure-like status for

Dillon and a diffusion status for Marcia as the respective model starting points). Yet, there are many similarities between these models, such as the value placed on the individual's search and co-construction of identity, the importance of the context for identity development, and optimal identity development involving as a sense of coherence and authenticity.

In Dillon and colleagues' (2011) model, sexual identity is viewed as multi-dimensional. At the individual personal identity level (i.e., at an intrapsychic level), sexual identity includes a person's sexuality, sexual orientation, and sexual orientation identity (Dillon et al., 2011). In terms of social identity, individuals can have an open or tacit identification and sense of belonging to a sexual identity-related social group(s) as well as holding beliefs/attitudes about such groups including an awareness of social power differentials between groups (Dillon et al., 2011). Individual and social identity come together to make up a person's sexual identity and change happens in the model through identity exploration and commitment, similar to how it is conceptualized by Erikson and Marcia's identity status model (Dillon et al., 2011).

It should be noted that in Dillon and colleagues' (2011, p. 658) model, there are identity statuses, and individuals' progress in their sexual identity development through these statuses is viewed in relatively malleable ways, in which:

> . . .there are opportunities for circularity and revisiting of statuses through-out the lifespan for a given individual. Thus, points in the model should be thought of as non-linear, flexible, and fluid descriptions of statuses through which people may pass as they develop their sexual identity over the lifespan.

In this model, people begin their first encounters with their sexual identity with an uncritical adoption of whatever is considered normative or expected in terms of sexuality in their culture (Dillon et al., 2011). Sexual identity is a unique domain of identity development in that socio-cultural pressures to conform to a particular sexual norm may be particularly potent and clearly communicated to youth early on in their development. Dillon and colleagues (2011) proposed that adoption of this unexamined default sexual identity (i.e., like the foreclosed status in Marcia's identity status model) is also likely to involve an uncritical acceptance of the status quo around social advantage and disadvantage for sexual identity-related groups, with the likely privileging of heterosexuality in many cultures. This start-ing point in sexual identity development is called compulsory heterosexuality by Dillon and colleagues (2011).

A moratorium-like period of active identity exploration can inspire a person out of compulsory heterosexuality and would involve trying out different ideas, behaviors, and preferences related to sexuality (Dillon et al., 2011). Active explo-ration is intentional and goes beyond what is the default or minimum in one's culture in terms of sexual identity exploration and does not have to just be limited to behaviors but can also include thinking (Dillon et al., 2011). It is also possible that a person can transition out of compulsory heterosexuality by adopting a type of diffusion orientation in which there is little attention and care paid to exploring or settling on a sexual identity (Dillon et al., 2011). A person can also move directly out of compulsory heterosexuality into a period of deepening commitment in relation to their sexual identity, where the sexual identity is solidified and incorporated into a person's identity (Dillon et al., 2011). Individuals with a heterosexual sexual orientation identity may come to this strengthening of who they are in terms of their sexuality after a period of active exploration or in the absence of exploration (Dillon et al., 2011). Those with an LGB sexual orientation identity are thought to come to a greater deepening and commitment to their sexual identity in combination with a period of active exploration, possibly moving back and forth between commitment and exploration (Dillon et al., 2011).

An optimal point in sexual identity development is characterized by the status called synthesis, in which the personal and social aspects of sexual identity are in harmony with each other, sexual identity is clear, authentic, and self-accepting (Dillon et al., 2011). Synthesis in terms of sexual identity development should be associated with a sense of integration between other aspects of identity that are relevant to sexuality (e.g., gender, religion; Dillon et al., 2011). Synthesis is not considered to be a permanent end state and, as noted earlier, this model has the possibility for movement back through the various statuses as the person goes through life and as societal conditions surrounding sexuality change (Dillon et al., 2011). A change-focused model that aims to encompass a diversity of experiences, such as that of Dillon and colleagues (2011) is a fitting theoretical example, given that a growing number of general population, longitudinal studies (primarily conducted in the United States) indicate that some individuals are likely to change and yet still others will show stability in aspects of sexuality (e.g., sexual attractions and behaviors) and sexual identity from adolescence into emerging adulthood (Morgan, 2013).[2]

Diversity in sexual and gender identity: beyond either/or conceptualizations

As noted, there is increasingly more emphasis on multi-dimensionality and diversity, when it comes to both gender and sexual identity (Bussey, 2011; Diamond et al., 2011). An implication of this change in perspective is that it is not assumed that gender and sexual identity are unmovably set at one time point in a person's life and remain that way until the end of life (Diamond, 2018; Morgan, 2013). As noted earlier, stability will be the case for some people but not all (Diamond, 2018). Further, when one reflects on the intersection of gender and sexual identity, consider the following:

> Historically, it was presumed that the link between gender identity and sexual identity/orientation was fairly straightforward: being attracted to women was a fundamental component of being a man, and being attracted to men was a fundamental component of being a woman ... Yet this simplistic model of the links between gender identity and sexual orientation simply does not fit

the empirical data . . . – after all, the very designation of a particular desire or behavior as "same sex" or "other sex" requires a stable appraisal of the gender status of everyone involved. Hence, although gender identity and sexual identity are separate phenomena, their relationship is dynamic and reciprocal, informed by an individual's personal sense of gender and his/her appraisal of the gender of social partners.

(Diamond et al., 2011, p. 26)

Ideas about what a person's physical sex is, the variations we have access to for gender and its expression, as well as conceptions of sexuality, sexual orientation, and sexual identity as ways that we make sense of ourselves as sexual beings, subjectively and in a wider societal context – are all in some regards essential pieces of the overall picture when it comes to understanding sexual and gender identity development in adolescents as well as in other developmental periods. Research efforts are now focused on better understanding how each of these separate pieces of a wider picture pattern themselves in unique ways depending on the interaction of the person and context. Gender and sexual identity development appear to be regularly intertwined, when individuals wish for and seek greater sexual and/or emotional intimacy with other people they are also likely to engage in more questioning around how gender enters into this equation as a matter of course (Diamond, 2018). Intersectionality and the concept of identity integration offer promising ways to bring the gender and sexual identity literatures into closer alignment and thereby provide a more holistic view of adolescent identity development.

Research exemplars

New frontiers for identity research involve realizing, in everyday research practice, all that is implied by bridging ideas like intersectionality and identity integration. Scholars have explored and documented how identity intersections are working across a variety of domains and with a diversity of methods (Syed & McLean, 2016). In this chapter section, the focus is on research studies that specifically concern the intersection between adolescent gender and sexual identity development. These research exemplars, in different ways, illustrate themes consistent with intersectionality (Cole, 2009) and identity integration (Syed & McLean, 2016). Here, we focus on two empirical examples.[3]

The White et al. (2018) study

The first research exemplar does not directly address identity development. However, this study is important because it was conducted with a sample of contemporary adolescents, and the study results illustrated some of the potential cultural and generational shifts that may be happening around the language used by some youth to describe their gender and sexual identity in the United States (White et al., 2018). The study is innovative in that network analysis was used to determine when labels for gender and sexual identity were used together by participants. The analysis allowed researchers to know what particular gender and sexual identity combinations were commonly endorsed by youth.

The study included 19,385 high school students living in the United States (average age was 16 years old) and study recruitment was school-based and via the internet, with an intention by the researchers to oversample youth with a sexual and/or gender minority identification (White et al., 2018). Interestingly, Lady Gaga, a singer, actor, and supporter of LGBQT rights, helped in the study recruitment by asking her social media followers to participate in the study. Surveys were completed on-line, and youth were asked to self-identify their gender and sexual identity with some pre-defined categories or with an open ended response. For gender, the pre-defined categories were as follows: *female, male, trans female, trans male*, as well as the option of *different* with space to write in one's own label(s). For sexuality, the pre-defined categories were: *heterosexual* or *straight, gay, lesbian, bisexual*, as well as the option of *other*, with space to write in one's own label(s) (White et al., 2018).

Study results showed that youth in this study commonly used traditional combinations of gender and sexual identity labels (White et al., 2018). Approximately 65% of co-occurring pairs given by participants were for *female and straight* or *male and straight*, as well as *female bisexual* or *male bisexual* as 9% and *female lesbian* or *male gay* as 6% of co-occurring pairs (percentages were rounded up). About 20% (approximately) of the remaining co-occurring pairs contained one or more write in labels, with one of the more frequently appearing combinations being female and pansexual (1.06% of co-occurring pairs). There was a great deal of variation in the write in labels (White et al., 2018). For gender identity, write in labels included: gender fluid, agender, non-binary, unsure, questioning. For sexual identity, write in labels included: asexual, unsure, questioning, demi-sexual, and queer. White et al. (2018) noted that some of the write in identity descriptions such as pansexual and queer allow sexual identity to be defined independent of the gender of a sexual/romantic partner and/or allow for more than two gender categories. Further, the researchers suggested that the identity labels written in by youth allowed them to self-identify in ways that transcended existing stereotypes about more long standing gender and/or sexual identity labels (White et al., 2018).

This study is a good example of how research practices consistent with an intersectional framework can advance knowledge about adolescent identity. The study recruitment was aimed at including underrepresented groups, the measurement allowed for input by study participants, and the analyses were open to potentially complex intersections between gender and sexual identity. This study was not aimed at multi-dimensional measurement of identity and did not speak to identity development in terms of how adolescents saw contextual or temporal identity integration. Yet, in a relatively straight forward manner, the study demonstrated how youth encountered existing societal expectations for gender and sexual identity development and how a sizable minority of youth showed some testing of the limits of such concepts as they related to their life experiences and identity.

The Diamond (2005, 2008) and Diamond and Butterworth (2008) studies

The second research exemplar is a study conducted by Diamond (2005, 2008). This was a 10-year longitudinal study (with five assessment time points) with 89 late adolescents/emerging adults who, at the time of the study launch/start, were an average age of 19 years and self-identified as women and had either rejected or were questioning a heterosexual sexual orientation (ten participants were not located for continued participation in the study; Diamond, 2008). Participants were recruited from a number of different organizations and settings, some of which were connected with sexual minorities (Diamond, 2005). Interviews were used to ask participants several questions about how they labelled and thought about their sexual identity as well as sexual attraction and behavior (Diamond, 2008). Study results indicated some variability in sexual attraction and behavior over time (Diamond, 2008). For example, one participant reported that her sexual attraction to women declined from 100% to 50% across four time points, and she stated in an interview the following:

> After I graduated from college . . . I found myself, not necessarily only attracted to both sexes, but also slightly more open-minded to the notion that maybe . . . maybe I can find something in just a person, that I don't necessarily have to be attracted to one sex verses the other . . . since then I've been in, let's see, a couple of different long-term relationships with women and I've had lots of sex with men and currently I'm in a long-term relationship with a man that I find very, very, very enjoyable and, um, ful- filling so it's hard for me to identify so therefore I kind of prefer to not identify or just kind of . . . kind of joke about it and say, "I am not bisexual or homosexual, I'm just sexual.
>
> (Diamond, 2005, p. 126)

Other study results showed that participants evidenced consistency with a homo- sexual, heterosexual, or bisexual orientation label/identity over the majority of time study points, and some individuals were moving between sexual orienta- tion labels/identities over time, from bisexual to unsure. But a general conclusion was that results did not support the idea that bisexuality represented a transition between heterosexual and homosexual orientations, but was relatively stable and viewed as a sexual orientation in its own right (Diamond, 2008).

Relevant to the intersection of gender and sexual identity, in particular, are findings reported by Diamond and Butterworth (2008) concerning four partic- ipants, who were part of this wider 10-year longitudinal study (i.e., Diamond, 2005, 2008). These four participants reported changes in both gender and sexual identity development over the course of the study. This subgroup and the wider study findings regarding the documentation of different trajectories in sexual identity development (Diamond, 2008) illustrated several ideas important to inter- sectionality, such as the non-homogeneity of groups. Diamond (2008) recognized that this study sample was likely to be diverse and searched for similarities as well as differences across the sample. There was also clarity and transparency about the study procedure, about how recruitment into the study was conducted and what that meant for the interpretation of study findings, and what the limits were on the generalizability of study findings (Diamond, 2008).

The subgroup results themselves (Diamond & Butterworth, 2008) also illustrated several substantive issues of importance. For participants in this subgroup, questioning and exploration around sexual attractions, behaviors, and sexual identity were associated with questioning and exploration around one's physical body/appearance and gender identity. Engaging in exploration in these areas would, in turn, later help to clarify participants' sexual attractions and behaviors as well as sexual identity. These subgroup findings also provided insight into the subjective experience of what it was like for participants to have gone from a birth sex assignment of female and heteronormativity to co-create a personally authentic combination of gender and sexual identity for themselves. These subgroup findings were also illustrative of how society and other people often push back against efforts to co-construct a meaningful and authentic gender and sexual identity, which is consistent with the idea of social location and power in the intersectionality framework and the notion of how people navigate person-society integration as was described by Syed and McLean (2016). A comment from a participant named Mark provides an example of how Mark experienced the reoccurring push back of society against having a more intermediate, rather than binary (i.e., female or male, heterosexual or homosexual) gender and sexual identity. Mark noted in an interview that:

> I'm not even going to tackle the pronoun thing because that's too confusing. And I find that "none of the above" pretty much is how I tend to label myself, only because I hate boxes. Hate them. Hate them. And I hate this whole like dichotomy paradigm that our society tends to revolve around. It's black – it's white/it's male – it's female/it's straight – it's gay/whatever. None of those fit.
>
> (Diamond & Butterworth, 2008, p. 374)

Other researchers who have conducted studies with adolescents and emerging adults in this topic area have also noted instances in which some youth are questioning and rejecting a societal status quo surrounding gender and/or sexual identity (i.e., rejecting heteronormativity, as well gender and sexual binaries) as part of their own identity development (e.g., Hammack & Cohler, 2011; Hammack, Thompson, & Pilecki, 2009; Savin-Williams, 2011).

Future identity research with the current generation of youth should take the implications of intersectionality for research practice seriously, as well as conduct more research on identity integration particularly in regards to gender and sexual identity development in different parts of the world, where norms and social practices surrounding gender, sexuality, ethnicity/culture, and religion vary (Bailey et al., 2016). The challenges for the future also include the need for more longitudinal empirical examples that have diverse multi-dimensional and mixed-method measurements of gender and sexual identity in the same study (Bowleg & Bauer, 2016). This type of research will allow for a better understanding of the conditions under which changes and stability in gender identity as well as sexuality, sexual orientation, and sexual identity are likely and for whom over time (Diamond, 2018; Morgan, 2013; Savin-Williams, 2011). Such research would also keep a focus on better ensuring equality and the creation of safe and resource-rich contexts for all youth.

Summary

Intersectionality and the concept of identity integration focus our attention on where important aspects of identity meet. These perspectives challenge us to embrace the complexity of identity and caution against the reduction of a person's identity down into its constituent parts (Cole, 2009; Parent et al., 2013). Intersectionality as a wider framework calls for recognition of how society works to offer opportunities or curtail life chances based on a person's identity and offers several important guidelines for research practice (Cole, 2009). The chapter uses the example of the intersection of gender and sexual identity to illustrate how the socially-recognized, two-gender only way of seeing the physical sex and gender of an adolescent does not encompass the bodies and life experience of all youths. Research presented describes cultural and generational shifts around the language used by many youths to describe their gender and sexual identity and how they label and think about their sexual identities and behaviors. Adult stakeholders in youth should be empowered and competent in their understanding of adolescent gender and sexual identity development.

Notes

1　See Bussey (2011) for more on how gender identity can be measured in ways that are consistent with this theory, as well as for an overview of research studies/findings related to this theory.
2　See Dillon et al. (2011) for more details on supporting measurement approaches and research studies/findings related to this theory about sexual identity development.
3　This chapter was not designed to provide comprehensive narrative summary of the research literature or an analysis of all theories relevant to adolescent gender and sexual identity development, but rather the aim of this chapter was to be illustrative and forward-looking. The reader interested in systematic narrative overviews of these research literatures is referred to several excellent articles and chapters cited in the reference list of this chapter.

References

Bailey, J. M., Vasey, P. L., Diamond, L. M., Breedlove, S. M., Vilain, E., & Epprecht, M. (2016). Sexual orientation, controversy, and science. *Psychological Science in the Public Interest, 17*, 45–101.
Bandura, A. (2008). Toward an agentic theory of the self. In H. W. Marsh, R. G. Craven, & D. M. McInerney (Eds.), *Self-processes, learning, and enabling human potential* (pp. 15–49). Charlotte, NC: Information Age Publishing.

Bem, S. L. (1981). Gender schema theory: A cognitive account of sex typing. *Psychological Review*, *88*, 354–364.

Bowleg, L. (2013). "Once you've blended the cake, you can't take the parts back to the main ingredients": Black gay and bisexual men's descriptions and experiences of inter-sectionality. *Sex Roles*, *68*, 754–767.

Bowleg, L., & Bauer, G. (2016). Invited reflection: Quantifying intersectionality. *Psychology of Women Quarterly*, *40*, 337–341.

Bussey, K. (2011). Gender identity development. In S. J. Schwartz, K. Luyckx & V. L. Vignoles (Eds.), *Handbook of identity theory and research* (pp. 603–628). New York, NY: Springer Science + Business Media.

Cole, E. R. (2009). Intersectionality and research in psychology. *American Psychologist*, *64*, 170–180.

Collins, P. H. (2000). *Black feminist thought: Knowledge, consciousness, and the politics of empowerment*. New York, NY: Routledge.

Crenshaw, K. (1991). Mapping the margins: intersectionality, identity politics, and vio-lence against women of color. *Stanford Law Review*, *43*, 1241–1299.

Diamond, L. M. (2005). A new view of lesbian subtypes: Stable versus fluid identity trajec-tories over an 8-year period. *Psychology of Women Quarterly*, *29*, 119–128.

Diamond, L. M. (2008). Female bisexuality from adolescence to adulthood: Results from a 10-year longitudinal study. *Developmental Psychology*, *44*, 5–14.

Diamond, L. M. (2018). Contemporary theory in the study of intimacy, desire, and sexu-ality. In N. K. Dess, J. Marecek & L. C. Bell (Eds.), *Gender, sex, and sexualities: Psychological perspectives; gender, sex, and sexualities* (pp. 271–294). New York, NY: Oxford University Press.

Diamond, L. M., & Butterworth, M. (2008). Questioning gender and sexual identity: Dynamic links over time. *Sex Roles: A Journal of Research*, *59*, 365–376.

Diamond, L. M., Pardo, S. T., & Butterworth, M. R. (2011). Transgender experience and identity. In S. J. Schwartz, K. Luyckx & V. L. Vignoles (Eds.), *Handbook of iden-tity theory and research* (pp. 629–647). New York, NY: Springer Science + Business Media.

Dillon, F. R., Worthington, R. L., & Moradi, B. (2011). Sexual identity as a universal pro-cess. In S. J. Schwartz, K. Luyckx & V. L. Vignoles (Eds.), *Handbook of identity theory and research* (pp. 649–670). New York, NY: Springer Science + Business Media.

Elder, G. H. Jr. (1998). The life course as developmental theory. *Child Development*, *69*, 1–12.

Erikson, E. H. (1968). *Identity: Youth and crisis*. New York, NY: Norton.

Fine, L. E. (2015). Penalized or privileged? Sexual identity, gender, and postsecondary educational attainment. *American Journal of Education*, *121*, 271–297.

Hammack, P. L. & Cohler, B. J. (2011). Narrative, identity, and the politics of exclusion: Social change and the gay and lesbian life course. *Sexuality Research & Social Policy*, *8*, 162–182.

Hammack, P. L., Thompson, E. M., & Pilecki, A. (2009). Configurations of identity among sexual minority youth: Context, desire, and narrative. *Journal of Youth and Adolescence*, *38*, 867–883.

Hegarty, P., Ansara, Y. G., & Barker, M. (2018). Nonbinary gender identities. In N. K. Dess, J. Marecek & L. C. Bell (Eds.), *Gender, sex, and sexualities: Psychological perspectives* (pp. 53–76). New York, NY: Oxford University Press.

Magnusson, E., & Marecek, J. (2018). Setting the stage: Gender, sex, and sexualities in psychology. In N. K. Dess, J. Marecek & L. C. Bell (Eds.), *Gender, sex, and sexuali-ties: Psychological perspectives* (pp. 3–28). New York, NY: Oxford University Press.

Marcia, J. E. (1966). Development and validation of ego-identity status. *Journal of Personality and Social Psychology*, *3*, 551–558.

McLean, K. C., Shucard, H., & Syed, M. (2017). Applying the master narrative framework to gender identity development in emerging adulthood. *Emerging Adulthood*, *5*, 93–105.

Morgan, E. M. (2013). Contemporary issues in sexual orientation and identity development in emerging adulthood. *Emerging Adulthood*, *1*, 52–66.

Parent, M. C., DeBlaere, C., & Moradi, B. (2013). Approaches to research on intersectionality: Perspectives on gender, LGBT, and racial/ethnic identities. *Sex Roles*, *68*, 639–645.

Rieger, G., & Savin-Williams, R. (2012). Gender nonconformity, sexual orientation, and psychological well-being. *Archives of Sexual Behavior*, *41*, 611–621.

Savin-Williams, R. (2011). Identity development among sexual-minority youth. In S. J. Schwartz, K. Luyckx & V. L. Vignoles (Eds.), *Handbook of identity theory and research* (pp. 671–689). New York, NY: Springer Science + Business Media.

Stewart, A. J., & McDermott, C. (2004). Gender in psychology. *Annual Review of Psychology*, *55*, 519–544.

Syed, M. (2010). Disciplinarity and methodology in intersectionality theory and research. *American Psychologist*, *65*, 61–62.

Syed, M., & McLean, K. C. (2016). Understanding identity integration: Theoretical, methodological, and applied issues. *Journal of Adolescence*, *47*, 109–118.

Tajfel, H., & Turner, J. (1986).The social identity theory of intergroup behavior. In W. Austin & S. Worchel (Eds.), *Psychology of intergroup relations* (pp. 7–24). Chicago, IL: Nelson-Hall.

White, A. E., Moeller, J., Ivcevic, Z., & Brackett, M. A. (2018). Gender identity and sexual identity labels used by U.S. high school students: A co-occurrence network analysis. *Psychology of Sexual Orientation and Gender Diversity*, *5*, 243–252.

7 Forging a brave new virtual identity

I really find out more about who I am by what my Facebook friends say to me. Sometimes it's so horrible to hear what they say about me, but they say good things too . . . My Mom helped me to think about whether I think the things people say about me are true or not. That's helped me a lot with the negative stuff – it really has.

(Elena, 14-year-old junior high school student)

The excitement and optimism as well as concern and trepidation over children and adolescents' social media and digital technology use are undeniable (e.g., UNICEF, 2017). For today's adolescents, the scope of their life context widens as technological innovations become more available (e.g., Pew Research Center, 2018). This chapter deals with an extension of identity research that concerns social media and digital technology use and how online spaces may alter the experience of adolescent[1] identity development. Many children and adolescents are online (e.g., Anderson & Jiang, 2018a). For example, "Youth (ages 15–24 years) are the most connected age group. Worldwide, 71 percent are online compared with 48 percent of the total population" (UNICEF, 2017, p. 3). In comparison to past generations, many in the current generation of youth were born as digital natives (Dimock, 2018) and have had exposure to a wide range of digital venues and experiences that have the potential to shift their identity development in a myriad of directions.

This chapter begins with a description of globalization in relation to adolescence and identity development. In the next chapter section, a summary of the digital landscape is provided by describing common forms of social media and digital technology used by present-day adolescents. These chapter sections are followed by a focus on research exemplars. In this section, four specific research studies are examined in detail in order to illustrate how researchers are working to better understand identity development in online contexts and to highlight future research priorities and innovations. A summary statement concludes the chapter.

Globalization, adolescence, and identity development

Globalization involves contact, exchange, and change between individuals and cultures (Berman et al., 2014). Globalization has also been described as follows:

the processes by which the constraints of geography on economic, cultural, and social organization progressively recede . . . Globalization has helped to transform businesses into multinational conglomerates and contributed to the growth of instant global communication, consumerism, and the dissemination of Western values. Globalization is also believed to have exacerbated economic segregation with and between nations, and reactions to globalization have contributed to the rise of fundamentalism and nationalistic and ethnic ferment.

(Thompson, 2012, p. 187)

Further, Rao and colleagues (2013) characterized globalization as an asymmetrical exchange. Indeed, the global youth culture is reflective of this lopsidedness, as it leans towards a preponderance of Western ideals, values, and products (Jensen, 2011). For example, in a focus group study with Indian urban middle-class adolescents, youth reflected on what they thought about the changes taking place in India in connection with globalization and said this:

Junk food is new! My grandmother says that 10 years ago food in India was very nutritious, but now Western food like burgers and pizza spoil our brains. (F)

Nowadays we only believe in purchasing costly bikes and buying branded stuff. (M)

Children are always talking in English rather than an Indian language. (M)

I think to some extent we've changed – like the music my friends and I listen to and the movies we watch are American. (F)

Now girls are equal to boys. (M)

(Rao et al., 2013, p. 15)

In the quote above F refers to female and M refers to a male study participant. These comments reflect how globalization and the Western leaning global youth culture are clearly present in the daily life of many adolescents as well as how adolescents may be aware and working to navigate and make sense of these trends in their own lives (Rao et al., 2013).

Globalization has direct implications for many facets of human development and identity. Here, the concept of cultural identity is used to provide a brief example of some of these implications. As noted in Chapter 5, cultural identity implies that there is a chance to consider various ways of life, ideas, and values, and one can make a psychological home in one or more cultural communities (Jensen, 2011). People may also come up with a creative workable fusion of different community values and practices (Jensen, 2011). Cultural identity is broadly relevant to everyone in that even for example youth who are in a sociocultural majority or mainstream in a given country may also have to navigate not only their local cultural context but also the global youth culture (Jensen, 2011). The use of social media and digital technology magnify the effects of globalization that have long been part of the human experience (Jensen, 2011). For example, the Silk Roads network was a conduit for globalization (UNESCO, n.d.).

These ancient trade routes connecting Asia (the far and near East) and parts of Europe were likely a much slower catalyst for exchange and change than the Internet is today. Consider what the Silk Roads meant to human history and then amplify that, and one can begin to appreciate the changes ahead as globalization takes greater hold across the continents. Indeed, Kay (2018, p. 267) stated that "We truly are in a social media world that affords possibilities and perils previously unknown to humankind."

Generation Z's digital landscape

Part of what makes the most recent generation of adolescents and young emerging adults distinguishable from other generations is defined by the way they use digital technology and social media. The post-Millennial generation, those who were 21 years old or younger in 2018, do not have an agreed upon name as yet (Dimock, 2018). However, some have begun to call this cohort Generation Z (Beall, 2017; Dimock, 2018) and have used the cut offs of birth between the late 1990s through the early 2000s to define who is in this generation (Beall, 2017; Miller & Lu, 2018). Although some uncertainty surrounds what to call this generation and who belongs to it, business-oriented circles have already characterized Generation Z as more "do it yourself" and nontraditional than the generation just before it (e.g., Millennials; Beall, 2017; Miller & Lu, 2018). Generation Z are extremely savvy at navigating the digital world, are globally tuned in, and take the use of digital technology as a seamless part of their lives (Beall, 2017; Miller & Lu, 2018). Further, members of Generation Z have also been described as continuously connected:

> Social media, constant connectivity and on-demand entertainment and communication are innovations Millennials adapted to as they came of age. For those born after 1996, these are largely assumed. The implications of growing up in an "always on" technological environment are only now coming into focus.
>
> (Dimock, 2018, n.p.)

What is the digital landscape like for the digital natives of Generation Z and for the rest of us? The term social media covers a great deal of ground and this term is used in this chapter to refer to the general online activities that people engage in for a diversity of reasons, such as entertainment, to participate in creative projects or activism, self-expression, and/or to connect with others (Manago, 2014; Rueda-Ortiz & Giraldo, 2016).

> Social media are defined as websites that facilitate the creation and exchange of user-generated content . . . social media include collaborative projects such as Wikipedia, social bookmarking websites . . . blogs and microblogs such as Twitter and Tumblr, content communities such as YouTube and Flickr, virtual game worlds such as World of Warcraft, virtual social worlds such as Second Life, and, of course, social networking sites such as Facebook.
>
> (Manago, 2014, p. 3)

People can engage in online activities by use of a diverse range of digital technologies such as smart phones and computers. The types of social media addressed in this chapter largely concern multiplayer online role-playing games and social networking sites (SNS). Online games can be played alone or with other players joining the same game. An example of multi-player online games is massively multiplayer online role-playing games (MMORPG). These games involve "virtual worlds in which players interact with each other in the online gaming environment" (Bacchini, De Angelis, & Fanara, 2017, p. 191). MMORPGs can have elements of SNS integrated within the game such as the ability to chat with other random players during game play, if one wishes to do so.

SNS and multi-player online game playing are distinct, but it should be noted that these media can overlap in some cases. For instance, many SNS (e.g., Facebook or Instagram) have no necessary connection to online games but can be shaped by users for that purpose. Players in addition to their game play may also be active on a SNS dedicated to the game (e.g., a Facebook group for players called the Fortnite Battle Royale Community). SNS have many possibilities and functions (Rueda-Ortiz & Giraldo, 2016). For instance:

> Seen as a personal diary, Facebook is a repository of moods and feelings. Seen as a gallery, Facebook is a place to exhibit their visual works. Seen as a blog, Facebook is a place to publish content, generate discussion and engage in activism.
>
> (Rueda-Ortiz & Giraldo, 2016, p. 56)

In SNS, people commonly make virtual profiles that contain images, entertainment, and other novel user-made content including information about one's mood, wishes, and opinions as well as reactions to what others have shared through the platform (Rueda-Ortiz & Giraldo, 2016). The profile itself and how it is created gives a constructed view of individuals and aspects of their life story at a glance (Larsen, 2016). An SNS profile page is an intentional construction that may or may not absolutely correspond to profile creators in actuality and what their lives are like offline (Manago, 2014). Because the audience for profile creators' content and activities are likely to include people known to them offline, there is typically at least some degree of correspondence between a person's on and offline SNS identity presentation (Manago, 2014). Yet, an SNS profile may allow people the possibility to accentuate dimensions of their identity that are not gross distortions of who they are, but are aspects that are not typically at the forefront or encouraged in their offline social interactions (Hughes et al., 2016). For example, a 12-year-old girl named Elyssa who was a participant in an ethnographic study of adolescents' interaction with a SNS called Ning commented as follows:

> On my profile, I made myself seem like the opposite of how my peers see me. On Ning, I seem like a colourful, bubbly girl who is very talkative and confident. This is because I designed my page with bright colours, joined multiple groups, gave gifts, and posted lots of comments.
>
> (Hughes et al., 2016, p. 9)

Elyssa also goes on to say:

> In real life, I am not very social, because I am quite shy and I tend to stutter A LOT. However, when I write, I do not stutter and I become creative and colourful in my writing. I feel more in control and confident when I am typing, because I don't get nervous . . .
>
> (Hughes et al., 2016, p. 11)

In relation to identity development, SNS offer opportunity for adolescents to experiment with differ presentations of themselves which may be ignored, dismissed, or affirmed by their contacts (Manago, 2014). Adolescent use of SNS is also thought to allow for a greater tailoring of adolescents' social environments on their own terms and without as much parental oversight as would be the case if the social contacts were taking place offline (Manago, 2014).

Adolescents' use of social media can also be an important venue for peer social interactions (Davis, 2013). Along with parents and other adults (e.g., teachers, coaches), peers can be important identity agents (Schachter & Marshall, 2010; Schachter & Ventura, 2008). The idea of an identity agent highlights how identity is developed in the context of relationships and how other people may knowingly, or work explicitly, to support another person's identity development (Schachter & Marshall, 2010). Identity agents can be a sounding board for adolescents' identity work (reinforcing and dismissing identity-related activities or decisions), and in the case of peers may also jointly engage in identity exploration and meaning making together (Schachter & Marshall, 2010). Thus, adolescents' social media use expands the field for peer social interactions and interaction with identity agents, particularly peers.

In the virtual social environment afforded by SNS, adolescents are most likely to participate in an online social network which reinforces ties to people that they already know offline (Manago, 2014). Studies have indicated thus far that the strengthening of connections to existing friends tends to be the primary reason why adolescents use SNS (Anderson & Jiang, 2018b; Borca, Bina, Keller, Gilbert & Begotti, 2015), and using SNS for this purpose has been associated with higher quality peer relationships that are characterized by more support and engagement (Larsen, 2016; Manago, 2014). For example, in a qualitative online survey of 2,400 Danish adolescents' SNS use (12–18-year-olds), online expressions of love and affection between friends that were perceived to be authentic were reported to be important to adolescents' happiness (Larsen, 2016). Responses from adolescents in this study that illustrate this point were as follows:

> It is always nice to know that someone loves you. And because I know that this person means it. (15-year-old girl)
> Because I know him, because I know he means it, and because I am just as fond of him . . . (13-year-old girl)
>
> (Larsen, 2016, p. 31)

Research evidence to date has supported the idea that SNS work best as an identity catalyst when used to better connect and deepen ties to offline friends, and SNS has also been associated with identity coherence (Davis, 2013; Manago, 2014). Emerging adults' use of SNS has also been shown to be an effective way to ease entry into new offline social contacts in the first years of university study (Manago, 2014). In addition to enriching offline friendships and thereby gaining greater exposure to potential identity agents, users of SNS also have the possibility of making completely new social contacts (Manago, 2014). Having a very wide network of contacts in SNS can present challenges in that maintenance of these relationships can take a great deal of energy and time for adolescents (Manago, 2014). Wide virtual social networks may also put quantity and a striving for popularity and/or notoriety ahead of the pursuit of establishing high quality relationships that afford psychological benefits (Manago, 2014).

Research exemplars

Many studies examine how social media fit into the life experience of adolescents and emerging adults (e.g., Hawley Turner et al., 2017). Even though the research literature on adolescents and their social media use is growing, it is premature to make conclusions about the associations between adolescents' digital life and their identity development. At the moment, longitudinal studies on social media use and adolescent identity development are sparse and researchers are just beginning to document associations between key constructs in this area,[2] largely

Table 7.1 Overview of selected features of research exemplars[3]

Study citation	Type of social media	Study design	Study sample
Crowe and Watts (2014)	Runescape, a MMORPG	Five year, ethnographic study	Child and adolescent players in UK and globally (estimated age 11–16 years old)
Davis (2013)	Use of online media (diverse types) with the intention to better connect to friends or identity expression/ exploration	Cross-sectional	2,079 adolescents living in Bermuda attending high school (average age 15)
Yang, Holden, & Carter (2018)	Use of social networking sites for social comparison of ability or opinion	Longitudinal	219 freshman university students in the United States (average age 18)
Bacchini et al. (2017)	Regular MMORPG players or not. Regular playing was 15 hours or more per week	Cross-sectional	415 Italian adolescents and emerging adults (average age 22 years old)

through the use of survey-based cross-sectional studies and/or ethnographic field work (Davis, 2013). The particular findings of the research exemplars in this chapter are noteworthy and begin to build up an evidence base, but the results of these individual studies should be viewed as in need of replication by future research studies. See Table 7.1 and note three at the end of this chapter for a concise overview of the selected research exemplars.

Research exemplar: the Crowe and Watts (2014) study

As a researcher, one can focus on a particular social media networking platform such as Facebook or Instagram or a given video game such as Undertale or Portal. The advantage of this approach is that knowing how an SNS or a video game is organized (how it is designed and what users are allowed to do) is important to attend to in the research process because the specific social media platform or tool will put constraints on how identity may be expressed or encountered and how connections to others are navigated in that digital space (Crowe & Watts, 2014; Wendler, 2014).

An ethnographic study conducted by Crowe and Watts (2014) offered an example of a research approach with a social media (i.e., game) specific focus. The online space for this study was a particular MMORPG called Runescape. This game involves role playing within the fantasy genre. The study focus was exploratory with the aim of mapping out how young people encountered this online space, what practices did they use, and how they formed a social community around Runescape. There are several interesting features of this study, such as the diversity of virtual and offline/material or real world data collection. For example, researchers noted that their field work across a five-year period consisted of the following data:

- 1628 separate recorded in-game virtual interaction/observation sessions;
- 3247 online in-game virtual interviews/interactions;
- 50 forum threads;
- 140 extended peer-to-peer virtual interviews/discussions;
- 20 material focus group interviews; and
- 23 game observations in the material world.

(Crowe & Watts, 2014, p. 219[4])

These researchers were based in the UK with some adolescents from the UK in the study and others from the global audience of Runescape players. Researchers observed that Runescape players (who were mostly children and adolescents) were sometimes flexible about taking on a gender different than their offline gender in the game (i.e., in the creation of their game avatar). This "gender bending" approach to the use of game avatars was interpreted by the researchers to be a function of the game design itself which allowed one to play as a girl or boy and yielded some perceived advantages to players in terms of game play, but also provided an opportunity for players' gender identity exploration (Crowe & Watts,

2014, p. 217). Two male adolescent players of Runescape who participated in this study said the following:

> I know plenty of guys that are girls and a few girls that are guys. No one cares who you are in RL [real life], it's who you are and what you do in Rune that matters.

> Why would I want to play as something I am in real life? I thought that was the whole point of it being a RPG!
>
> (Crowe & Watts, 2014, p. 223)

In the quote above, RPG refers to role playing game. A female adolescent player described the advantages of playing Runescape with a male avatar as follows: "Playing as a guy lets you just get on with the game. If I wanna feel sexy I just go back to the face-mage and swap back" (Crowe & Watts, 2014, p. 225).

The study by Crowe and Watts (2014) on Runescape is valuable in that it is documenting the intriguing phenomenon of gender bending with game avatars which shows the ways that adolescents through their game play may question the utility of the gender conventions common in fantasy-oriented video games and in other media in which female and male physical features in this genre are regularly exaggerated or differentially portrayed (e.g., in the game, female avatars lack similar amounts of clothing and armor relative to male avatars; Crowe & Watts, 2014). This study is also illustrative of the ethical considerations and best practices that researchers will have to develop when conducting virtual ethnography with children and adolescents. It would be a promising future study to longitudinally examine changes in players' gender identity (which was not measured in the Crowe & Watts study) relative to changes in players' game play over time as it relates to gender. Researchers could also have an intentional systematic recruitment of participants from a few different online multiplayer role playing games that treat gender in the game story line, activities, and avatar possibilities in different ways. While the Crowe and Watts (2014) study is clearly interesting and important to a field in which few studies exist, the study also raises the ethical concern about the full scope of what researchers should consider when conducting online virtual ethnography with children and adolescents and how research findings generated from a game-specific study can remain relevant as adolescents' online tastes and game activities change over time.

Research exemplar: the Davis (2013) study

Some researchers are attempting to circumvent the limitations of the short shelf life of particular types of social media by taking an approach that combines a user focus with an informed appreciation of the types of media and digital technology being used by study participants. In other words, in the case of adolescent identity development, there should be emphasis both on what the social media use means to the adolescent along with an awareness of what particular media and/or digital technology is being used by adolescents and how these types of media and digital technology allow for similar and/or different online experiences.

These research priorities are well illustrated by a survey-based cross-sectional study conducted by Davis (2013) with 2,079 adolescents in Bermuda. This study sample impressively represented approximately 80% of the total population of high school students living on the Island. Participants' average age was 15 years old. Self-concept clarity was the identity-related index measured in this study, and this construct represented facets of identity coherence (Davis, 2013). More specifically, self-concept clarity was reflective of the integrative work that people do to understand who they are across varied aspects of themselves and across time (Campbell et al., 1996). Other important study constructs were adolescents' perceptions of their relationship with their friends and mother (i.e., relationships with important identity agents; Davis, 2013).

Exemplifying researchers' attempts to better understand why youth go online and what experiences they have in digital spaces, the study conducted by Davis (2013) had several survey questions that concerned adolescents' views about how they approach online contexts and if they have the expectation that they would be more likely to be able to express themselves more freely online and if they see online contexts as a place where they can better craft a presentation of their identity in ways that they desire – this scale was called online identity expression/ exploration. Other survey questions concerned adolescents' motivations to use online contexts to improve their connections with already existing offline friends. This scale was called online peer communication (Davis, 2013).

Descriptive study results indicated that the vast majority of adolescents in this sample had and kept up a Facebook profile (90%), owned a cell phone (94%), owned a laptop computer (83%), instant messaged (87%), and watched YouTube (96%). Many adolescents in this sample also played video games on a console (59%) or played single player online/cell phone games (50%) and fewer adolescents played multiplayer online games (30%). The main study results showed that having a good relationship with one's mother and friends was positively associated with more self-concept clarity. A good relationship with one's mother was also connected to a good relationship to one's friends (Davis, 2013).

Other results indicated that going online to strengthen one's existing friendships was related to better relationships with friends, which was also associated with more self-concept clarity (Davis, 2013). Conversely, going online to express one's identity was associated with less friendship quality and less self-concept clarity. Thus, supportive friendships, connection to one's mother, and going online to shore up existing friendships were all connected to more self-concept clarity. A searching more experimental use of online contexts was indicative of less self-concept clarity (Davis, 2013). The content of items used to measure identity expression/exploration in this study had a mix of item prompts which could be indicative of authentic identity exploration (e.g., "I enjoy using the Internet to try out different ways of expressing myself") to item content that may reflect a search for affirmation from others (e.g., "I can show a better version of myself

online . . . When I'm online, I can present myself how I want others to view me";
Davis, 2013, p. 2290). Other studies have measured different aspects of online
experiences and self-concept clarity but a synthesis of these study findings relative to the Davis (2013) study are hampered in some cases by differences in how
online experiences were conceptualized and measured across these other studies that concerned online experiences and self-concept clarity (e.g., Israelashvili,
Kim, & Bukobza, 2012).

In short, the Davis (2013) study exemplified what can be gained by attending
to the reasons why adolescents go online while also paying empirical attention,
at least descriptively, to the types of media and digital technology adolescents are
using. Importantly, future research should seek to replicate the Davis (2013) study
findings in other samples as well as determine if the type of identity expression/
exploration that adolescents were doing online may have longer-term implications
for identity development or if this type of engagement in online spaces (which
appeared to not be beneficial to adolescents) indicated a transitional moment that
would be followed by different online activities and resultant identity development changes. Further research studies along the lines of the Davis (2013) study
would be of particular value with the addition of a longitudinal design, and this
would add to what can be learned about how certain online activities (and the
intentions and motivations behind this engagement in online spaces) relate to
identity development and how such activities interface with relations and actions
of identity agents such as adolescents' parents and friends.

Research exemplars: the Yang et al. (2018) and Bacchini et al. (2017) studies

Because the Yang et al. (2018) and Bacchini et al. (2017) studies have similar-
ity in their main implications, these studies are described together in this chapter
subsection. The Yang and colleagues' (2018) study concerns social comparison.
The type of social comparison that people do off and online appears to matter
very much. The more beneficial type of social comparison is observation of the
ways in which other people meet life's challenges or solve problems and this
could include issues of connected to identity (i.e., this type of social comparison is called opinion comparison; Yang et al., 2018). On the other hand, social
comparison of ability is a competitive observation of what others may excel at or
have relative to one self (Yang et al., 2018). Such comparisons have been found
to leave most individuals clearly worse off in terms of self-evaluation and mood
(Yang et al., 2018).

One of the few longitudinal studies of social media use and identity was conducted by Yang and colleagues (2018). This was a short-term longitudinal study
(approximately one year) with 219 entering university students in the United
States who reported regular SNS use (at least once a week, e.g., Facebook,
Instagram, Twitter, and/or Snapchat). Participants were on average 18 years old.
Surveys were used to measure several constructs. The identity-related constructs
were identity processing style, which is an information processing-oriented index

of how people approach identity questions/issues (Berzonsky, 1989), as well as identity coherence as measured by the Erikson Psychosocial Stage Inventory and global self-esteem. The online constructs measured concerned participants' engagement in social comparison of ability or opinion when using SNS. Across the two time points, 62% of the sample remained in the study (136 participants; Yang et al., 2018).

Main study results indicated that participants who engaged frequently in social comparison of ability while using SNS were likely to also have a diffuse-avoidant identity style (i.e., those forestalling identity work; Yang et al., 2018). Social comparison of ability and a diffuse-avoidant identity style at time one were prospectively related to less identity coherence at time two (i.e., at the longitudinal follow up). Further, social comparison of opinion on SNS was not significantly associated with changes in identity coherence or global self-esteem (Yang et al., 2018). The Yang and colleagues' (2018) study is clearly valuable given that it is one of the first longitudinal studies in this area.

The Bacchini et al. (2017) study was cross-sectional and included Italian adolescents and emerging adults. The study recruitment was designed in such a way as to include two subgroups within the sample, namely participants who were regular MMORPG players who played at least 15 hours a week and participants who did not play MMORPGs. Surveys were used to measure internet addiction as well as identity processes such as commitment, in-depth exploration, and reconsideration of commitment as measured by the Utrecht-management of identity commitments scale (U-MICS; Crocetti, Schwartz, Fermani, & Meeus, 2010) in the domains of education/job and best friend. Main study results indicated that participants who were in the process of questioning or letting go of prior commitments across the measured identity domains were likely to be regular MMORPG players and were elevated on internet addiction (Bacchini et al., 2017). Those participants involved in deep and active forms of identity exploration tended not to be regular MMORPG players (Bacchini et al., 2017).

Considering intersections across the results in three of the research exemplars, namely the studies by Davis (2013), Yang et al. (2018) and Bacchini et al. (2017), it is evident that adolescents' and emerging adults' use of online spaces are indeed associated with facets of identity development. It can also be concluded from these research exemplars that this was clearly a timely and rich line of inquiry that should continue. As previously noted, the findings from the research exemplars require further testing and replication before substantive conclusions can be made. However, these studies themselves represent the empirical work needed to identify online activities that can serve as catalysts or put the brakes on identity development. Advances in this type of knowledge will provide a sound empirical basis for the development of future identity intervention efforts.

Research exemplars: research priorities and innovations

A research priority that has already become evident from these early studies is that it is vital to unpack what social media use actually means to the young person. Why do adolescents go online? What are their intentions, expectations, and goals when they go online? What actually happens once they are there? Do they get what they set out to find? Simply documenting the amount of time that adolescents spend online and attempting to link that to identity, but not seeking answers to the aforementioned questions, falls short of insightful research at this point in time and does not advance knowledge in this field. Wider recommendations regarding adolescents' digital life are consistent with the need to unpack adolescents' motivations to use, and the experiences they have with, social media. For example, Middaugh, Schofield Clark, and Ballard (2017, p. S130) in a research review noted that caring professionals' interactions with adolescents should "Change the focus from time with screens to the quality of activities which youth engage in digital spaces."

In terms of innovation, these study exemplars are of value in their own right even though it is early days in this field of research, because these studies show where the state-of-the science is and also point to future research priorities. These research exemplars also highlight innovations in the methods used, how research questions are being refined, and demonstrate how researchers are encountering and working to solve many practical research problems. Future research is likely to stand on the shoulders of these early innovators (i.e., the research exemplars described in this chapter) in the digital identity research field.

Summary

Some virtual spaces are thought to encourage the spread of a global youth culture, individual self-expression, and the enhancement of social networks (Manago, 2014). An adolescent's interaction with social media can serve as a context for identity development. In this virtual space, people can access and provide information (fact and opinion) as well as encounter a range of values and lifestyle possibilities (Kay, 2018; Manago, 2014). Related to this topic, Anthony Lake, the executive director of UNICEF stated the following:

> The internet is all of these things, reflecting and amplifying the best and the worst of human nature. It is a tool that will always be used for good and for ill. Our job is to mitigate the harms and expand the opportunities digital technology makes possible.
>
> (UNICEF, 2017, p. 2)

Indeed, social media have diverse uses and meanings to people. Because of this diversity, how development unfolds in relation to social media and digital technology use is likely to be complex (Manago, 2014). Research studies and theory specifically about adolescent identity development in digital landscapes are few in number but are likely to grow in the future. Much more research is needed to determine how positive forms of identity development interface with digital life. As these associations are clarified in future research studies, new ways to leverage online social interactions and experiences to the benefit of adolescent identity development should be at the forefront of research efforts. The digital adolescent identity field is an exciting work in progress, with researchers launching novel studies to show proof-of-concept and expand the field.

Notes

1 One may ask how relevant is the Internet and online settings for adolescents from a global perspective? To get a sense of scale, first consider Internet use among adults globally. The vast majority of adults who live in developed nations are Internet users. More than 80% of adults in countries such as France, Israel, South Korea, the United States, and Sweden say they use the Internet at least sometimes or have a smart phone that can connect to the Internet (Pew Research Center, 2018). In comparison to adults' use of the Internet in developed nations, Internet use rates are lower in developing nations such as India and sub-Saharan Africa (Pew Research Center, 2018). However, the rate of Internet use is growing by leaps and bounds in developing nations. Take as a case in point several nations in sub-Saharan Africa such as South Africa, Nigeria, Kenya, and Ghana. These nations have seen a substantial recent increase in Internet use (Pew Research Center, 2018). Rates of smartphone ownership among people living in several nations in sub-Saharan Africa have doubled since 2014 and are likely to double again by 2025 (Pew Research Center, 2018). Young people in sub-Saharan Africa and across the globe are more likely than older people to have a smart phone and to be online (Pew Research Center, 2018; UNICEF, 2017). Yet, there are still disparities in access to and use of the Internet. For young people, such disparities may be associated with living in particular nations where Internet access is limited in general, gender, access to a smartphone and not a computer (which provides different opportunities online) as well as not having the financial means to buy technology that allows access to the Internet (UNICEF, 2017). Population trends which put the fastest growing parts of the world population and adolescents in developing nations, as well as trends towards increased Internet use and access to digital technology in developing nations and high levels of Internet use already reached in many developed nations (UNICEF, 2017), all point towards the importance of digital life to many present-day adolescents and even more so in the future. In this chapter, phrases such as "adolescent Internet use is . . ." appear frequently and in these cases, we typically specify which adolescents we are referring to and where they live, if that information was available in the primary source of information.

2 An examination of existing empirical studies using a search engine often used in psychology called PsycINFO yielded 32 results or hits when the search criteria required that the word "identity" was the document title and the word "Internet" was referenced anywhere in the abstract. Other search criteria were that the search result be a peer-reviewed empirical study with a child or adolescent study sample. We used these search criteria because there are many theoretical and conceptual chapters on this topic and many empirical studies on adolescents' use of online spaces in general but those studies do not address identity development directly, even using a broad theoretical umbrella for the conception of identity. Studies about this topic can use differing terms and constructs and also appear in disciplines outside of psychology. Even with the noted limitations to this literature search, this survey of what PsycINFO had to offer on this topic in terms of empirical studies is informative because it gives the reader a sense of the evidence base within this emerging field.

3 In reference to the research exemplars described in Table 7.1, other information about the research exemplars that is noteworthy but did not fit into Table 7.1 are the following reflections about the pattern of findings across the studies. The results of the Crowe and Watts (2014) study are unique relative to the other research exemplars. This study was exploratory and valuable in highlighting the practice of gender bending by players, illustrated an interesting on and offline data collection approach,

but did not have direct assessment of participants' identity development. The Davis (2013) study showed that using online activities to build better relationships with peers and parents may support optimal identity development (e.g., more self-concept clarity). From the Yang et al. (2018) and Bacchini et al. (2017) studies, results showed that when individuals were delaying identity work (diffuse-avoidant identity style or loosing identity commitments) they may also be using online spaces (e.g., use of SNS for comparisons of ability or regular MMORPG playing) in ways that may not ultimately serve them in terms of moving towards more optimal identity outcomes. These are initial findings and require replication.

4 Bullet points were in the original quoted text by Crowe and Watts (2014).

References

Anderson, M., & Jiang, J. (2018a). Teens, social media & technology 2018. Pew Research Center, May 31. Retrieved from www.pewinternet.org/2018/05/31/teens-social-media-technology-2018

Anderson, M., & Jiang, J. (2018b). Teens' social media habits and experiences. *Pew Research Center*, November 28. Retrieved from www.pewinternet.org/2018/11/28/teens-social-media-habits-and-experiences

Bacchini, D., De Angelis, G., & Fanara, A. (2017). Identity formation in adolescent and emerging adult regular players of massively multiplayer online role-playing games (MMORPG). *Computers in Human Behavior, 73,* 191–199.

Beall, G. (2017). 8 key differences between gen Z and millennials. *Huffington Post,* November 6. Retrieved from www.huffingtonpost.com/george-beall/8-key-differences-between_b_12814200.html?guccounter=1

Berman, S. L., Ratner, K., Cheng, M., Li, S., Jhingon, G., & Sukumaran, N. (2014). Identity distress during the era of globalization: A cross-national comparative study of India, China, and the United States. *Identity: An International Journal of Theory and Research, 14,* 286–296.

Berzonsky, M. D. (1989). Identity style: Conceptualization and measurement. *Journal of Adolescent Research, 4,* 267–281.

Borca, G., Bina, M., Keller, P. S., Gilbert, L. R., & Begotti, T. (2015). Internet use and developmental tasks: Adolescents' point of view. *Computers in Human Behavior, 52,* 49–58.

Campbell, J. D., Trapnell, P. D., Heine, S. J., Katz, I. M., Lavallee, L. F., & Lehman, D. R. (1996). Self-concept clarity: Measurement, personality correlates, and cultural boundaries. *Journal of Personality and Social Psychology, 70,* 141–156.

Crocetti, E., Schwartz, S., Fermani, A., & Meeus, W. (2010). The Utrecht Management of Identity Commitments Scale (U-MICS): Italian validation and cross-national comparisons. *European Journal of Psychological Assessment, 26,* 169–183.

Crowe, N., & Watts, M. (2014). "When I click 'ok' I become sassy – I become a girl." Young people and gender identity: Subverting the "body" in massively multi-player online role-playing games. *International Journal of Adolescence and Youth, 19,* 217–231.

Davis, K. (2013). Young people's digital lives: The impact of interpersonal relationships and digital media use on adolescents' sense of identity. *Computers in Human Behavior, 29,* 2281–2293.

Dimock, M. (2018). Defining generations: Where Millennials end and post-Millennials begin. Pew Research Center, March 1. Retrieved from www.pewresearch.org/fact-tank/2018/03/01/defining-generations-where-millennials-end-and-post-millennials-begin

Hawley Turner, K., Jolls, T., Schira Hagerman, M., O'Byrne, W., Hicks, T., Eisenstock, B., & Pytash, K. E. (2017). Developing digital and media literacies in children and adolescents. *Pediatrics*, *140*, S122–S126.

Hughes, J., Morrison, L., & Thompson, S. (2016). Who do you think you are? Examining the off/online identities of adolescents using a social networking site. In M. Walrave, K. Ponnet, E. Vanderhoven, J. Haers & B. Segaert (Eds.), *Youth 2.0: Social media and adolescence: Connecting, sharing and empowering* (pp. 3–19). Switzerland: Springer International Publishing.

Israelashvili, M., Kim, T., & Bukobza, G. (2012). Adolescents' over-use of the cyber world: Internet addiction or identity exploration? *Journal of Adolescence*, *35*, 417–424.

Jensen, L. A. (2011). Navigating local and global worlds: Opportunities and risks for adolescent cultural identity development. *Psychological Studies*, *56*, 62–70.

Kay, A. (2018). Erikson online: Identity and pseudospeciation in the internet age. *Identity: An International Journal of Theory and Research*, *18*, 264–273.

Larsen, M. C. (2016). An "open source" networked identity. On young people's construction and co-construction of identity on social network sites. In M. Walrave, K. Ponnet, E. Vanderhoven, J. Haers & B. Segaert (Eds.), *Youth 2.0: Social media and adolescence: Connecting, sharing and empowering* (pp. 21–39). Switzerland: Springer International Publishing.

Manago, A. M. (2014). Identity development in the digital age: The case of social networking sites. In K. C. McLean, & M. Syed (Eds.), *The Oxford Handbook of Identity Development* [E-reader version] (pp. 1–33). New York: Oxford University Press. doi: 10.1093/oxfordhb/9780199936564.013.031

Middaugh, E., Schofield Clark, L., & Ballard, P. J. (2017). Digital media, participatory politics, and positive youth development. *Pediatrics*, *140*, S127–S131.

Miller, L. J., & Lu, W. (2018). Gen Z is set to outnumber millennials within a year. *Bloomberg News*, August 20. Retrieved from www.bloomberg.com/news/articles/2018-08-20/gen-z-to-outnumber-millennials-within-a-year-demographic-trends

Pew Research Center (2018). Internet connectivity seen as having positive impact on life in sub-Saharan Africa, but digital divides persist. Pew Research Center, October 9. Retrieved from www.pewglobal.org/2018/10/09/internet-connectivity-seen-as-having-positive-impact-on-life-in-sub-saharan-africa

Rao, M. A., Berry, R., Gonsalves, A., Hastak, Y., Shah, M., & Roeser, R. W. (2013). Globalization and the identity remix among urban adolescents in India. *Journal of Research on Adolescence*, *23*, 9–24.

Rueda-Ortiz, R., & Giraldo, D. (2016). Profile image: Ways of self-(re-)presentation on the Facebook social network. In M. Walrave, K. Ponnet, E. Vanderhoven, J. Haers & B. Segaert (Eds.), *Youth 2.0: Social media and adolescence: Connecting, sharing and empowering* (pp. 41–60). Cham, Switzerland: Springer International Publishing

Schachter, E. P., & Marshall, S. K. (2010). Identity agents: A focus on those purposefully involved in the identity of others. *Identity: An International Journal of Theory and Research*, *10*, 71–75.

Schachter, E. P., & Ventura, J. J. (2008). Identity agents: Parents as active and reflective participants in their children's identity formation. *Journal of Research on Adolescence*, *18*, 449–476.

Thompson, R. A. (2012). Changing societies, changing childhood: Studying the impact of globalization on child development. *Child Development Perspectives*, *6*, 187–192.

UNESCO (n.d.) World heritage list. *Silk roads:* The routes network of Chang'an-Tianshan Corridor. Retrieved from https://whc.unesco.org/en/list/1442

UNICEF (2017). *Children in a digital world: The state of the world's children 2017*. New York: UNICEF Division of Communication.

Wendler, Z. R. (2014). "Who am I?": Rhetoric and narrative identity in the Portal series. *Games and Culture, 9*, 351–367.

Yang, C., Holden, S. M., & Carter, M. D. K. (2018). Social media social comparison of ability (but not opinion) predicts lower identity clarity: Identity processing style as a mediator. *Journal of Youth and Adolescence, 47*, 2114–2128.

8 Identity beyond adolescence

What comes next?

> I think since adolescence, my sense of identity has only grown stronger and more solid over time. There haven't been any earth-shattering changes along the way. It's just now I'm far less concerned about what others might think of me and far more trusting of myself and doing what feels right.
>
> (John, 51-year-old teacher)

> For me, the accidental death of my older brother when I was 21 just completely shattered my sense of myself and my certainty about the way the world was "supposed" to be. You just aren't supposed to die so young. That single event has, to this day, made me so very aware of just how fragile life is and how I can never take anything for granted.
>
> (Sarah, 30-year-old computer programmer)

Many years ago, when I (JK) first began teaching a university course on life-span development, a 19-year-old student came up to me after class one day and asked why she had to learn about adult development – why didn't the class just end at that "terminal point of marriage"? After all, not much of consequence really happened after that, she pointed out. (And whatever really *did* happen to Cinderella through those many years of life after she met her prince charming and lived happily ever after?) The formation of identity is not restricted to adolescence, as Erikson (1980, p. 122) pointed out: "[I]dentity formation neither begins nor ends with adolescence: it is a lifelong development . . ." This final chapter will focus on some of the normative changes in identity that are likely to occur beyond adolescence, through ongoing phases of adult life. The chapter will also address how adolescent identity resolutions are also likely to impact major psychosocial challenges of adulthood.

The primary reason for the focus of the final chapter is to help readers anticipate what may lie ahead – to appreciate how initial identity resolutions formed at the end of adolescence/emerging adulthood can have rather long-term consequences. Certainly, identity-defining choices and life directions can change over time, but beyond emerging adulthood, major identity changes become far less common (as the research presented ahead will show). For some individuals, there may be just a growing sense of internal coherence or self-certainty that characterizes identity as it evolves beyond adolescence, while for others, there may be more dramatic "life course changes" to one's understandings of oneself and one's place in the world. These individual differences in the identity formation process beyond adolescence lead to a number of identity-related questions. What dimensions of one's identity formed during adolescence and young adulthood are likely to remain stable over time and what dimensions are likely to change? Are there different types of contexts that may be associated with different patterns of identity stability or change during adult life? Where identity does markedly change, are there particular types of events generally associated with specific identity change pathways during adult life? And how are adolescent resolutions to identity related to one's capacity for intimacy, generativity, and integrity during adulthood?

It is theory and research originating in the psychosocial framework of Erik Erikson that has perhaps offered the most prolific insights into ongoing identity development beyond adolescence. Erikson took special care to emphasize how identity, once formed and stabilized by the end of adolescence, will likely continue to develop through young, middle, and later adulthood years as well:

> Such a sense of identity [developed during adolescence], however, is never gained nor maintained once and for all. Like a "good conscience," it is constantly lost and regained, although more lasting and more economical methods of maintenance and restoration are evolved and fortified in late adolescence.
>
> (Erikson, 1980, p. 128)

Erikson also wrote extensively about how adolescent identity resolutions may become re-activated and revised during post adolescent phases of the life-span. Indeed, Erikson and his colleagues have devoted an entire book to examining the ways in which identity resolutions of adolescence become reconsidered particularly during later adulthood: "Old age's reconciling of the tension between identity and identity confusion reinvolves the individual in the psychosocial process that dominated adolescence" (E. H. Erikson, J. M. Erikson, & Kivnick, 1986, p. 129). It is thus important to appreciate the impact that identity resolutions undertaken during adolescence may have on various dimensions of adult life in the years beyond identity's primary time of formation.

This volume has reviewed different perspectives on how identity forms and develops during adolescence and emerging adulthood in preparation for entry into adult life, and research from within these varied traditions has begun to supply answers to some of the questions noted above. In this final chapter, we explore these questions and conclude with reflections on how identity-related research and practice might be optimized for future developments in the field.

Stability and change in identity beyond adolescence: theory

Erikson (1968, 1980; Erikson et al., 1986) has given considerable attention to the epigenesis of identity beyond adolescence through the ensuing psychosocial tasks of adult life. Among the important themes Erikson discussed in identity's onward journey were the importance of identity continuity and the preservation of a sense of self-sameness through the inevitable biological, psychological, and social changes that life invariably brings. In the words of one research participant I (JK) interviewed as a mid-life adult:

> [O]h, I am the same person who I was when I was 7. To other people, my body has changed, and their expectations of me have changed, but I feel the same. Except now I do behave as I feel . . . and people sometimes find it a little odd. But in the long run it's better to be true to yourself than to be true to other people's expectations of you.
>
> (Kroger, 1993, p. 213)

Erikson et al. (1986, p. 130) also made general comments about ongoing identity development through mid-life: "During adulthood, the individual struggles to balance a faithfulness to some commitments with an inevitable confusion and abandonment of others, all the while living a life that, in turn, both represents and reflects an underlying sense of self." And Erikson himself continued to highlight resolutions to the *identity versus role confusion* task of adolescence as the foundation for working through the psychosocial tasks of *intimacy versus isolation, generativity versus stagnation,* and *integrity versus despair* during adult life.

With these comments by Erikson in mind, Marcia (2002) developed a cyclical model of ongoing identity development during adulthood. He proposed that following initial identity resolutions of adolescence and young adulthood, there were likely to be normative life events that could shake people at their psychological foundations (i.e., cause disequilibrium), and such life experiences would be associated with some kind of identity reformulation. He conceptualized a conical structure, whereby the phases of adolescence, early adulthood, middle adulthood, and late adulthood represented increasingly large elliptical cycles within the cone (pointed downwards), as one re-experienced one or more ongoing, disequilibrating cycles of identity foreclosure (and/or diffusion) through moratorium through achievement during each subsequent phase of adulthood, as one grappled with issues of *intimacy versus isolation, generativity versus stagnation,* and *integrity versus despair*. Marcia noted that in the case of adults exhibiting stable foreclosure patterns, where the identity structure was designed to prevent disequilibrium, these ongoing cycles of identity development might or might not occur. Where development did occur for the foreclosed individual, the disequilibrium experienced was likely to be quite shattering. Identity diffuse adults were also unlikely to experience identity disequilibrium during ongoing phases of adult life, according to Marcia, because they lacked a solid identity structure at the outset. Marcia and colleagues (Stephen, Fraser, & Marcia, 1992) had initially proposed a sequence of moratorium-achievement-moratorium-achievement (MAMA) cycles through adult life, in which one might regress to earlier modes of functioning at times of identity distress. Through his later model, Marcia tried to capture in more detail the cycles of identity disequilibrium and reconstruction that had the potential to emerge through ongoing phases of identity development over the course of adulthood. In order for a new identity structure to emerge, an old one needed to disintegrate, which was likely to be a very confusing and painful experience. Given Marcia's theoretical propositions, what does the research show about ongoing patterns of identity development beyond adolescence? While adult identity research having origins in Erikson's and Marcia's models has now produced a number of investigations, findings from other theoretical models discussed in this volume will also be presented, where possible, to detail ongoing changes in identity through adulthood.

Stability and change in identity beyond adolescence: research

In order to address the question of stability and change in identity's evolution beyond adolescence, one must look, ideally, to longitudinal studies of identity over time as well as cross-sectional and retrospective studies (important but not as ideal as longitudinal studies). Marcia's identity status approach, described in Chapter 2, has been used extensively to identify various pathways that identity status change may take over the course of adulthood. The direction of change and/or stability that these pathways take have now been the focus of a number of longitudinal, cross-sectional, as well as retrospective studies. Findings from studies in the next sections generally illustrate the following trends:

- Where identity status change does occur, the most common pathway of movement is from foreclosure to moratorium to achievement.
- The highest probability of identity status change occurs during adolescence and emerging adulthood in comparison with the later part of young adulthood and midlife.
- Different types of life-style contexts appear associated with different patterns of identity development from adolescence/emerging adulthood through midlife.
- Identity achievement remains elusive for approximately half of individuals as they enter adult life, at least among those sampled from research conducted in primarily Western contexts.
- The likelihood of movement from the identity diffusion status between the end of adolescence and young to middle adult life is low.
- Narrative studies point to increasing levels of meaning-making over adolescence/young adulthood and of increasing self-concept clarity from adolescence though adulthood.

Longitudinal studies

Several longitudinal studies of identity status change over various phases of adult life now exist. In Finland, Fadjukoff, Pulkkinen, and Kokko (2016) evaluated identity status patterns of stability and change at ages 27, 36, 42, and 50 years old in a representative sample of 172 adults from the general population of a large Finnish city. Findings showed considerable variation in identity status ratings given across identity domains. However, the developmental trend from age 27 to age 50 was moderately progressive toward identity achievement within all but the religious identity domain. Remaining stable for the ideological domains across the four data collection times of young and middle adulthood was characteristic of the identity diffusion status only. Cramer (2017) also conducted a longitudinal study evaluating identity status at ages 18, 22, and 35 years among a sample of individuals initially drawn as part of a random sample of entering freshmen at a small American college. Results showed a modest increase in identity achievement scores over this time interval as well as a large decrease in moratorium scores. Group mean scores showed little change in diffusion status scores over the 17-year time interval (although there was individual variability in this status).

Whitebourne and colleagues (Sneed, Whitbourne, & Culang, 2006) used a paper and pencil measure of identity achievement and diffusion only to study identity status stability and change between college and age 54 years, with data collected every 11 years, at ages 20, 31, 42, and 54. Results indicated a general increase in identity achievement scores between the ages of 20 and 31; additionally, the rate of increase to the *identity versus role confusion* resolution slowed at each data collection point between the ages of 31 and 54. Helson, Stewart, and Ostrove (1995) assessed three cohorts of women who had been young adults in the 1950s, early, and late 1960s through to their mid adulthood years with a Q-sort measure of identity status. While it was not possible to follow individual pathways of identity status change over time in this study, there was high stability in all of the women's identity status vectors from their early forties throughout mid adulthood, suggesting that major identity changes were primarily a phenomenon of late adolescence and emerging adulthood. *Thus, these longitudinal studies all point to identity showing generally progressive trends toward achievement, primarily from late adolescence through emerging adulthood.*

Several narrative studies have also made use of Marcia's identity status groupings and followed individuals over young and middle adulthood. Josselson (2017) reported on the lives of 25 college women over the course of 35 years (interviews were conducted around the time of their graduation from college at 21 years, and again at ages 33, 43, and 55 years). Josselson documented how most of these women went about finding and revising their identities over time, and noted how late midlife often brought subtle but important changes to how the women came to see and understand themselves and the world. She noted that in their twenties and early thirties, most women focused on trying to develop a sense of competence in the world, while their later thirties and early forties brought concerns with whether or not they were really pursuing the identity-defining directions they had envisaged and becoming the people they wished to be; the decade of their forties often became the time of major identity revisions for those who achieved a sense of their own identities by young adulthood. By their mid-fifties, these women were reaping the benefits of their earlier identity work and enjoying an "age of fulfilment."

Josselson commented, however, on the patterns for several women she identified as drifters (diffusions) as they left college with no clear goals for the future, living entirely in the moment; if they imagined any futures for themselves at all, their hopes were fantasies, and they had no clear thoughts of how to actualize these "dreams." Although there was individual variation among the drifters in college, most by mid-life were feeling battered and chastened by their circumstances, drifting in and out of places, relationships, endeavours, and holding more jobs, using more drugs and alcohol, and trying more religions as they continued to struggle with feelings of frustration and disappointment across their adult lives.

A further narrative longitudinal study of identity status change from the mid- to late twenties by Carlsson, Wängqvist, and Frisén (2015) attempted to learn more about continuity in identity development after initial identity commitments had been undertaken as well. Some 124 Swedish men and women were given an identity status interview at age 25 and again at age 29, with the four identity statuses similar in frequency at the two ages; stability was a typical pattern for all identity statuses except that of moratorium. Despite the relative high rates of identity status stability, however, identity narratives indicated important changes in the ways individuals approached changing life conditions, the extent to which they engaged in ongoing meaning-making, and how they continued to pursue different life directions. It seems that an identity achieved stance was necessary for a solid sense of identity to stay adaptive and flexible over time. A further investigation of those who remained in the diffusion status from their mid to late twenties (seven of 124 participants), found a pattern of keeping their lives on hold through decreased or haphazard activity in relation to changing life circumstances, few attempts to make meaning of these situations, and attempts by some to try to "dissolve" their personal life directions (Carlsson, Wängqvist, & Frisén, 2016).

Several additional dimensions of identity change and stability have also been examined longitudinally from late adolescence over the course of adult life. Pals (2006) studied narrative identity processes for women from the Mills Longitudinal Study (Helson, 1967). Data collection for these women began in 1958 when the women were 21 years of age, and they were subsequently studied at ages 27, 43, 52, and 61 years. At age 52 years, some 83 of these women provided a narrative of their most difficult time since college, and Pals used additional personality data from the age 21, 52, and 61 assessments in her study of identity narratives over time. She assumed that difficult life experiences were identity challenging, and she wanted to learn more about how participants responded to their difficult challenges through their narrative processing and their resolutions. In general, Pals found that changes and new ways in how people interpreted their lives and life experiences were likely to trigger new but enduring identity-related patterns of thinking, feeling, and behaving in adult life over time. More specifically, two important findings emerged:

1 Individuals high in "coping openness" embraced the narrative challenge of addressing their difficult life experiences and engaged in exploratory narrative processing of their situations that allowed for greater levels of wisdom, self-understanding, and emotional complexity over time.
2 A coherent positive resolution to the challenging event predicted increasing ego resiliency over the course of adult life.

Issues of identity clarity and content in adulthood have also been examined longitudinally over a three-year time span during adulthood with a sample of individuals aged 19–86 years at the start of the study (Lodi-Smith, Cologgi, Spain, & Roberts, 2017). The study found that changes in self-concept clarity over time corresponded to changes in identity contents and role engagements (sometimes brought about by increasing health limitations). Self-concept clarity appeared, from this study, to be an integral marker of identity maturity in adulthood. *Thus, the longitudinal narrative studies cited above showed ongoing adaptive changes in the ways that many individuals approach changing life conditions and challenges, engage in reflective meaning-making, and continue to pursue different life directions beyond adolescence with increased self-concept clarity; however, some individuals (diffusions) continued to flounder in their life directions well beyond the adolescent years to lead, at best, chaotic, frustrating, and disappointing lives.*

Cross-sectional and retrospective studies

A large, meta-analytic study of identity status stability and change over the course of young and middle adulthood was undertaken by Kroger, Martinussen, and Marcia (2010). While this study also included identity status patterns of development during adolescence that have been reviewed in Chapter 2, the larger investigation also included material on young adult development during the ages of 22–36 years. It is interesting that while the likelihood of being identity achieved was 34% at age 22 (across eight studies and 247 participants) and 31% from 23 to 29 years (across 11 studies with 253 participants), the 30 to 36 year time span showed approximately half (47%) of the participants to be identity achieved (across nine studies with 310 participants). Noteworthy, however, is the fact that well into the thirties, the incidences of identity achievement were not higher. Subsequent to this work, a cross-sectional study of identity status change from adolescence into middle adulthood in Trinidad found that the achieved identity status was most common in middle age, compared with adolescence, emerging, and young adulthood years, while moratorium and diffusion statuses were more characteristic of the younger age groups (Arneaud, Alea, & Espinet, 2016). Again, approximately half of individuals in this study were identity achieved by midlife, according to the mean ages of participants who had experienced various adulthood transitions (to marriage, parenting, becoming employed, etc.).

When exploration and commitment variables are considered separately and cross-sectionally across late adolescence and the early years of adulthood, Luyckx and colleagues (Luyckx, Klimstra, Duriez, Van Petegem, & Beyers, 2013) found that despite some minor fluctuations, identity commitment processes increased in a linear fashion for a sample of Flemish high school, university, and working individuals aged 14 to 30 years of age. Exploration in breadth and exploration in depth were highest among those in their early to mid-twenties. Additionally, exploration in breadth and depth were strongly related to commitment processes in late adolescence and young adulthood but became increasingly linked with ruminative exploration and depression by the late twenties. It remains unknown at present how these patterns of identity exploration and commitment evolved over the course of adulthood beyond age 30. *Thus, cross-sectional studies of identity status change over time point to remarkably low levels of identity attainment by midlife (only about half of those samples studied); identity exploration in breadth and depth seem to peak from the early to mid-twenties.*

Cross-sectional narrative studies of adult identity development also provide some insights into identity from adolescence through adulthood. McLean (2008) examined narrative identity in two age groups of individuals: those from late adolescence through young adulthood (age 17–35 years) and older adults (age 65–85) years. In an interview, participants reported three self-defining memories – memories that were vivid, emotional, personally important, and/or highly memorable in that they powerfully conveyed how one came to be the person one currently was. After interviews, participants were asked to report their age at the time of the memory and what it meant to their sense of identity. Findings showed that through their memories, younger individuals constructed themselves more in terms of change, while older participants presented themselves more in terms of stability. McLean concluded that although the mechanisms for developing narratives about the self and identity may be similar from late adolescence over adulthood, the functions of creating narratives may be quite different. For late adolescents and young adults, narratives appeared to provide a vehicle for self-exploration and understanding, while for older adults; narratives provided a sense of stability and resolution. For both age groups, however, there was a striving toward identity continuity over time.

Pasupathi and Mansour (2006) also cross-sectionally examined adult differences in autobiographical reasoning about identity-related issues through narratives. They undertook two studies. The first, an interview study, examined memories of significant life events – turning points or crises – for adults, diverse both ethnically and in terms of social class. Approximately half were under the age of 65 years old and the remainder over age 65. The second study extended the first study using a different sample of adults, aged 18–89 years, as well as requesting a written rather than verbal form of presentation for their autobiographical memories. Results from the two studies indicated that middle aged and older adults were more likely than younger adults to demonstrate explicit autobiographical reasoning when constructing their personal, identity-related narratives. The two studies also found age-related increases in the likelihood of autobiographical reasoning into middle age. It may be that there is an increasing emphasis on remembering more meaningful life experiences as well as an increasing need to remember in order to integrate identity elements across one's life with age.

Cross-sectional and retrospective studies of additional identity-related variables have also been undertaken through the adulthood years. For example, Zucker, Ostrove, and Stewart (2002) used cross-sectional samples of college educated young, middle, and late adulthood women to find higher levels of self-certainty with age. An additional retrospective study of identity certainty among a group of highly educated women aged 30 to 50 years old also found this variable to increase with age (Stewart, Ostrove, & Helson, 2001). Higher levels of self-certainty in identity-related issues do appear to be one concomitant of aging beyond adolescence. *Thus, these cross-sectional identity-related narrative studies again showed higher levels of self-certainty with age, as well as more stability and resolution of identity concerns over time, alongside the ability to remember more meaningful life events; strivings for identity continuity, however, were present from adolescence through adulthood.*

Retrospective accounts of identity stability and change over adulthood have been relatively uncommon. However, despite the issues that accurate recall may bring to remembered life transitions, Kroger and Haslett (1987, 1991) undertook a series of identity status interviews with 100 mid-life men and women aged 40–63 years from upper-middle class backgrounds in an effort to examine patterns of stability and change in identity status over the time since mid-adolescence. Analyses revealed different identity status transition pathways for individuals who had selected different life-style options, even when age, education level, parental and marital status and identity domain were held constant. For example, while men who were full-time workers throughout their adult lives had about a 50% probability of being identity achieved in the vocational domain by age 43, women who were full-time homemakers since having children in young adult life had only about a 12% probability of being identity achieved by age 43 within this vocational domain. By contrast, women who had worked full time outside the home throughout their childrearing years as well as women who had returned to full time work following their childrearing years both had about a 95% chance of being identity achieved by age 43 years. The probability of change from foreclosure and diffusion statuses was very low across all lifestyle groups beyond age 25 years in this vocational identity domain. Additionally, ongoing MAMA cycles of moratorium-achievement were present during young and middle adulthood across all life-style subgroups, after initial identity commitments had been chosen for those initially rated as identity achieved. This retrospective study offers important insights into the relationships between life style contexts and various identity status transition patterns and change rates from adolescence through young and middle adult life.

In sum, one thread that runs through all the longitudinal, cross-sectional, and retrospective accounts of identity development during and beyond adolescence presented above is that there is no reason to expect initial identity interests and commitments adopted by the end of adolescence to see one through one's adult life. Limited research into events associated with identity changes from a variety of perspectives have all pointed to the continued testing, refinement, and overcoming of obstacles in forging an identity from adolescence through adult life. It is difficult to give a definitive statement about the types of events that may be associated with specific types of identity changes over the course of adulthood. While some studies have examined potential precipitators of identity change during late adolescence and young adult life (reviewed in Chapter 2), there is far less information about factors potentially associated with identity change during middle and late adulthood. Some research does suggest, however, that for the identity achieved, it is often internally driven events (e.g., new insights, deepened awareness or understandings about one's identity-related life circumstances that may lead to change; Josselson, 2017; Pals, 2006). Identity clarity does appear to increase with age. Furthermore, where an initial identity has not been formed during adolescence or young adulthood, the likelihood of this development occurring during adulthood is limited. It is not possible to comment on identity stability or change during *later* adulthood at this time, since so few studies have been undertaken exploring identity in this phase of the life cycle.

Adolescent identity resolutions and the psychosocial tasks of adulthood: theory

What are the relations between identity resolutions formed by the end of adolescence or emerging adulthood to the ongoing psychosocial tasks of adult life that Erikson (1968) identified? In his epigenetic scheme, Erikson emphasized the interrelationships among all psychosocial tasks of development. With reference to adolescent identity, Erikson noted how resolutions to the *identity versus role confusion* task consolidated during adolescence or young adulthood would continue to impact ongoing psychosocial tasks of *intimacy versus isolation, generativity versus stagnation,* and *integrity versus despair* over the course of early, middle, and later adulthood. Erikson (1985, n.p.) also suggested that identity beyond adolescence was likely to remain under the dominance of psychosocial tasks of adulthood: "Once ascended from its precursors in earlier stages . . . each [identity] quality must be renewed in subsequent stages under the dominance of later crises." Friedman (1999), however, criticized Erikson for failing to clearly elucidate ongoing developments of identity during adulthood.

Recently, I (JK) began to explore what the epigenesis of identity might actually entail during adult development through the examination of individual case studies during each post-adolescent psychosocial phase (Kroger, 2018). These case studies suggested that identity, once attained, and ongoing psychosocial stages of adulthood may continue to co-develop over time. Much remains to be learned about how identity continuity is both retained and transformed through normative psychosocial developments of adulthood. Below is an overview of research that has explored the relationship between identity and each of Erikson's psychosocial tasks of *intimacy versus isolation, generativity versus stagnation,* and *integrity versus despair* during adulthood. Results point to identity's evolution in the tasks of psychosocial development beyond adolescence.

Adolescent identity resolutions and the psychosocial tasks of adulthood: research

Identity and intimacy

As noted in Chapter 2, *intimacy versus isolation* is a key psychosocial task of young adulthood, with optimal resolution producing the capacity to genuinely love.

Erikson (1968) proposed that in order to experience mature forms of intimacy, resolutions to questions of identity needed to be reasonably well consolidated; otherwise, close relationship with another was most likely to be in the service of addressing identity needs of the individual partners. At the same time, however, Erikson suggested that women may need to hold identity resolutions in abeyance until a suitable partner could be found around which to consolidate one's sense of identity. While Erikson's (1968) ideas on identity development among women fell by the wayside long ago, women, nevertheless, have shown more diverse patterns in their associations between identity and intimacy than men in contemporary research.

A meta-analysis of 21 studies examining the relationship between identity and intimacy among late adolescent and young adult men and women was undertaken by Årseth, Kroger, Martinussen, & Marcia (2009). For men, there was a strong sequential relationship between identity and intimacy, as Erikson (1968) had suggested. Results for women were more mixed, however. About two-thirds (65%) of identity achieved and moratorium women were high in intimacy, like the men; however, foreclosed and diffuse women were almost equally likely to be in low as well as high intimacy groups. This finding suggests that for some women, identity and intimacy are co-developing. One subsequent study, however, has supported the sequential ordering of identity and intimacy in late adolescence and young adulthood for both genders (e.g., Beyers & Seiffge-Krenke, 2010). Further work is needed to understand more fully the relationships between identity and intimacy for both men and women.

There have been additional studies examining links between identity and intimacy further into adult life. For example, Sneed, Whitbourne, Schwartz, and Huang (2012) undertook a longitudinal investigation of identity and intimacy and their associations with subjective well-being among 182 individuals who were alumni of the University of Rochester between the 1960s and 1980s. Individuals were studied every 11 years at ages 20, 31, 42, and 54 years to examine the predictive power of identity and intimacy to each other over time as well as their associations with feelings of well-being at mid-life. Results generally showed strong positive links between identity and intimacy over the course of adult life. Identity issues were likely to be revisited in early mid-life, and successful, intimate partnerships during young adulthood were strongly linked with a fulfilling sense of identity during mid-life as well as feelings of well-being. The study also pointed to the notion that resolution to the task of *intimacy versus isolation* is critical not only for developing relationships in young adulthood, but also for sustaining these relationships through midlife.

In Canada, Beaumont and Pratt (2011) used a measure of identity style (closely associated with the identity statuses) to investigate links between identity and intimacy. Samples of early and mid-life individuals, comparable in educational and ethnic background, were examined in terms of identity style, intimacy, and generativity. Here, identity style was differentially associated with intimacy resolutions. The informational identity style (comparable to identity achievement) positively predicted intimacy resolutions for the two age groups, while the normative identity style (comparable to foreclosure) in young adulthood predicted a type of pseudointimacy (a partnership more stereotypic in nature, lacking genuine intimacy) with a partner at mid-life. These latter studies supported Erikson's (1968) suggestion of an epigenetic relationship between identity and intimacy during young and middle adulthood, although longitudinal studies of these variables for both genders are in great need.

Identity and generativity

As noted in Chapter 2, Erikson described the task of *generativity versus stagnation* as a key focus for midlife adults. Generativity refers to the desire to genuinely care for and guide the next as well as future generations through such activities as parenting, mentoring those outside the immediate family through work and other social contexts, volunteering in one's community, and wanting to leave behind some kind of legacy or impact on the world in ways small or large. The counterpoint to generativity is stagnation – self-absorption or self-indulgence – so that little, if any, energy is expended in service to the well-being of others. An optimal resolution to this task is the ability to genuinely care, both for the self and for others, across times and places, both near and far. While much research during midlife has examined the relations between generativity and mental health outcomes, investigations that examine the direct association between identity and generativity have been far fewer in number. However, these studies have generally shown increasingly positive connections between identity and generativity through mid-life.

Bradley and Marcia (1998) were early investigators who looked at the importance of ego development (related to identity) to generativity status, finding a moderately positive association between generativity and ego development and a moderately negative association between conventional forms of generativity (caring for members of their own group or those of similar backgrounds only) and rising levels of ego development. A longitudinal study in Finland by Fadjukoff, Pulkkinen, Lyyra, and Kokko (2016) examined parental identity status over 14 years during mid-adulthood (ages 36, 42, and 50 years) and found that parental identity achievement increased from ages 36 to 42 and remained stable thereafter. Neither early parenthood nor number of children was related to parental identity status at any age. Parental identity achievement was also more common among women and foreclosure among men throughout midlife. An achieved parental identity status was also linked with higher generativity scores for both men and women at age 42, and this same association between parental identity status and generativity held for the women but not for men in this sample at age 50. Non-committed parental identity status (diffusion or moratorium) was linked with the lowest levels of nurturance for both genders at ages 36 and 42, when nurturance scores were measured. Beaumont and Pratt (2011) also found that mid-life adults scored higher on a measure of generativity than younger adults; there was also a direct positive relation between identity and generativity using a measure of identity style in a cross-sectional sample of early and midlife adults. Those normative in identity style (similar to those in the foreclosed identity status) were likely to be conventional in their generativity (restricted in their caring to those in their immediate social groups or having similar interests and values). A further study by James and Zarrett (2006) pointed to a similar association among participants from the Sears, Maccoby, and Levin (1951) study over time, where identity that was assessed in 1951 predicted generativity in 1996.

Several narrative studies have also explored the relations between identity and generativity. McAdams, Diamond, de St. Aubin, and Mansfield (1997) found that adults aged 25–72 years old who scored high on a measure of generativity were also more likely to narrate life stories with content that showed commitment to personal ideologies and prosocial behaviors than those were those scoring low on generativity. Merrill and Fivush (2016) turned to intergenerational family narratives, or stories that parents and grandparents shared with their children about their own experiences growing up. These researchers showed that intergenerational narratives and the process of sharing these life stories by elders influenced the psychosocial development of both adolescents and the adults in their families. These narratives helped to create a sense of identity and generativity among younger generations, contributing both to family identity as well as individual well-being. A further narrative study undertaken in Canada examined the relations between trajectories of generative concerns and environmental narrative identity over the course of young adulthood at ages of 23, 26, and 32 years old (Jia, Soucie, Alisat, & Pratt, 2016). Among the findings, were increased generative concerns through early adulthood. Additionally, those who developed higher levels of generative concern by age 32 years also had more salient environmental narratives at age 32 (salient environmental narratives were stories told by participants that depicted turning points in their environmental concerns, coded according to the breadth and sophistication of reasoning, vividness, and impact). *Thus, ego development, identity style, and narrative reviews all illustrate increasing levels of generative concerns with age as well as generativity's positive links with identity during early and mid-adulthood, in line with Erikson's (1968) predictions.*

Identity and integrity

Erikson's (1968) final psychosocial task of *integrity versus despair* normatively has been a primary focus of concern during late adulthood. During this phase, questions commonly have arisen about the meaning that one's life has had, and many identity questions may become reactivated as the end of life feels somewhat more imminent. As noted in Chapter 2, Integrity involves the ability to accept the life one has lived with peace and satisfaction, rather than enormous regrets about the roads not taken. Despair refers to a general attitude of unhappiness or despondence over the life course one has taken and dread at the way it is ending. Optimal resolution to this final life task resulted in what Erikson termed wisdom, or the ability to integrate resolutions of all previous life phases to involve a deeper understanding of the human condition and a connection with those of different places and generations, without fear of death.

After her husband's death, Joan Erikson made use of her husband's annotations on an earlier edition of *The Life Cycle Completed* to suggest that with the increasing number of years one is likely to spend in late adulthood, a ninth stage of development may be needed to capture the psychosocial challenges of very late adulthood (E. H. Erikson & J. M. Erikson, 1997). This stage captured the struggle that growing mental and physical declines may bring to retaining a sense of integrity. Indeed, an investigation of the two phases of *integrity versus despair* has found some age group distinctions (Brown & Lowis, 2003). Those in their sixties were primarily focused on traditional integrity concerns, while those in their eighties and nineties were preoccupied with concerns of physical and/or mental decline.

Although Erikson et al. (1986) wrote extensively about the theoretical links between identity and integrity in late adulthood, there has been very little longitudinal or cross-sectional research undertaken to examine this relationship. On a longitudinal basis, Sneed et al. (2006) documented that integrity scores increased and identity scores decreased during mid-life, in their study of individuals at age 20 years and subsequently every 11 years until age 54 years. However, Marcia and his colleagues were among the few research teams who have directly examined the relations between integrity and identity in late adulthood (Hearn et al., 2012). The researchers validated a measure integrity status (the Self Examination Interview) for late life adults and examined, cross-sectionally, how integrity was associated with participants' identity status. Participants were in their sixties, seventies, and eighties (mean age approximately 75 years). A significant association between integrity and identity status was found, with some 86% of integrated late life adults found to be identity achieved, while no despairing persons were identity achieved. Those participants who were non-exploring (i.e., had not examined questions of personal meaning in their lives) and pseudo-integrated (i.e., fit the world into simplistic templates and clichéd meanings) in integrity status tended to be foreclosed in their identity status.

Predictors and precursors to resolutions of *integrity versus despair* have also been undertaken in several studies. James and Zarrett (2006), in their longitudinal study over 45 years of adult women found that while identity directly predicted generativity over time, it was generativity scores alone that predicted integrity scores in late adulthood; integrity scores were also negatively related to depression during the final assessment of these women when they were 70 years of age and over. Hannah, Domino, and Hendrickson (1996) also examined predictors of *integrity versus despair* in a sample of adults. In their regression analyses, they found that the most parsimonious model for predicting *integrity versus despair* scores were generativity, trust, intimacy, identity, and autonomy, with no meaningful gender differences.

Considered together, studies of this major section that have examined relations between identity and subsequent psychosocial tasks of adult life have pointed toward the epigenetic nature of ongoing identity development during adulthood. Research has shown that optimal resolution to the *identity versus role confusion* task of adolescence and young adulthood is associated with optimal resolutions to *intimacy versus isolation, generativity versus stagnation,* and *integrity versus despair* through the years of adult life. Identity seems to be a strong predictor of ongoing development in the psychosocial tasks of adult life.

Summary and conclusions: identity as the balance between self and other

I (JK) once overheard a well-liked teacher in a quiet moment of reflection comment to a distraught 16-year-old that there is no map when it comes to matters of maturing; even Frost's road not taken, described in his well-known poem by that name, is more defined in form than the course this teenager needed to plot. While there are undoubtedly no detailed relief maps laying out the finer contours of our individual identity pathways, there do appear to be some major general thoroughfares in the identity formation process that, when recognized, might have given both the adolescent wayfarer and sympathetic bystander above some assurance of a future for this teenager that would once again cohere, albeit in a new way. Mappings of general normative routes provided by Erikson, Blos, narrative psychologists, and sociocultural psychologists not only allow us to glimpse the next developmental roadside resting points on the adolescent identity journey into adult life but also provide guides as to the most useful means of unblocking developmental arrest as well as assisting the already engaged traveler on his or her own life journey. Having studied the roadmaps of these general approaches to the formation of identity primarily through adolescence and emerging adulthood, what general directions for future identity research and practice might best advance our understanding of this complex process?

The approaches to understanding identity development during adolescence and young adulthood that have been reviewed in this volume have *all* recognized the importance of both individual as well as contextual factors in charting identity's developmental course. However, different emphases have been placed on the role of the individual – biological and socially constructed factors (such as gender, ethnicity, physical strengths and limitations) as well as personal psychological factors (individual needs, conscious and unconscious, wishes, preferences) – and the role of the context (familial, social, cultural, national) across the identity approaches reviewed in this volume, generating different understandings of identity balances between self and other in resultant research.

One obvious recommendation for future research would be to combine forces and integrate the strengths of as many of the general perspectives on identity as are practical into future studies of identity's formative process. Earlier chapters have also called for an integrated model to study identity in context (e.g., Galliher, McLean, & Syed, 2017). Here, we would support such recommendations and ask that researchers frame their studies of identity with an awareness of national, regional, and more immediate social contexts and smaller group influences as well as potential historical/cohort effects on an individual's identity development. Additionally, individual variables involving both the process of identity development as well as other dimensions of identity that are important to maintaining a sense of personal continuity over time be examined through a combination of research methods.

Longitudinal studies of identity's structure, content, and process evolution over time should be encouraged; at the same time, such work should aim to address these variables at relatively frequent time intervals. During adolescence and young adulthood, studies are beginning to undertake identity evaluations in a greater variety of national settings than a decade ago. However, beyond adolescence, the norm of 10–11-year time intervals between data collection points makes it difficult to follow some of the more nuanced threads of identity formation and revision over time in any meaningful way. Additionally, the dearth of identity studies, longitudinal or otherwise, for late adolescents in relation to late life adults (when many identity issues are likely to re-emerge) make these interesting comparative life phases for future research.

Further exploration of circumstances associated with the developmental arrest of identity is also essential to undertake, such that contexts may be structured to facilitate development in optimal ways. Steps toward how one might best support identity exploration in contexts where this process is adaptive are also important to undertake in future identity research. Ultimately, however, it is only one's own ease with that process of change that will allow one to aid and not hinder others on their own life journeys. Michener (1972) noted that the most important journey a person will make in life is to find his or her own identity – for if one fails in this task, it really doesn't much matter what else one finds.

References

Arneaud, M. J., Alea, N., & Espinet, M. (2016). Identity development in Trinidad: Status differences by age, adulthood transitions, and culture. *Identity: An International Journal of Theory and Research, 16*, 59–71.

Årseth, A. K., Kroger, J., Martinussen, M., & Marcia, J. E. (2009). Meta-analytic studies of identity status and the relational issues of attachment and intimacy. *Journal of Adolescence, 9*, 1–32.

Beaumont, S., & Pratt, M. (2011). Identity processing styles and psychosocial balance during early and middle adulthood: The role of identity in intimacy and generativity. *Journal of Adult Development, 18*, 172–183.

Beyers, W., & Seiffge-Krenke, I. (2010). Does identity precede intimacy? Testing Erikson's theory on romantic development in emerging adults of the 21st century. *Journal of Adolescent Research, 25*, 387–415.

Bradley, C., & Marcia, J. E. (1998). Generativity-stagnation: A five category model. *Journal of Personality, 66*, 39–64.

Brown, C., & Lowis, M. J. (2003). Psychological development in the elderly: An investigation into Erikson's ninth stage. *Journal of Aging Studies, 17*, 415–426.

Carlsson, J., Wängqvist, M., & Frisén, A. (2015). Identity development in the late twenties: A never ending story. *Developmental Psychology, 51*, 334–345.

Carlsson, J., Wängqvist, M., & Frisén, A. (2016). Life on hold: Staying in identity diffusion in the late twenties. *Journal of Adolescence, 47*, 220–229.

Cramer, P. (2017). Identity change between late adolescence and adulthood. *Personality and Individual Differences, 104*, 538–543.

Erikson, E. H. (1968). *Identity, youth and crisis*. New York, NY: W.W. Norton & Company.

Erikson, E. H. (1980). *Identity and the life cycle*. New York, NY: W.W. Norton & Company.

Erikson, E. H. (1985). Fragments, unsorted. Folder 2, *85M-41. *bMS AM* 2031 (1725). Erikson Harvard Papers.

Erikson, E. H., & Erikson, J. M. (1997). *The life cycle completed (extended version)*. New York, NY: W. W. Norton.

Erikson, E. H., Erikson, J. M., & Kivnic, H. Q. (1986). *Vital involvement in old age*. New York, NY: W. W. Norton & Company.

Fadjukoff, P., Pulkkinen, L., & Kokko, K. (2016). Identity formation in adulthood: A longitudinal study from age 27 to 50. *Identity: An International Journal of Theory and Research, 16*, 8–23.

Fadjukoff, P. Pulkkinen, L., Lyyra, A. L., & Kokko, K. (2016). Parental identity and its relation to parenting and psychological functioning in middle age. *Parenting: Science and Practice, 16*, 87–107.

Friedman, L. J. (1999). *Identity's architect: A biography of Erik Erikson*. New York, NY: Scribner.

Galliher, R. V., McLean, K. C., & Syed, M. (2017). An integrated developmental model for studying identity content in context. *Developmental Psychology, 53*, 2011–2022.

Hannah, M. T., Domino, G., Figueredo, A. J., & Hendrickson, R. (1996). The prediction of ego integrity in older persons. *Educational and Psychological Measurement, 56*, 930–950.

Hearn, S., Saulnier, G., Strayer, J., Glenham, M. Koopman, R., & Marcia, J. E. (2012). Between integrity and despair: Toward construct validation of Erikson's eighth stage. *Journal of Adult Development, 19*, 1–20.

Helson, R. (1967). Personality characteristics and developmental history of creative college women. *Genetic Psychology Monographs, 76*, 205–256.

Helson, R., Stewart, A., & Ostrove, J. (1995). Identity in three cohorts of midlife women. *Journal of Personality and Social Psychology, 69*, 544–557.

James, J. B., Zarrett, N. (2006). Ego integrity in the lives of older women: A follow-up of mothers from the Sears, Maccoby, and Levin (1951) Patterns of Child Rearing Study. *Journal of Adult Development, 12*, 61–75.

Jia, F., Soucie, K., Alisat, S., & Pratt, M. (2016). Sowing seeds for future generations: Development of generative concern and its relation to environmental narrative identity. *International Journal of Behavioral Development, 40*, 466–470.

Josselson, R. (2017). *Paths to fulfillment: Women's search for meaning and identity*. New York: Oxford University Press.

Kroger, J. (1993). On the nature of structural transition in the identity formation process. In J. Kroger (Ed.), *Discussions on ego identity*. Hillsdale, NJ: Lawrence Erlbaum Associates.

Kroger, J. (2018). The epigenesis of identity: What does it mean? *Identity: An International Journal of Theory and Research, 18*, 334–342.

Kroger, J., & Haslett, S. J. (1987). A retrospective study of ego identity status change by midlife adults. *Social and Behavioral Sciences Documents, 17*, Ms. no. 2797 (52pp.).

Kroger, J., & Haslett, S. J. (1991). A comparison of ego identity status transition pathways and change rates across five identity domains. *International Journal of Aging and Human Development, 32*, 303–330.

Kroger, J., Martinussen, M., & Marcia, J. E. (2010). Identity status change during adolescence and young adulthood: A meta-analysis. *Journal of Adolescence, 33*, 683–698.

Lodi-Smith, J., Cologgi, K., Spain, S. M., & Roberts, B. W. (2017). Development of identity clarity and content in adulthood. *Journal of Personality and Social Psychology, 112*, 755–768.

Luyckx, K., Klimstra, T. A., Duriez, B., Van Petegem, , S., & Beyers, W. (2013). Personal identity processes from adolescence through the late twenties: Age differences, functionality, and depressive symptoms. *Social Development, 22*, 701–721.

Marcia, J. E, (2002). Identity and psychosocial development in adulthood. *Identity: An International Journal of Theory and Research, 2*, 7–2.

McAdams, D. P., Diamond, A., de St. Aubin, E., & Mansfield, E. (1997). Stories of commitment: The psychosocial construction of generative lives. *Journal of Personality and Social Psychology, 72*, 678–694.

McLean, K. C. (2008). Stories of the young and the old: Personal continuity and narrative identity. *Developmental Psychology, 44*, 254–264.

Merrill, N., & Fivush, R. (2016). Intergenerational narratives and identity across development. *Developmental Review, 40*, 72–92.

Michener, J. (1972). *The fires of spring.* New York, NY: Random House.

Pals, J. L. (2006). Narrative identity processing of difficult life experiences: Pathways of personality development and positive self-transformation in adulthood. *Journal of Personality, 74*, 1079–1110.

Pasupathi, M., & Mansour, E. (2006). Adult age differences in autobiographical reasoning in narratives. *Developmental Psychology, 42*, 798–808.

Sears, R., Maccoby, E., & Levin, H. (1951). *Patterns of child-rearing.* Stanford, CA: Stanford University Press.

Sneed, J. R., Whitbourne, S. K., & Culang, M. E. (2006). Trust, identity, and ego integrity: Modelling Erikson's core stages over 34 years. *Journal of Adult Development, 13*, 148–157.

Sneed, J. R., Whitbourne, S. K., Schwartz, S. J., & Huang, S. (2012). The relationship between identity, intimacy, and midlife well-being: Findings from the Rochester Adult Longitudinal Study. *Psychology and Aging, 27*, 318–323.

Stephen, J., Fraser, E., & Marcia, J. E. (1992). Lifespan identity development: Variables related to Moratorium-Achievement (MAMA) cycles. *Journal of Adolescence, 15*, 283–300.

Stewart, A. J., Ostrove, J. M., & Helson, R. (2001). Middle aging in women: Patterns of personality change from the 30s to the 50s. *Journal of Adult Development, 8*, 23–37.

Zucker, A. N., Ostrove, J. M., & Stewart, J. J. (2002). College educated women's personality development in adulthood: Perceptions and age differences. *Psychology and Aging, 17*, 236–244.

Index

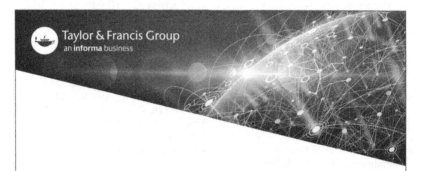

Made in United States
North Haven, CT
16 January 2024

47561163R00128